# ABSOLUTE BEGINNER'S GUIDE

(TO)

Microsoft®
# Office 2003

Jim Boyce

800 East 96th Street,
Indianapolis, Indiana 46240

# Absolute Beginner's Guide to Microsoft® Office 2003

International Standard Book Number: 0-7897-2967-9

Library of Congress Catalog Card Number: 2003103660

Printed in the United States of America

First Printing: October 2003

06   05   04   03          4   3   2   1

## Trademarks

## Warning and Disclaimer

## Bulk Sales

Que Publishing offers excellent discounts on this book when ordered in quantity for bulk purchases or special sales. For more information, please contact

**U.S. Corporate and Government Sales**
**1-800-382-3419**
**corpsales@pearsontechgroup.com**

For sales outside the U.S., please contact

**International Sales**
**1-317-428-3341**
**international@pearsontechgroup.com**

**Associate Publisher**
Greg Wiegand

**Acquisitions Editor**
Angelina Ward

**Development Editor**
Howard Jones

**Managing Editor**
Charlotte Clapp

**Project Editor**
Tonya Simpson

**Copy Editor**
Kitty Jarrett

**Indexer**
Chris Barrick

**Proofreader**
Kathy Bidwell

**Technical Editor**
Karl Hilsmann

**Team Coordinator**
Sharry Gregory

**Interior Designer**
Anne Jones

**Cover Designer**
Dan Armstrong

**Page Layout**
Bronkella Publishing

# Contents at a Glance

# Table of Contents

# About the Author

**Jim Boyce** has authored and co-authored more than 50 books on computers and technology, and he specializes in Microsoft Office, Windows Server, Windows client operating systems, and a handful of other technologies and applications. In addition to writing books, Jim also frequently writes for techrepublic.com and other online technical sites, including OfficeLetter.com, on a variety of topics.

Some of Jim's other recent books include *Microsoft Outlook 2003 Inside Out* (Microsoft Press), *Windows XP Power Tools* (Sybex), and *Windows Server 2003 Bible* (Wiley).

In past lives Jim has been an engineering technician at a shipyard, a college instructor, a Unix system administrator, and most recently, owner of an Internet access and Web development company.

You can email Jim directly at `jim@boyce.us`. His Web site is located at `www.boyce.us`.

# Dedication

*With love to my wife, for putting up with me for more than 25 years.*

# Acknowledgments

It has been a while since I wrote for Que, and this book has been a great reintroduction to the Que staff. I particularly want to thank Greg Wiegand and Angelina Ward for bringing me this opportunity. Thanks also to Tonya Simpson for a great job of managing the project, and to Howard Jones and Kitty Jarrett for their help in editing. I also thank Chris Barrick, Kathy Bidwell, the grahpics department, and Kelly Maish for their help in developing and producing the book.

I'd also like to offer a special thanks to Blair Rampling, Bill Zumwalde, and Scott Backstrom for helping with this and other projects so we could meet our deadlines and still end up with a quality product. I promise to take Bill and Scott flying as a bonus, but I don't guarantee to stay right-side-up. Blair, you can go, too, but it's much safer on the ground—trust me.

# We Want to Hear from You!

As the reader of this book, *you* are our most important critic and commentator. We value your opinion and want to know what we're doing right, what we could do better, what areas you'd like to see us publish in, and any other words of wisdom you're willing to pass our way.

As an associate publisher for Que, I welcome your comments. You can email or write me directly to let me know what you did or didn't like about this book—as well as what we can do to make our books better.

*Please note that I cannot help you with technical problems related to the topic of this book. We do have a User Services group, however, where I will forward specific technical questions related to the book.*

When you write, please be sure to include this book's title and author as well as your name, email address, and phone number. I will carefully review your comments and share them with the author and editors who worked on the book.

Email:  feedback@quepublishing.com

Mail:  Greg Wiegand
   Associate Publisher
   Que Publishing
   800 East 96th Street
   Indianapolis, IN 46240 USA

For more information about this book or another Que title, visit our Web site at www.quepublishing.com. Type the ISBN (excluding hyphens) or the title of a book in the Search field to find the page you're looking for.

# Introduction

I began using Microsoft Word with version 1.0, when it ran only on DOS—before Windows even existed! In the many years since, Microsoft Office has become the most popular productivity suite.

You've probably turned to this book because you need to get up to speed with some or all of the programs in the Office suite. Each of these programs offers lots of features, but you'll find that most people—even computer professionals like me—often use only a fraction of each program's capabilities. That's all most people need.

This book focuses on the core features in each of these Office applications: Outlook, Word, Excel, PowerPoint, and Access. Rather than inundate you with lots of facts about features you'll never use, I've focused on the features you will use most often with each one. With this book in hand, you should have no trouble quickly becoming proficient with each one.

# How This Book Is Organized

You might want to focus on one particular Office application at first because it's the one you think you will use the most. You'll find that easy to do because this book separates each program into its own part. This book is organized into eight main parts:

- **Part I, "Getting Your Feet Wet,"** introduces you to Microsoft with a quick tour of its main programs and features. Part I also explains how to install Office, work with Office programs and documents, and get help when you need it. In this part you'll learn how to keep Office up to date and what to do if a program crashes.

- **Part II, "Contacts, Email, and Lots More with Outlook,"** covers Microsoft Outlook 2003, the program in Office that helps you work with email, manage contacts, plan a schedule, and generally keep track of your work day. In this part you'll learn how to work with email, appointments, contacts, tasks, and notes, and also how to keep track of events by using the Journal folder.

- **Part III, "Writing with Word,"** explores Word in detail. Word is the program you use to write letters, proposals, brochures, and other documents. You'll learn in Part III not only how to create a document in Word but also how to add graphics, add character and paragraph formatting, use templates and styles, check your spelling and grammar, create mailing lists and mail-merge form letters, and more.

- **Part IV, "Number-Crunching with Excel,"** provides an introduction to Excel, Office's spreadsheet program. In this part you'll learn how to create and enter numbers, text, formulas, and other information into a worksheet and how to format that information to add impact and make the worksheet more useful. Part IV also explains how to work with multiple worksheets, move information from one worksheet to another, add charts and graphs, and print and save Excel documents.

- **Part V, "Creating Presentations in PowerPoint,"** takes you on a guided tour of PowerPoint, which enables you to create presentations for meetings, classes, or even online delivery across the Internet. In this part you'll learn how to start a new presentation, add slides, add text and graphics to slides, and even add music, video clips, and other data to your presentation.

- **Part VI, "Organizing Data with Access,"** focuses on Access, the database program in Office. In this part you'll learn how and why to use a database, how to create databases in Access, and how to enter data. Part VI also explains how to query the database to look up information and create reports, sort and filter records, and perform calculations. You'll also learn how to create forms to simplify entering and viewing data.

By the time you finish all the chapters in this book, you'll be well on your way to becoming an expert with Microsoft Office.

# Conventions Used in This Book

I hope that this book is easy enough to figure out on its own, without requiring its own instruction manual. As you read through the pages, however, it helps to know precisely how I've presented specific types of information.

## Web Page Addresses

There are a lot of Web page addresses in this book. They're noted as such:
`www.boyce.us`

Technically, a Web page address is supposed to start with `http://` (as in `http://www.boyce.us`). Because Internet Explorer and other Web browsers automatically insert that piece of the address, however, you don't have to type it—and I haven't included it in the addresses in this book.

## Special Elements

This book also includes a few special elements that provide additional information not included in the basic text. These elements are designed to supplement the text to make your learning faster, easier, and more efficient.

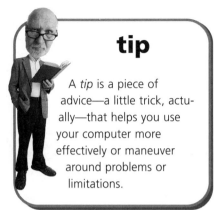

**tip**

A *tip* is a piece of advice—a little trick, actually—that helps you use your computer more effectively or maneuver around problems or limitations.

**note**

A *note* is designed to provide information that is generally useful but not specifically necessary for what you're doing at the moment. Some notes are like extended tips—interesting, but not essential.

**caution**

A *caution* tells you to beware of a potentially dangerous act or situation. In some cases, ignoring a caution could cause you significant problems—so pay attention to them!

## Let Me Know What You Think

I always love to hear from readers. If you want to contact me, feel free to email me at jim@boyce.us. I can't promise that I'll answer every message, but I will promise that I'll read each one!

If you want to learn more about me and any new books I have cooking, check out my Web site, at www.boyce.us. You'll find searchable databases containing tips on Office and Windows, with information about many of my other books. Also check out www.officeletter.com for more helpful tips about Microsoft Office.

# PART I

# GETTING YOUR FEET WET

1

# A QUICK TOUR OF OFFICE

It's a safe bet that because you're reading this book, you have little or no experience with Microsoft Office. You likely have at least some experience with Windows, and you might even be an advanced user, but you're just not familiar with Office.

The best way to get a good feel for what an application can do is to take a quick look at its main features. That's what you'll do in this chapter. First, let's take a look at some reasons you're working with Microsoft Office in the first place.

# Why Office?

There are a handful of key tasks that most people want to accomplish with a computer, particularly in a business setting, and this is probably true of you. For example, it's a good bet that you need to manage your email and contacts, work with letters and other documents, and maybe even keep track of some information in a database. There are no doubt several other tasks you need to perform on a regular basis with your computer.

Microsoft Office is a suite of applications designed to give you the programs you need to accomplish most of your tasks. If you're not familiar at all with Microsoft Office, you might think it's mainly for creating documents. Although Office does include Word to help you create, view, and modify documents, it also includes several other applications, each with a specific purpose. These productivity applications include the following:

- **Word**—You can use Word to create and manage documents such as reports, letters, research papers, and signs.

- **Outlook**—You can use Outlook to manage your email, contact list, to-do list, schedule, and other personal or business-related information.

- **Excel**—You can use Excel to store and analyze mainly numeric information, such as sales, grades, bills, and so on.

- **Access**—You can use Access to create, view, and modify relational databases. For example, you might track inventory, customers, students, or similar information with a database.

- **PowerPoint**—You can use PowerPoint to create presentations for meetings, sales calls, classes, and the Web.

There are certainly other programs that let you accomplish these tasks. For example, Microsoft's own Works application suite offers some of the same capabilities as Word, Excel, and Access. Applications from other vendors also offer the same or more advanced features.

So why choose Microsoft Office? Although some would argue that popularity is not a good reason to pick a particular application or suite, Microsoft Office is by far the most popular productivity suite. Why do I think that's important? If you change jobs, it's a good bet that the next company will be using Microsoft Office, so you won't have to learn a new set of applications. If you're a student, learning Office is important because that first job will probably require that you use at least one Office application. It's also likely that the people with whom you need to share documents—whether in your own company or another—will be using Microsoft Office because of its popularity. What's more, Office can import and export in several popular formats to help you share documents with others who do not use Office.

Another important reason Office is a good choice is the integration between the programs. You can easily use data from one Office program in another. For example, you can create a mass mailing in Word by using contacts you have stored in Outlook or in an Access database.

Over the many years it has been in development, Office has become easier to use. That's particularly true with this latest edition. Lots of wizards, a streamlined user interface, good Help documentation, and other features (not to mention this book!) will help you get up to speed with all your Office applications.

Although Microsoft Office doesn't do everything, it can probably handle a big portion of the things you need to do in a given day. Add in a few special-purpose applications, including a nice streaming audio player for your favorite online radio station, and your day is set!

# Tips for Upgrading from Previous Versions

You might have a copy of Office installed on your computer already, perhaps because it came with your computer. You don't need to remove it before you install Office 2003. Instead, you can upgrade the existing copy to Office 2003. The following sections offer some tips to help you through a successful upgrade.

## Back Up Anything You Can't Lose

Unless you haven't used your old copy of Office, you probably have at least some documents on the computer that you wouldn't want to lose. Maybe they are letters or reports you created in Office, email messages or contacts stored in Outlook, or Access databases. Whatever the case, you should back up these documents. It's unlikely that upgrading to Office 2003 will cause any of those documents to be lost, but why take the chance?

The documents can be almost anywhere on your computer, so unless you've been really conscientious about organizing your documents, you should search the hard disks for them. Here's a list of the file types for which you should search:

- **.DOC and .DOT**—.DOC files are documents, and .DOT files are templates that help define the look and content of a .DOC file. Both are created with Word.

- **.XLS**—These are Excel spreadsheet files.

- **.PPT**—These are PowerPoint presentation files.

- **.PST and .OST**—.PST files are personal folder files that store Outlook data (email, contacts, and so on). .OST files are offline store files used in conjunction with Exchange Server mailboxes. They enable you to work with Outlook data when you can't connect to your Exchange Server.

- **.MDB**—These are Access database files. You'll probably find a few .MDB files on your computer that you didn't create. Many programs, Office included, use Access databases to store content and other information.

In general, you can back up to any medium, including another hard disk, a floppy disk, ZIP media, and recordable CD (CD-R). If you back up to a CD-R and later have to restore the files from the CD to your hard disk, you just need to remember to change the file attributes so that the files are no longer read-only. You right-click a file or folder and choose Properties to change the read-only attribute.

> **note**
>
> In Windows 2000, you can select Start, Search, For Files or Folders to begin searching for files on your computer. In Windows XP, you can select Start, Search to open the Search Companion pane, and then click All Files and Folders to begin searching for document files.

## Clean Up the Computer

No, this doesn't mean wiping the grime off the top of the monitor, although that's not a bad idea. Before installing Office, you should take the time to *defragment* the computer's hard disk. Setup is going to copy a ton of files to your computer, and having the disk in good shape will make for a faster installation and better performance afterward.

You can find the Disk Defragmenter by selecting Start, All Programs, Accessories, System Tools. You can also right-click a drive in My Computer, choose Properties, and click the Tools tab in the System Properties dialog box to access the Disk Defragmenter.

> **tip**
>
> A disk that is *fragmented* has pieces of its files scattered across the hard disk. Defragmenting a drive rewrites the files into contiguous space on the disk, providing quicker disk access and ultimately better performance.

## Be Prepared for the Unexpected

After any program upgrade, you're likely to find features that no longer work as you think they should. In some cases it's intended, and in others it isn't. Before you upgrade to Office 2003, you should check to see if there are any patches available for Office 2003 by visiting the Microsoft Office Web site at `www.microsoft.com/office`. If there are no updates or installing an update doesn't solve a problem you're having, you can search the Windows Knowledge Base for articles that might explain the cause of your problem. You can find a search link for the Knowledge Base at `http://support.microsoft.com`.

# Working with Letters and More with Word

Letters, reports, and similar correspondence are the mainstay of business, and creating them is one of the most common tasks you're likely to perform with Office. I've been using Word since version 1, which first saw the light of day around 1983. Figure 1.1 shows Word 20 years later, as Word 2003.

**FIGURE 1.1**

You can use Word to create all kinds of written documents.

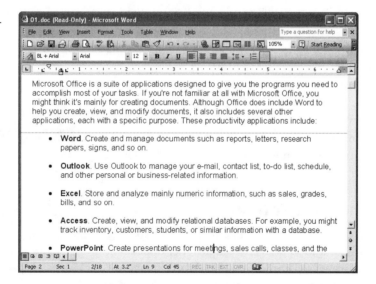

Word isn't limited to creating just letters and boring, dry reports. Word includes several templates and wizards to help you quickly and easily create legal pleadings, faxes, Web pages, memos, agendas, resumes, brochures, manuals, directories, and lots more. Anything that gets read on paper or online can probably be created with Word. For example, Figure 1.2 shows a brochure created with Word.

**FIGURE 1.2**

You can create
many kinds of
documents with
Word.

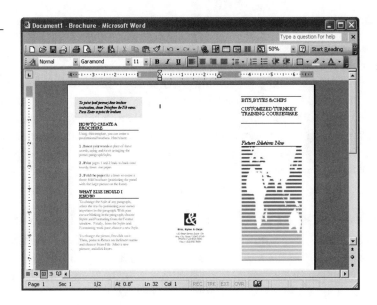

⇨    See Chapter 9, "Creating and Editing Word Documents," to learn how to create
documents with Word.

As Figure 1.2 shows, you can easily include graphics
in documents you create with Word. In fact, you can
also include video clips, audio clips, spreadsheets,
charts, graphs, and many other types of data,
thanks to the object linking and embedding (OLE)
technology in Windows. I cover how to include
other data types in Word documents in Chapter 12,
"More Than Just Words."

## Document and Font Formatting

Word gives you control over almost every aspect of
how a paragraph or even a single letter appears in
a document. You can control paragraph spacing,
indents, justification, and more. You can use different fonts, colors, sizes, and other properties for
characters in a document. The result is that you

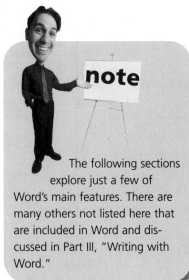

**note**

The following sections
explore just a few of
Word's main features. There are
many others not listed here that
are included in Word and discussed in Part III, "Writing with
Word."

have the ability to control to a fine degree how a document looks onscreen as well as how it looks on paper or online.

⇨   Chapter 10, "Adding Pizzazz," explains how to add formatting to a document.

Word also makes it easy to add tables and columns to a document. Figure 1.3 shows both of these elements in a document. You can draw tables with the mouse or simply tell Word how many columns and rows you want and let it do the work for you. In either case, you can merge table cells, change cell width and height, and make lots of other changes after the fact. You can also use Word's AutoFormat features to automatically format the appearance of a table.

**FIGURE 1.3**

Columns and tables are easy to create in Word.

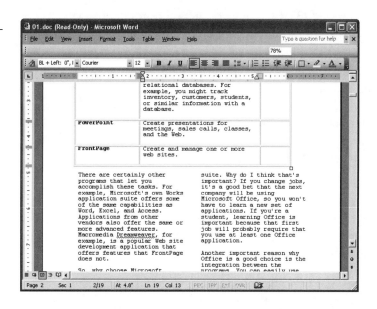

⇨   See Chapter 11, "Organizing with Tables and Columns," to learn about tables and columns in Word.

## Styles

If you frequently work on a particular type of document, you'll find that *document styles* are a very handy Word feature. Styles let you apply complex formatting to a paragraph and its contents with just a few mouse clicks. For example, this book was written with Word, and the different visual styles you see in the book—such as bullets, different font types and sizes, and special notes and tips—were defined in Word. You can create a collection of styles and save them as a template, which you can then use to create documents. Templates make it easy to create and use styles in multiple documents, such as one book to another.

⇨   See Chapter 10 to learn about templates and styles.

## Spelling and Grammar

Some people are whizzes at spelling; others find it a real challenge. Everyone has problems with certain words. With Word, you can concentrate on writing and let Word concentrate on spelling. Word has an extensive dictionary and can check your spelling for you as you type, underlining in red words it doesn't recognize. Word can also correct misspelled and mistyped words automatically to save you time.

Word can also check your grammar and prose style, offering suggestions about sentence fragments, awkward sentence structure, and so on. Word underlines in green words or phrases for which it has grammar suggestions.

➪    Chapter 13, "Checking Spelling and Grammar," explains how to set up and use Word's spelling and grammar features.

If you work in a field that has special terminology, you'll be happy to know that Word can use custom dictionaries to help you with spelling of words that are not contained in the default dictionary. You can also create your own dictionary entries and control lots of other aspects of how Word checks spelling and grammar (including turning off both features).

## Outlining and the Document Map

Working with a long document can be a real chore if there's not a good outline. Word offers some great features that help you create an outline and work within a long document. Figure 1.4 shows an outlined document. The left pane is the Document Map, which helps you quickly navigate through a long document by using its outline levels.

**FIGURE 1.4**

You can use the Document Map to navigate through a long document.

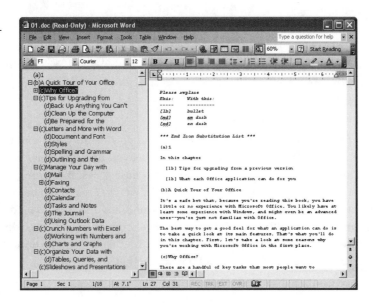

▷ See Chapter 9 to learn how to create and work with outlines.

Word offers several shortcuts for creating an outline. For example, you can press Ctrl+Alt+*<arrow>*, where *<arrow>* is the left or right arrow key, to promote or demote an outline head. Word also provides paragraph styles for easy outlining, the ability to automatically number an outline by using different numbering styles, and the ability to easily expand and collapse the outline to navigate through it and work with specific sections.

# Managing Your Day with Outlook

In a nutshell, Outlook is a personal information manager (PIM), but Outlook goes far beyond the pop-up PIMs that were so popular in the early 1990s. Most Office users spend a large portion of their time in Outlook.

## Using Mail

One of the main (but certainly not only) uses for Outlook is to manage email. Outlook 2003 can handle Exchange Server, Post Office Protocol (POP3), Internet Mail Access Protocol (IMAP), and Hypertext Transfer Protocol (HTTP) based mail accounts. It offers one-click configuration for Hotmail and MSN HTTP mail accounts, but it also supports other HTTP-based accounts.

Support for a large range of account types and the fact that you can use multiple accounts in Outlook at one time mean that Outlook can serve as your only email application, regardless of the number or type of accounts you use. Figure 1.5 shows the Outlook Inbox.

▷ See Chapter 5, "All Your Email in One Handy Spot," to learn how to start sending and receiving email.

You can use Outlook's built-in message form to create and read messages, or you can use Word, which offers more formatting options. Most people don't need all that formatting in email messages, so my choice is to use the built-in form, which is shown in Figure 1.6.

**tip**

Outlook used to support Microsoft Mail and cc:Mail, but support for these programs was dropped in Outlook 2002. However, the Transcend MAPI Provider for cc:Mail still works with Outlook. (MAPI stands for Mail Application Programming Interface.) You can find more information at www.transend.com/datasheet.html.

**FIGURE 1.5**

You use Outlook
to manage
email.

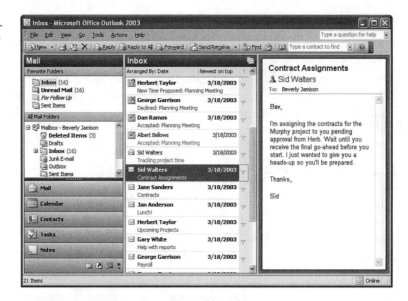

**FIGURE 1.6**

It's easy to cre-
ate a new email
message in
Outlook.

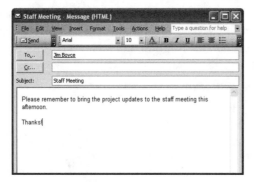

Outlook makes it easy to address email. You can select an address from the Contacts folder, address books on an Exchange Server, or the Windows Address Book, or you can enter an address manually. You can easily attach documents or other files, insert hyperlinks in messages, use stationery to control the appearance of a message, and more.

Outlook creates several default folders to contain messages, and you can create additional folders to further organize messages. For example, new messages arrive in the Inbox, but you might create a folder to contain messages you receive from family members.

⇨ See Chapter 5 to learn how to create mail folders and use rules to process mail.

Outlook offers easy-to-create rules that further help you organize messages. You can use the rules to route messages to different folders when they arrive, automatically reply to messages, delete unwanted messages, and perform almost any other message-processing task. Outlook includes built-in filters to help you block junk mail and messages that have adult content.

## Faxing

Outlook 2003 and earlier versions of Outlook can work in concert with the Windows Fax service included with Windows 2000 to deliver incoming faxes to the Outlook Inbox folder. Microsoft decided to drop support for that feature in Windows XP. That's too bad because it is a handy feature that Windows XP users will miss.

> **tip**
>
> You can create custom forms for Outlook items and use those forms instead of the default form. You can also create Outlook *templates*, which are Outlook items (such as a contact or a message) stored on disk, and use those templates to automate repetitive tasks. For example, you might create a message template to use when you submit a weekly report in which some of the information is the same from week to week.

You can send faxes from almost any application, and in most cases you'll be sending them from an application other than Outlook. For example, you can fax a document directly from Word by printing it to the Fax printer device.

⇨ Chapter 14, "Saving, Printing, and Emailing Documents," explains how to fax a document.

However, you'll probably store fax numbers for your contacts in the Outlook Contacts folder, in addition to their email addresses, phone numbers, and so on. You can select the recipient from your Contacts folder when you send the fax.

Although Outlook 2003 doesn't accept incoming faxes from the Windows XP Fax service, it does work with many third-party fax applications, such as WinFax, to provide that capability. Windows 2000 users can take advantage of the Windows 2000 Fax service to deliver incoming faxes to their Inboxes.

## Using the Contacts Folder

The Outlook Contacts folder (see Figure 1.7) is the place to store your contacts—friends, family members, business associates, clients, and so on.

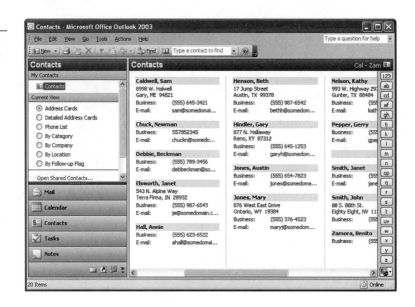

You can include lots of information about a contact: name, address, phone number, email addresses, fax number, personal information, and lots more. Figure 1.8 shows the Contact form to give you an idea of some of the information you can include.

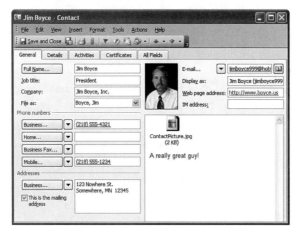

Outlook gives you several ways to view the Contacts folder, and you can also create custom views. You double-click a contact to open a contact's form to view additional information or make changes. You can also right-click a contact to perform certain actions, such as create a new email message or meeting request. You can also start a phone call (Outlook dials for you) and perform other tasks.

As mentioned earlier in this chapter, the Contacts folder is handy for addressing email messages and sending faxes. When you click one of the recipient buttons (To, Cc, or Bcc) on a message form, the Select Names dialog box appears (see Figure 1.9). You can select a name from the Contacts folder and other locations, depending on Outlook's configuration.

**FIGURE 1.9**

You can use the Select Names dialog box to add recipient addresses to a message.

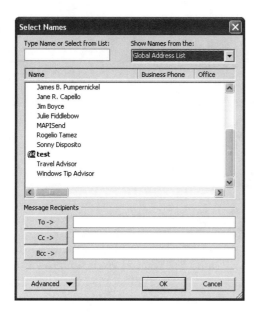

⇨   See Chapter 4, "Keeping Track of People and Places by Using Contacts," to learn how to use the Contacts folder.

## Using the Calendar Folder

The Calendar folder (see Figure 1.10) helps you manage your schedule. You can easily enter appointments and other events in the calendar, and Outlook optionally displays a reminder for each one a set time before the event (using the lead time for the reminder that you specify).

As with its other folders, Outlook gives you several ways to view your calendar. You can view a single day, the work week, or a month, or you can create custom views to suit your needs.

**tip**

You can use the Date Navigator—the small calendar at the top of the Navigation pane—to quickly select a date and change months.

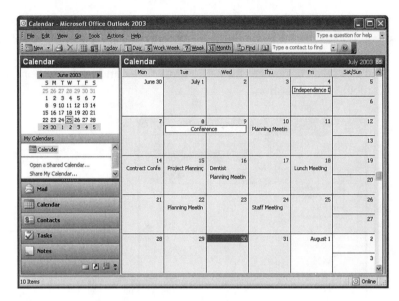

## Using the Tasks and Notes Folders

The Tasks folder (see Figure 1.11) lets you keep track of the tasks you need to perform, much like an electronic to-do list. You can create your own tasks and also create and assign tasks to others. The task list shows the task name, its due date, and the completion status. You just place a check mark beside a task, and Outlook marks it as completed, striking through it to indicate that it is complete.

**FIGURE 1.11**

You can use the
Tasks folder to
manage your
pending tasks.

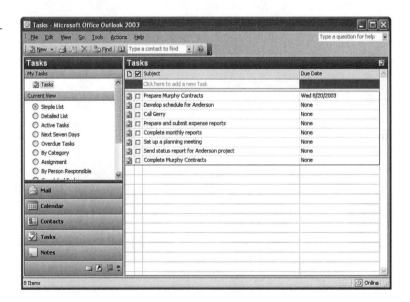

You can add other fields to the Tasks folder views, such as Percent Complete, Date Completed, and several others. You can also set a reminder for tasks to help you remember when you need to work on them or when they are due.

➪   Chapter 7, "Managing a To-Do List," explains how to work with the Tasks folder.

The Notes folder (see Figure 1.12) gives you a place to keep notes that don't really belong as other Outlook item types. For example, you might use the Notes folder to store information about tasks before you're ready to actually create a task. Or you might use it for a shopping list. Whatever the case, it's easy to use the contents of your notes in other Outlook items or other applications. For example, you can easily copy the text from a note to a task or to an email message.

**FIGURE 1.12**

You can use the Notes folder to keep information that doesn't really fit other Outlook item types.

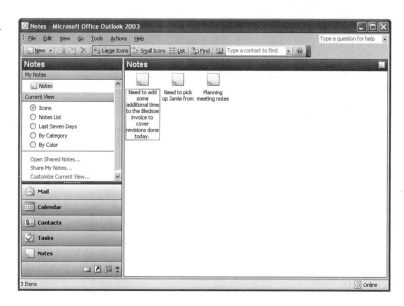

## Using the Journal Folder

Like a paper journal, the Outlook Journal folder lets you keep track of events, the time you spend on a project, phone calls, and other events. Figure 1.13 shows the Journal folder's default view.

You can add items to the Journal folder yourself or let Outlook add certain types of items. For example, when you make or receive a phone call, you can enter the start and end times for the call, as well as notes regarding the conversation (see Figure 1.14).

**FIGURE 1.13**

You can keep track of phone calls, documents, and other events with the Journal folder.

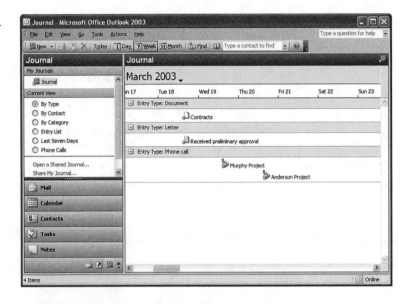

**FIGURE 1.14**

You can keep notes about phone calls in the Journal folder.

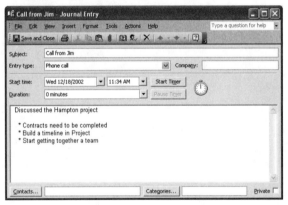

If you need to track the amount of time you work on a document—for example, because you need to bill your time to a client—you can let Outlook automatically add document times to the Journal folder. As you work with a document, Outlook keeps track of the time spent and creates Journal folder entries accordingly.

➪ See Chapter 6, "Keeping Track of Appointments and Other Big (or Small) Events," for an explanation of how to use the Journal folder.

## Using Outlook Data Elsewhere

As you become experienced with Outlook you'll probably come to realize that much of your information is stored there. Fortunately, you can use that information in other Outlook items and other applications. For example, maybe you want to send out a holiday letter to all your friends, and you have their addresses stored in your Contacts folder. It's a simple matter to create a mail-merged letter that inserts the recipient's address in the letter and then prints the letter (or creates a new document on disk).

Throughout the rest of the book I explain how you can use not only Outlook items, but other Office data in other applications.

# Crunching Numbers with Excel

Microsoft Excel is a *spreadsheet* application. You mainly use Excel to keep track of and analyze numeric information such as grades, sales figures, budgets, bills to pay, and so on. However, you can also use Excel to store and sort other types of information.

## Working with Numbers and Formulas

The thing you'll most often do with Excel is enter numbers and then use formulas to analyze those numbers. A very simple example is adding a column of numbers to determine the total value of some office assets, as shown in Figure 1.15.

**FIGURE 1.15**

You can use Excel to analyze numeric information.

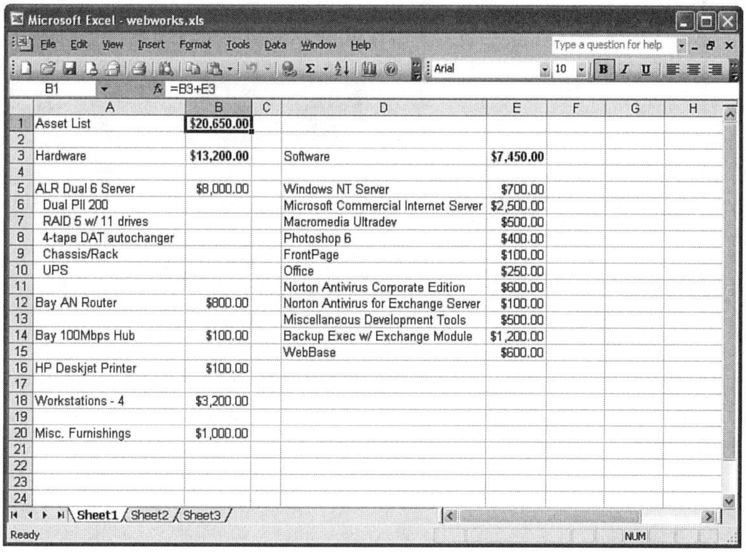

Excel makes it easy to enter information and perform math operations and other manipulation on the information. It gives you quick access to common operations such as Sum, Average, Count, and many more in several different categories, including Financial, Date & Time, and Math & Trig. You can quickly add simple calculations or build very complex formulas to analyze or process information in the way you need.

⇨ Chapter 17, "Once Around the Worksheet," introduces you to spreadsheets, and Chapter 18, "From Simple Addition to What-ifs: Formulas," explains how to add formulas to spreadsheets.

## Using Charts and Graphs

Excel isn't limited to just numbers. You can also add text and other types of data, including charts and graphs. Excel offers some great charting and graphing features that make it easy to add those elements to a spreadsheet. In most cases, you just highlight a range of information, select a command from the menu, and set a few options, and you have a great-looking chart or graph (see Figure 1.16).

**FIGURE 1.16**

You can easily add charts and graphs to a spreadsheet.

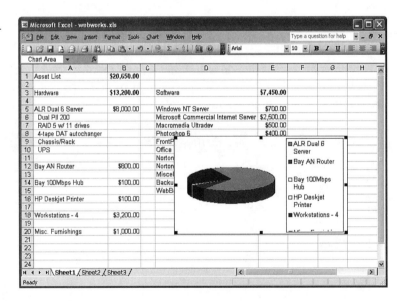

The charts and graphs you create in Excel don't have to stay in Excel. You can easily import them into Word or other applications to create reports, Web pages, and other types of documents.

# Organizing Data with Access

Microsoft Access lets you create and manage relational databases. A *relational database* is a collection of data stored in related tables. A relational database offers flexible and powerful search and query capabilities, particularly compared to a *flat-file database*. An example of a flat-file database is a text file that contains names, one per line.

You can do relatively little with a flat-file database, but a relational database such as Access (see Figure 1.17) offers the capability to store data in multiple tables and extract information in an almost unlimited number of ways. Here are some examples of information you might store in a database:

- Contact information for family members, friends, or customers
- Information on video or audio collections
- Information on antiques or collectibles
- Demographics information
- Inventory information
- Product lists

**FIGURE 1.17**

You can use a database to track and query data of any kind.

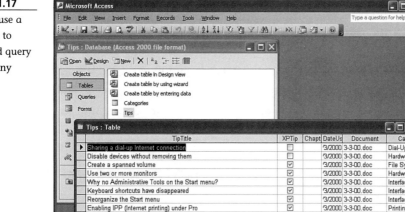

## Tables, Queries, and Reports

You can easily create a blank database in Access, add a table, and then add fields to the table. The *fields* are the individual items of information that make up one *record* in a table. For example, let's say you create a database to keep track of the products you sell. You create a table called Products, and each product is a record in that table. Here are some fields you might have in the Products table:

- **Name**—This text field stores the product's name.
- **PN**—This text field stores a unique part number that identifies the part or product.
- **Cost**—This number field stores the item's manufacturing cost.
- **Price**—This number field stores the item's selling price.
- **Color**—This text field stores the available colors of the item.
- **InStock**—This Yes/No field indicates whether the item is in stock.

**note**

A Yes/No field is also called a *Boolean* field. Boolean values describe logic such as Yes/No, True/False, Or, And, and a few others.

A *query*, which you can build easily with Access, lets you search a database for records that meet some search conditions. For example, you might create a query to search the Products database for products that are out of stock to help you quickly figure out what you need to manufacture or order. You can build a query manually or use the Simple Query Wizard provided by Access to quickly create one.

At some point you'll probably want to print some data from a database, and that's where reports come into play. A *report* is a bit like a query, except it ends up on paper rather than onscreen. That's a bit simplified, but the general idea is correct.

⇨    See Chapter 27, "Database Basics," for an introduction to Access and databases.

# Using Slide Shows and Presentations with PowerPoint

PowerPoint, another of the applications included with Microsoft Office, helps you create presentations and slide shows for meetings, classes, sales presentations, and so on. Figure 1.18 shows PowerPoint with a sample presentation started.

Each slide in a presentation can contain text, images, and even rich media such as video and audio clips. By supporting these types of media, PowerPoint makes it possible to create rich, professional-looking presentations that you can present to a live audience or broadcast across a local network or the Internet. PowerPoint is also a handy tool when you just want to create a set of printed handouts.

**FIGURE 1.18**

You can use PowerPoint to create slide show presentations.

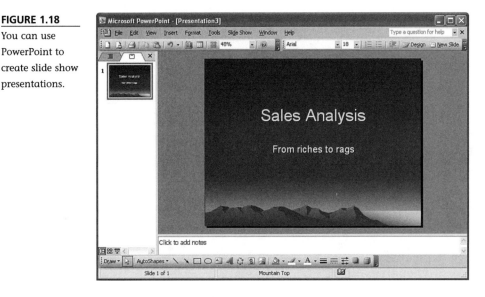

PowerPoint includes lots of templates with predefined backgrounds and themes that you can use to create presentations with very little effort. You can also create and use your own themes.

⇨   See Part V, "Creating Presentations in PowerPoint," to learn how to create presentations by using PowerPoint.

# THE ABSOLUTE MINIMUM

Microsoft Office is by far the most popular productivity suite on the market, and it has been for a long time. Understanding how to use Office applications is probably not only important to you today, but it could be important in the future if you change jobs. Most jobs involve using at least one Office application.

Each of the applications in the Office suite is geared toward a particular type of task. For example, you might use Word to create a written report, Excel to analyze sales figures, and PowerPoint to present information in a sales meeting. One of the best things going for Office is the ease with which it enables you to use the same data in different ways and different applications.

The rest of the chapters in Part I, "Getting Your Feet Wet," explain how to install, start, and begin using Office. They also explain how to get help when you get stuck. The other parts in the book each focus on a particular Office application.

Now, flip that page, and let's get Office installed on your computer!

2

# OFFICE BASICS

Office applications share some common features with other Windows applications and with each other, and there is a common set of tasks you'll perform in each Office application. After you learn these basic tasks, you'll be able to work in one Office application as well as the next.

This chapter covers those common tasks and also explains how to install and start Office. It also gives you some tips on using the keyboard and mouse with Office to speed things up a bit. Best of all, this chapter tells you how to undo changes you make to a document, which could really save your bacon!

# Installing Office

Before you can start using Office applications, you need to install Office. Microsoft has made some pretty decent strides in the last several years toward simplifying application installation by standardizing on a setup utility called the Microsoft Installer. That's what Office uses to install its applications. You shouldn't have much trouble installing Office, so I don't cover Setup in detail. Instead, I give you a good overview of the process, and I give you some tips on ways you can fine-tune Setup in certain situations.

## Simple Installations

If your computer's CD-ROM drive has AutoPlay enabled, all you need to do to start Office Setup is pop in the CD, and Setup should start automatically. If it does not start by itself, you need to open My Computer, open the CD-ROM drive, and double-click Setup.exe.

Setup starts a Setup Wizard that helps you perform the Office installation. The wizard first asks for the Office product key, which you find on the back of the CD case or on the Certificate of Authenticity, which is probably the case, if Office came bundled with your PC. Setup then prompts for user information and asks you to accept the end user license agreement (EULA).

Next, Setup lets you choose an installation type:

- **Typical**—Choose this option to install the most commonly used Office applications and components.

- **Complete Install**—Choose this option to install all applications and optional components.

- **Minimal Install**—Choose this option to install a bare minimum set of applications and components if you don't have much space available on your hard disk.

- **Custom Install**—Choose this option if you want to choose which applications and optional components to install.

If you choose the Custom Install option, the wizard prompts you to select the applications you want to install. You need to place a check mark beside each of the ones you want and click Next. If you want to specify which components Setup installs, you need to choose the option Choose Advanced Customization of Applications and click Next. You then see the page shown in Figure 2.1.

**FIGURE 2.1**

You use the
Advanced
Customization
page to choose
which compo-
nents to install.

You can click the arrow to the left of a component and then choose one of the following four options:

- **Run from My Computer**—Install the components listed for a Typical
  installation now, and install all other subcomponents the first time you try to
  use them.
- **Run all from My Computer**—Install all subcomponents on the computer.
- **Installed on First Use**—Don't install the component until you try to use it
  the first time.
- **Not Available**—Don't install the component and don't make it available in
  Office.

The third option, Installed on First Use, lets Setup perform a just-in-time installation
of the component. For example, if you don't know if you are going to use
PowerPoint, you can select this option, and Setup will make it look like PowerPoint is
installed on your computer. However, the files won't be copied to your computer
until you actually try to use PowerPoint for the first time.

I like to have everything available, and I usually have plenty of disk space, so I typically install everything. If you're concerned about the amount of space available on
your disk, choose the Typical or Minimal options or select Installed on First Use for
any applications and components you're not sure you'll need.

The rest of the installation process is pretty straightforward, so you shouldn't have
any problems with it. If you need to add or remove applications or components, you
can insert the CD and run Setup again. As Figure 2.2 shows, Setup gives you the
option to add or remove components, reinstall or repair Office, or remove Office.

## Tips for Installing Office

Installing Office on a single computer isn't a tough task, so I don't go into any more detail on that topic. If you're looking at installing Office on several computers, however, check out the following sections, which explain ways to install Office for multiple users. The following sections don't go into a lot of detail because this is an introductory book, but they do point you to some good tools and resources to get you started.

### Customizing an Installation

There are a handful of tools you can use to customize an Office installation. Using these tools is not worth the trouble for just a couple installations, but they are great when you need to install Office for a whole department, for example.

The *Office Resource Kit*, available by download from Microsoft at www.microsoft.com/office, includes a tool called the *Custom Installation Wizard (CIW)*. The CIW presents several pages where you preconfigure various Office options such as which applications and components to install, installation location, organization name, and most Office application settings. The result is an *MST* (that is, transform) file. You can add the MST file to a network share or CD and have Setup customize the installation based on the settings you provide in the MST file.

**tip**

You should use the Reinstall or Repair option if you're having problems with Office and want to restore it to its original installation state.

The *Resource Kit* also includes the Profile Wizard, which you can use to create an Office profile (that is, application settings and options) to apply to other computers. You can also use the Profile Wizard to move a user's Office settings from one computer to another, such as when the user upgrades to a new system.

## Installing from a Network Server

One of the easiest ways to install Office to several computers is to put the Office files on a network server and let the users install from there. To use this method, you need to create an Office *installation share*. You create a folder on the server and share it, giving users read access. Then you pop in the CD, open a command prompt, change to the CD drive, and run the command **SETUP.EXE /A**. Setup copies the needed files to the folder you specify.

When users need to install Office, they can connect to the shared folder and run Setup.exe. If you want to customize the installation, you can run the CIW, edit the PRO.MSI file in the shared folder, and place the resulting MST file in the same folder. When the users run Setup, the customized settings apply.

**note**

You can install a retail copy of Office for only one user. You need to purchase an Open License version of Office if you need to install for multiple users and/or customize the installation. With an Open License version, you receive one set of software media (CDs) and client licenses for as many clients as you purchase, along with one product code that doesn't require activation.

## Using Other Tools

If you need to roll out Office to a really large number of users, you should consider using *group policy*. This section provides an overview without getting too deep into group policy.

Users in a Windows 2000 Server or Windows Server 2003 domain can receive group policies from the server when they log on. Group policies can apply at the site, domain, organizational unit (OU), or local level, depending on where you define them. These group policies do such things as define the user's working environment and restrict the actions the user can perform. Group policy can also cause applications to install automatically for users.

You can deploy (that is, install) an application in one of two ways by using group policy:

■ **Publish**—When you publish an application, the application appears in a user's Add or Remove Programs applet in the Control Panel, enabling the user to add the application when he or she needs or wants it.

■ **Assign**—When you assign an application, the application appears as if it is installed on the user's computer. For example, the user sees shortcuts to the Office applications in his or her Programs menu. When the user tries to open an application or a document associated with the application, Setup performs a just-in-time installation of the application.

In both cases, the application installs from a network installation share, so before you deploy an application by using group policy, you need to first create the share and optionally customize it with the CIW.

➪ To learn more about group policy and deploying applications with it, check out Microsoft's Web site, at www.microsoft.com/windows2000/ techinfo/howitworks/management/grouppolicyintro.asp.

> **tip**
>
> When you combine group policy–based application installation with Remote Installation Services (RIS) to install the operating system, you have relatively painless disaster recovery. If a user's computer crashes, you can plug a new one into the network and let RIS and group policy re-create the user's computer with almost no effort other than logging in.

# Starting Office Programs When and How *You* Want

When you start Office for the first time, it generally wants to activate itself, which means it needs to send a small amount of information to Microsoft. You don't need to include any personal information or even register. The activation wizard looks at your computer's hardware and creates a key to identify it. It then sends the key to

Microsoft and retrieves an activation code. If you don't want to use the Internet, you can call Microsoft at the phone number provided by the wizard, read the key, and retrieve your activation code.

When you start an Office application, you usually see the Office Language Bar, shown in Figure 2.3. The Language Bar gives you access to dictation, voice commands, and a small number of other functions that vary a bit, depending on whether an Office application is running.

> **tip**
>
> If you install an Open License version of Office, no activation is required.

**FIGURE 2.3**

The Language Bar gives you quick access to voice commands and dictation.

I don't cover using the Language Bar in detail in this book, but if you want to use its features, you need to train it for your voice. To do so, you select Tools, Training to start the Voice Training Wizard. The wizard asks you to read documents so that it can train itself to your voice.

If you don't want to use the Language Bar, you can just turn it off! You click the small down arrow at the right side of the Language Bar and choose Settings. Then you click Language Bar in the Settings dialog box, clear the option Show the Language Bar on the desktop, and click OK. Then you click OK on the Settings dialog box, and the Language Bar disappears.

## Starting Office Applications

Setup places a shortcut for each of the Office applications in your Programs menu, so you can select Start, Programs (or All Programs), Microsoft Office, and then select the program you want to use.

> **tip**
>
> When you realize you like the Language Bar and say, "Hey, I want that back!" you can easily turn it back on. You just choose Tools, Speech, Speech Recognition. The Language Bar reappears, and you can change its settings as needed.

You don't even have to open an Office application directly. You can just double-click an Office document, and its application opens, with the document you selected open within it.

## Starting Office Applications Automatically

I use some Office applications—mostly Word and Outlook—all day long. I hardly ever log off my computer, and I never turn it off, but if I did, I'd want those applications to start automatically.

The easiest way to make a program start automatically when you log on is to add it to your Startup folder. To do this, you open the Start menu, right-click the icon of the application you want to start automatically, and drag it to the Startup folder. Then you release the mouse button and choose Copy Here to create a shortcut in the Startup folder.

**tip**

If you like really easy access to the one or two Office applications you use most, you can place a shortcut on the desktop. To do this, you right-click the application's icon in the Programs menu and drag it to the desktop. Then you choose Copy Here to copy the shortcut.

## Using Switches to Control Startup

In some situations, you might need to use a switch to start an office application. A *switch* is an option you include on an Office application's command line that basically tells the application to do something it wouldn't normally do. For example, maybe you're getting tired of seeing the Word splash screen every time Word starts. Maybe you'd like to prevent the Normal.dot template from loading. Or maybe you want to start Outlook with a particular profile or folder.

**tip**

What if you use more than one Outlook profile and have Outlook configured to ask you to choose a profile at startup? In this case, you can use a command-line option with the shortcut in the Startup folder to specify the profile. The next section explains how.

There are several optional switches for each Office application. You could open a command prompt and start the application by using a switch, but it's easier to create a shortcut, particularly if you want to use the switch in a shortcut in the `Startup` folder. Here's how you do it:

1. Right-click the desktop and choose New, Shortcut to start the Create Shortcut Wizard.

2. Click Browse and browse to the folder that contains Office (probably `C:\Program Files\Microsoft Office\Office11`).

3. Select one of the following files:

   - **Word**—`winword.exe`
   - **Outlook**—`outlook.exe`
   - **Access**—`msaccess.exe`
   - **Excel**—`excel.exe`
   - **PowerPoint**—`powerpnt.exe`

   Click OK. The Create Shortcut dialog box reappears.

4. Click at the end of the text box and outside the quote and then type a space, followed by the switch or switches.

5. Click Next, enter a name for the shortcut, and click Finish.

You can use the shortcut where you created it, or you can drag it to the `Startup` folder in the Start menu if you want the application to start automatically at logon, using the specified switch.

# Working with the Navigation Pane

The Navigation pane, shown in Figure 2.4, is the main tool for navigating Outlook's folders. The contents of the Navigation pane change depending on which folder is open. The buttons near the

> **tip**
>
> If you have trouble picking out the correct file (in some cases, more than one file has the same name but different file extensions), look for the icon that matches the one shown in the Start menu. Or you can right-click the file, choose Properties, and make sure the Type of File field says `Application`.

bottom of the Navigation pane are the gateway to your Outlook folders. For example, you can click the Mail button to open the Inbox folder, or click the Calendar button to open the Calendar folder.

**FIGURE 2.4**

You can use the Navigation pane to navigate through your Outlook folders.

Mailbox folders

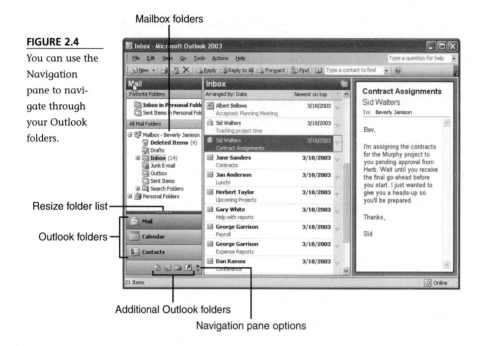

Resize folder list

Outlook folders

Additional Outlook folders

Navigation pane options

When you open the Calendar folder, the Navigation pane shows a *date navigator*, which is simply a calendar, at the top of the Navigation pane. Click the left or right arrow on the calendar to change months, and click a date to view that date in the Calendar folder.

Other folders change the Navigation pane contents in other ways. For example, as Figure 2.4 shows, the Navigation pane shows a folder list when you open the Inbox. The remaining folders show a list of available view types. Figure 2.5 shows how the Navigation pane looks when the Calendar folder is open.

If you need to see more buttons on the Navigation pane, click and drag the resize bar shown in Figure 2.4. You can also click Configure Buttons at the bottom right of the Navigation pane and choose Enlarge Button Bar or Shrink Button Bar to change the size. This pop-up menu also gives you some additional options, such as the capability to add or remove buttons from the Navigation pane and set options for it.

You'll learn more about using the Navigation pane in Part II, "Contacts, Email, and Lots More with Outlook."

**FIGURE 2.5**

The Navigation pane looks a bit different when the Calendar folder is opened.

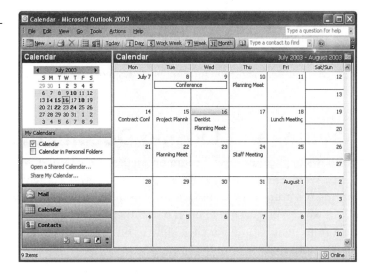

# Working with More Than One Document at a Time

Some of the Office applications let you open more than one document at a time, and that can really be handy when you need to compare documents or just have a lot going on! For example, you might open a letter in Word and also open a report so you can work on both. Word, Excel, and PowerPoint all let you open multiple documents. To do so, you just click File, Open and open a document. These applications open a new *instance* of the program (that is, another application window) to display the document.

When you open another database in Access, however, the current one closes. If you want to have two databases open at one time, you need to open the first one and then open another copy of Access from the Start menu and open the second database in *that* copy.

Outlook is a bit different from the other Office applications. You can work with only one profile at a time. If you try to open another instance of Outlook with a different profile (by using the /Profile command-line switch), Outlook ignores the specified profile and just opens another copy with the current profile.

An Outlook *profile* stores account and data file information and controls what accounts and data you see when you open Outlook.

⇨ You can open someone else's mailbox in Outlook if you need to work with it along with your own. I explain how to do that (and why you'd want to) in Chapter 5, "All Your Email in One Handy Spot." In Chapter 5, I also explain how to open two or more Outlook windows, each showing a different Outlook folder.

# Opening, Saving, and Closing Documents

Most Windows applications use a common method for opening, saving, and closing documents. Word, Excel, and PowerPoint all start a new document by default when you start the program. They, along with Access, also display the task pane (refer to Figure 2.3), which you can use to open a document. You can select a recently used document from the task pane or click More or one of the other links to open a document that is not listed.

To open a file without using the task pane, you can choose File, Open to display the standard Office Open file dialog box (see Figure 2.6).

⌐My Places Bar

**FIGURE 2.6**

You can use the Open dialog box to open documents.

The Open dialog box is simple to use, so I don't cover it in detail. Note that the My Places Bar at the left edge of the dialog box contains icons for some common places you're likely to find documents. You can just click an icon to open the folder it represents. You can also choose a folder from the Look In drop-down list box. You can use the Files of Type drop-down list box to choose the type of document you want to open, although you need to understand that you must open a document meant for the current application; you can't simply open any Office document from any Office application.

When you've finished working with a document, you can close it but keep the program open. To do so, you can choose File, Close or you can click the Close Window button at the right edge of the menu bar to close the document. It's the smaller × icon beneath the program's Close (×) button (see Figure 2.7).

**tip**

You can add to the My Places Bar your own icons for frequently used folders. You just browse to the appropriate folder and then choose Tools, Add to My Places.

Close Window button

**FIGURE 2.7**

You can close a document window without closing the application.

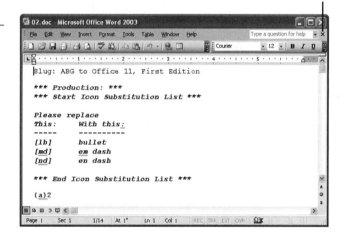

As you work on documents, you'll no doubt want to save them to disk. You can click the Save button on the toolbar or choose File, Save to save a document using its current name. If you haven't saved the document before, the program displays the Save As dialog box, in which you enter the pathname and filename for the document. You don't have to include the file extension; the program does that for you.

In the Save As and Open dialog boxes is a toolbar that has some useful features (see Figure 2.8).

**tip**

You can save an existing document to a new file by choose File, Save As and specifying a new name.

For example, you can click the Create New Folder button to quickly create a new folder. You can use the Views drop-down list box to choose the type of view you want for a folder. The Tools menu offers several related commands that are discussed elsewhere in the book where appropriate.

**FIGURE 2.8**

You can use the toolbar in the Open and Save As dialog boxes to access additional tools and features.

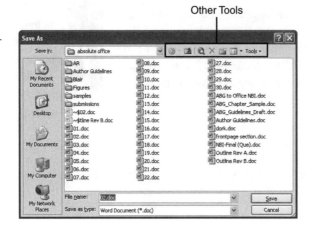

Most Office programs give you the ability to save a document using more than one format. For example, you can save a Word document as a DOC file or as an HTML file (that is, Web page), Extensible Markup Language (XML) document, text-only file, and so on. You can use the Save As Type drop-down list box to choose the desired format. The options you see in this drop-down list box vary from one Office program to another.

# Using Handy Mouse and Keyboard Tips

I've been using computers since the early 1980s, and because I type all day long, I can type pretty fast. So, it's easier for me to use the keyboard for several tasks than it is to use the mouse. This section discusses some of the keyboard shortcuts you might find handy, and then it explains some mouse tips that can save you time.

First, you can press Ctrl+O to display the Open dialog box to open a file. Ctrl+P opens the Print dialog box that you use to print a document.

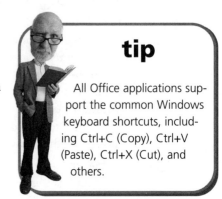

**tip**

All Office applications support the common Windows keyboard shortcuts, including Ctrl+C (Copy), Ctrl+V (Paste), Ctrl+X (Cut), and others.

Each Office program has preassigned *shortcut keys* that make the program perform specific actions. For example, in Word Ctrl+N starts a new, blank document. Ctrl+R right-justifies the current paragraph. Ctrl+Alt+left arrow promotes an outline heading, and Ctrl+Alt+right arrow demotes an outline heading.

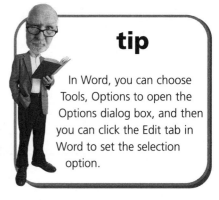

**tip**

In Word, you can choose Tools, Options to open the Options dialog box, and then you can click the Edit tab in Word to set the selection option.

To learn about shortcut keys for a particular program, you can search the program's Help document by using the keyword *shortcut keys*.

I also have a few mouse tips for you. First, you can often right-click in an Office program to bring up a context menu that lets you access certain common tasks. In Word, for example, the context menu that appears when you right-click lets you choose font or paragraph formatting, look up synonyms, and more.

In Word, the option When Selecting, Automatically Select Entire Word causes Word to select the whole word when you highlight just a portion of it. You can also move the mouse to the left of a paragraph until the pointer changes to a right-facing arrow if you want to select an entire line.

You'll learn other mouse shortcuts as you become more familiar with each Office program. You should experiment with the mouse to learn more.

# Undoing Changes

Unless you're the kind of person who doesn't have erasers on your pencils, sooner or later you're going to say, "Whoops! I didn't want to do that!" Maybe you accidentally deleted a whole paragraph, cut an image you didn't want to cut, or simply changed your mind about an edit. No problem! Office lets you undo changes to your heart's content.

**note**

If you can't undo the last edit, or if there are not any edits to undo, the command changes to Can't Undo.

You can find an Undo command in each Office application's Edit menu. In some cases the command is slightly different, such as Undo Typing. In any case, choosing Edit, Undo undoes the last edit that you made to the document. You can also press Ctrl+Z to undo changes; Ctrl+Z is the shortcut key for Edit, Undo.

In most cases the Office application keeps track of multiple edits, and you can undo more than once. For example, let's say you open a document in Word and make several edits to it. You then decide you want to undo most, but not all, of them. You can repeatedly press Ctrl+Z to undo the changes until you get the document back where you need it.

You can also find a Redo command in the Edit menu of each Office application. Redo is the reverse of Undo. For example, let's say you make some changes to a paragraph in Word and then you press Ctrl+Z to undo the changes. You decide you want to put the paragraph back the way it was, so you choose Edit, Redo or press Ctrl+Y to restore the change. Think of it this way: Ctrl+Z moves backward through a list of edits, and Ctrl+Y moves forward through them.

> **tip**
>
> You can usually undo even after you save a document. For example, you might make some changes, save the document, and then use Ctrl+Z or the Undo command to undo a number of changes that you made before saving. The copy on disk keeps the changes until you resave the document.

# Saving Office Settings

At first you probably won't spend a lot of time changing settings in Office applications, but over time you'll certainly customize them to suit your needs and preferences. If your computer crashes and you need to reinstall your operating system and applications, you'll lose your customized settings. And if you move to a new computer, you'll probably want your existing Office application settings to move to the new computer, as well.

There are some ways to manually move Office application settings between computers or save and restore them, but I prefer to take the easy route. The Save Your Settings Wizard that is included with the *Office Resource Kit* takes a snapshot of the settings on a computer and saves them to a file. You can then run the wizard again to import the settings after you restore the computer following a crash, or you can run the wizard to import the settings to a new computer.

For more information about the *Office Resource Kit*, point your browser to www. microsoft.com/office. Click Technical Resources and choose Resource Kits. You can find the *Office Resource Kit*, as well as additional resource kits with handy tools and add-ons, on the resulting page.

# THE ABSOLUTE MINIMUM

Installing Microsoft Office is easy, thanks to the simple wizard provided by Setup. After you have Office installed, you can start each of the Office programs from the Start menu or simply double-click an Office document to open the document with its program. You can also create shortcuts on the desktop or in other folders for quick access to the Office programs you use often.

This chapter explains how to create new Office documents, open existing ones, and save them. You have also learned some useful mouse and keyboard tips to help you save time working with each program, what to do when an Office program crashes, and how to configure a handful of common Office settings.

Before you jump into Office, you should take the time to read Chapter 3, "Help!" which explains how you can get help in each Office application when you need it.

# 3

# HELP!

Chapters 1, "A Quick Tour of Office," and 2, "Office Basics," provide a quick tour of Office's features and offer a brief look at how to perform some basic tasks in the individual Office applications. Now you're probably ready to dive in and start learning and using each of the applications.

As you get a bit deeper into Office, it's a sure bet that sooner or later you will need some help with a feature or experience a problem with one of the Office applications.

This chapter explains how to use the Help features that are built into Office and Windows. They also explain where to find additional information about Office, how to update it, and how to recover from a crash if (more likely, *when*) it occurs.

# Getting Quick Help

Microsoft has built a large Help content base for Office applications over the years. Microsoft has also simplified the content to a degree, which is both good and bad. It's good in that inexperienced users can often find quick answers to simple questions, but it's bad in the sense that some of the higher-level content has been eliminated. Office 2003 applications merge this lower-level content with additional content on the Internet to provide a more balanced approach. The following sections describe the ways you can quickly get help in an Office application.

## Clicking the Question Mark

You can find quick help for commands and options with relative ease. In a dialog box, for example, you can click the Help button (the question mark button, which is beside the dialog box's Close button) to view information about the options in the dialog box. When you click this button, the application opens the Help window for the application and displays the Help information for that dialog box (see Figure 3.1).

**FIGURE 3.1**

The Help window shows information about the selected dialog box.

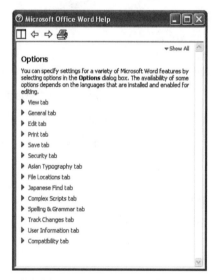

## Searching for Specific Topics

Besides clicking the Help button, another way to get quick help about a command or feature is to enter a search keyword or phrase in the Type a Question for Help search text box, which appears at the right edge of the application's menu bar (see Figure 3.2).

Search box

**FIGURE 3.2**

You can click in the Type a Question for Help search text box, type a question, and press Enter to get help.

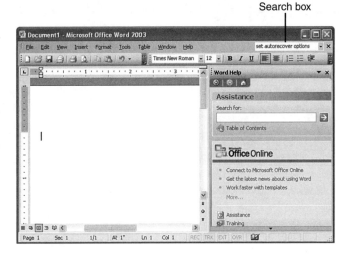

You type a keyword or phrase in the text box and press Enter. If the application determines that you are connected to the Internet, the application searches the Microsoft Web site for Help information, as shown in Figure 3.3.

**FIGURE 3.3**

Word searches the Microsoft Web site for more information.

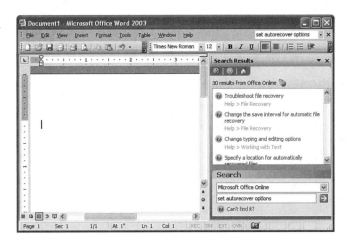

If the computer is not connected to the Internet, the application searches its local Help documentation for topics that meet the search conditions, as shown in Figure 3.4.

To view a Help topic, you just click the topic link. The application then displays the Help information in a Help window (see Figure 3.5).

**FIGURE 3.4**

An application can display Help information from its local Help content.

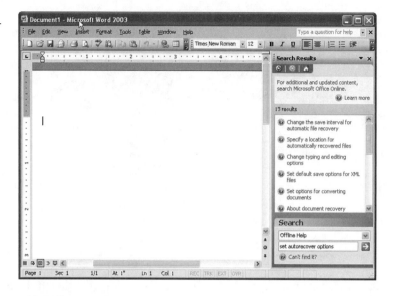

**FIGURE 3.5**

The application displays Help information in a Help window.

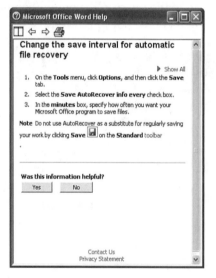

# Pressing the F1 Key

Pressing the F1 key on the keyboard is another option for obtaining quick help. When you press F1, the Office application provides help. The Help content the application provides depends on the application and what you are doing in the application when you press F1. For example, the application might open an Assistance pane, as shown in Figure 3.6.

**FIGURE 3.6**

The Assistance
pane provides
links to various
types of Help
content and
other resources.

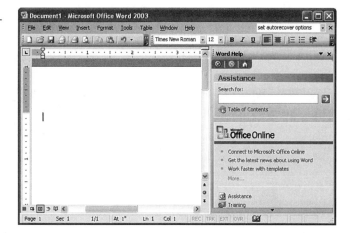

In many cases, the application opens context-sensitive Help content. *Context-sensitive Help* is tied to the context of what you're doing in the application at the moment. For example, you can choose Format, Paragraph in Word to open the Paragraph dialog box. When you press F1 with this dialog box open, Word displays Help content for formatting paragraphs (see Figure 3.7).

**FIGURE 3.7**

Word can dis-
play context-
sensitive Help for
formatting para-
graphs.

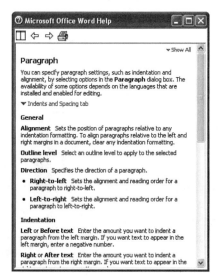

## Using the Help Menu

You can use the Help menu in an application to get help in the application. The Help menu provides the same basic Help content that you can access by pressing F1, and it also provides links to the Microsoft Web site and other resources. It also provides options for detecting and repairing problems with the application, an option to check for application updates on Microsoft's Web site, and an option to activate the application.

The About command on the Help menu doesn't offer help for the application itself, but it does provide access to related information (see Figure 3.8).

**FIGURE 3.8**

The About dialog box for an application displays the version and other information.

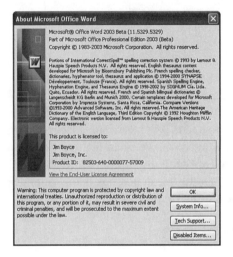

You can view the application version on the About dialog box. If you call Microsoft for help with an application, in many cases the technicians want to know what version of an application you are using and whether any service packs or other updates are installed. You can find this information in the About dialog box.

You can click System Info on the About dialog box to view information about the computer's configuration, Office application settings, and other information, as shown in Figure 3.9. Support technicians sometimes have you open the system information to check settings or computer configuration.

When you need to call Microsoft for help, you don't need to rummage in your closet or desk drawer for the phone number. You can just click Tech Support on the About dialog box to open the Help pane and display product support information, including links to the Microsoft Web site and support options.

**note**

The About dialog box also includes a Disabled Items button. If the application experienced a problem and started in Safe mode, you can click Disabled Items to view the application features and add-ins that are disabled in Safe mode.

**FIGURE 3.9**

You can use the System Information window to get information about the application and the system in general.

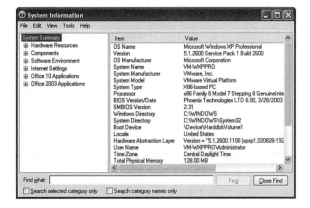

# Meeting (and Changing) the Office Assistant

In this and the previous version of Office, Microsoft publicly stated its intention to cut out the Office Assistant, an animated Help feature that has been in the product for quite some time. However, the Office Assistant is alive and well in Office 2003. The default character, Clippit, is an animated paper clip (see Figure 3.10).

**FIGURE 3.10**

You can ask questions of the Office Assistant.

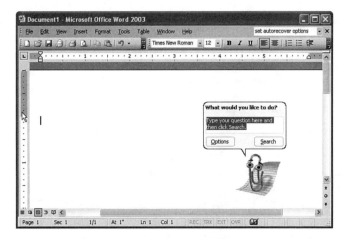

The Office Assistant can display alert messages and serve as the means by which you submit questions about program features. The Office Assistant can also offer tips about a range of topics and offer help using the various wizards in Office programs.

The Office Assistant is hidden by default in a typical installation of Office 2003. To view the Office Assistant, you choose Help, Show the Office Assistant. Setup installs the Office Assistant if it is not already installed.

To use the Office Assistant to query the Help documentation, you just double-click the Office Assistant and enter a word or phrase in the resulting dialog box, as shown in Figure 3.10.

Some people really like the Office Assistant, and others can't stand it. However you feel, the Office Assistant can be a helpful tool, particularly when you are just learning to use Office.

To configure options for the Office Assistant or choose an assistant other than Clippit, you can display the Office Assistant by choosing Help, Show the Office Assistant. Then you right-click the Office Assistant and choose Options to display the Office Assistant dialog box (see Figure 3.11).

**note**

This is a bit trivial, but Office refers to the character as Clippit, but Microsoft's Web site refers to him as Clippy. If you need a few minutes of distraction, point your Web browser to www. microsoft.com/office/clippy.

**FIGURE 3.11**

You use the Options tab of the Office Assistant dialog box to configure Office Assistant options.

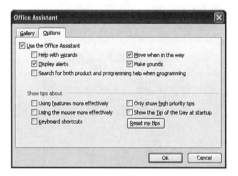

The Options tab of the Office Assistant dialog box, which is shown in Figure 3.11, enables you to specify what actions the Office Assistant will perform and what types of information it will offer.

You can click the Gallery tab (see Figure 3.12) to view the other characters you can choose as the Office Assistant.

If you want to turn off the Office Assistant temporarily and use the other Help features

**tip**

For a bit more diversion, you can right-click the Office Assistant and choose Animate to put the Assistant through its paces. If you do this several times, the animation changes each time.

instead, you right-click the Office Assistant and choose Hide. To turn it off altogether, you right-click it and choose Options. On the Options tab, you clear the Use the Office Assistant option and click OK.

**FIGURE 3.12**

You can choose a different Office Assistant character if you want.

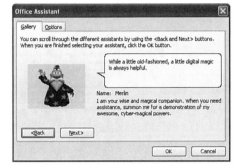

# Working with Help Documents

When you open general Help, the application opens the Assistance pane, which looks as shown in Figure 3.13.

**FIGURE 3.13**

You can use the Assistance pane to search for help on specific topics.

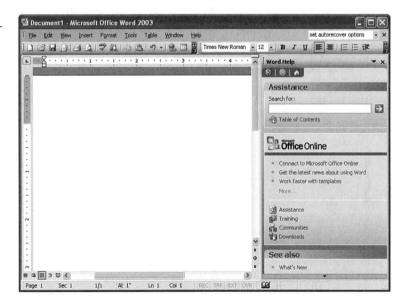

You can click in the text box, type a search word or phrase, and click the Go button to search for help on the specified feature or topic. You can also click the Table of Contents link to open Help's table of contents, as shown in Figure 3.14.

**FIGURE 3.14**

You can use the table of contents to browse the Help system.

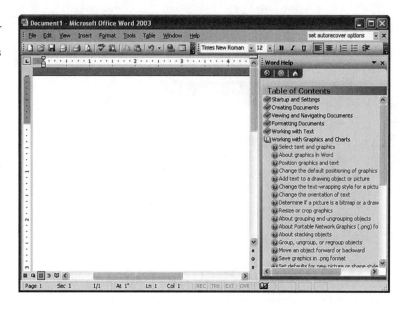

The table of contents is expandable and collapsible, enabling you to browse through the Help content to locate specific topics. You can click a topic to open a separate window in which to view the topic, as shown in Figure 3.15.

**FIGURE 3.15**

Help displays a topic in a separate window.

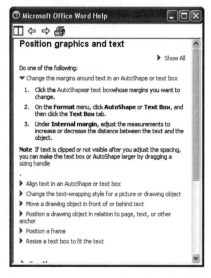

# Updating Office

Microsoft occasionally publishes updates to Office applications to fix bugs or, less often, add features. If you work in a large organization, your network administrators might install these updates to your computer automatically. Whether you use Office at home or in a Fortune 500 company, you can download and install updates yourself.

One way to search for updates for Office is to choose Help, Check for Updates. Your Web browser opens at the Microsoft Office Web site on the Downloads page, which provides a link to help you quickly locate updates and add-ons.

You can also open a Web browser, enter the URL `http://office.microsoft.com`, and then click the Product Updates link in the navigation bar at the left.

# Getting More Help on the Web

Several Web sites are devoted to Microsoft Office. I've already mentioned the Office site at `http://office.microsoft.com`, which provides direct access to lots of resources for Microsoft Office.

If you need to research a problem you're having or want more information about a particular feature, you can search Microsoft's Product Support Services site for more information. In this case, you point your Web browser to `http://support.microsoft.com`. The Support site includes a Product Support Centers section that offers links to support areas for specific applications, including Office. For a more general approach, you can click the Search the Knowledge Base link, which opens a Search the Knowledge Base page (see Figure 3.16). You can use this page to perform keyword searches for specific applications and operating systems.

Another site to which I am partial is The Office Letter. I regularly contribute to the tips section of the site. You can find the site at `www.officeletter.com` (see Figure 3.17).

For broader searches on other technology issues, and to find more information about using Microsoft Office, you can check out the sites `www.informit.com` and `www.techrepublic.com`. Each of these sites offers an excellent range of information on a variety of operating systems and applications, including Office.

**tip**

For tips on using Windows and links to other books on a variety of topics, see my Web site, at `www.boyce.us`.

**FIGURE 3.16**

You can search Microsoft's Knowledge Base for technical information about Office and its individual applications.

**FIGURE 3.17**

You can look for helpful Office tips on the Web site The Office Letter.

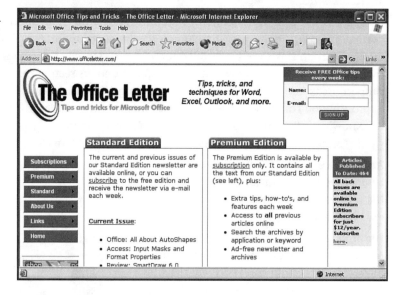

# What to Do When Office Crashes

Office applications are relatively stable, but sooner or later, one will crash while you are using it. When an application crashes, it generally locks up and becomes unresponsive. You can click the application all you want, but it remains frozen.

You can use the Microsoft Office Application Recovery tool, shown in Figure 3.18, to make sure your work is saved in the event that the Office application you are working in hangs. In Office 2003 you use Application Recovery instead of the old method of ending processes from the Windows Task Manager.

**FIGURE 3.18**

Application Recovery enables you to close a hung Office application without losing your work.

To use Application Recovery, you select the hung application from the list of running Office applications and click either Recover Application or End Application. Clicking Recover Application forces the hung application to close, at which point you can choose to send a report to Microsoft about the crash. Application Recovery then automatically recovers the document you were working on and opens it in the application again. Clicking End Application button simply forces the hung application to close. In either case, Application Recovery closes automatically when it's done.

What happens to your data when an application crashes depends in part on the application and in part on how the application is configured. For example, Access saves most changes as you make them, so you are not likely to lose any data if Access hangs. Outlook is similar, in that changes typically take place immediately, so there is little chance of data loss if Outlook hangs.

Word, Excel, applications and PowerPoint include an AutoRecover feature that by default saves recovery information every 10 minutes. When the application restarts after a hang, it displays an AutoRecover pane that enables you to select the document to recover. The most you lose is the work done on the document since the last AutoRecover save. You can configure the AutoRecover period on the Save tab of the application's Options dialog box (which you open by choosing Tools, Options).

In many cases, a hung Office application will restart in Safe mode, which disables certain features that could have caused the application to hang and enables the application to start. The application prompts you to verify that you want it to open in Safe mode; you click Yes to do so or No to open the application normally.

If you are unable to open an application or if it crashes repeatedly, you can open the application in Safe mode and repair it. When you do this, any missing or corrupted application files are replaced:

1. Hold down the Ctrl key when you start the application to start it in Safe mode.

2. Choose Help, Detect and Repair to open the Detect and Repair dialog box (see Figure 3.19).

3. Click Start to start the repair process.

**FIGURE 3.19**

You can choose options for repairing an application.

# THE ABSOLUTE MINIMUM

All the Microsoft Office applications provide a consistent Help interface that gives you information about each program feature and how to accomplish specific tasks. In almost every case, Help is just a key away—you can just press F1 to open Help.

This chapter lists other sources of information to help you learn to use Office effectively and what to do when an Office application crashes so you don't lose your document.

Now that you have a good understanding of how to work in Office applications and get help when you need it, you're ready to dive right in. Chapter 4, "Keeping Track of People and Places by Using Contacts," introduces you to Microsoft Outlook, which you can use to manage email, contacts, a calendar, and more.

# PART

# CONTACTS, EMAIL, AND LOTS MORE WITH OUTLOOK

# 4

# KEEPING TRACK OF PEOPLE AND PLACES BY USING CONTACTS

One of the tasks for which you can use Outlook is to keep track of your *contacts*, the people—friends, co-workers, clients, and so on—whose address and other information you need to keep and use. You can include lots of information for each contact, including the mailing address, phone number, and email address. Outlook goes a lot further, however, enabling you to include such things as spouse's name, anniversary, birthday, and other information. Outlook 2003 even lets you include a photo with each contact.

Outlook makes it easy to accomplish certain tasks by using contacts. For example, you can easily send an email message or dial a contact's phone number by using the Contacts folder. You can use your contacts for a mail-merge, to send a letter to a selection of your contacts. To do this, you create one letter, and Outlook and Word take care of customizing the address, salutation, and other items automatically for each printed copy.

This chapter explains how to add contacts to the Contacts folder, change the way you view contacts, and use contacts in common and useful ways.

# Adding People to Your Contacts Folder

You just click Contacts in the Navigation pane to open the Contacts folder. You can also choose Go, Contacts to get the same result. By default, the Contacts folder displays contacts by using the Address Cards view, as shown in Figure 4.1.

**FIGURE 4.1**

The Address Cards view shows name, address, and other basic contact information.

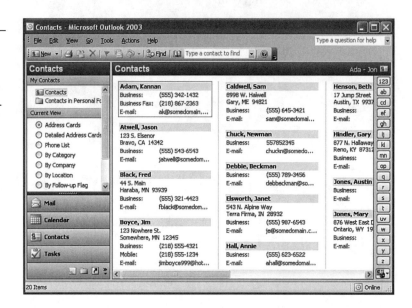

Now let's add some contacts. With the Contacts folder open, you click the New button on the toolbar. Outlook opens the Contact form shown in Figure 4.2.

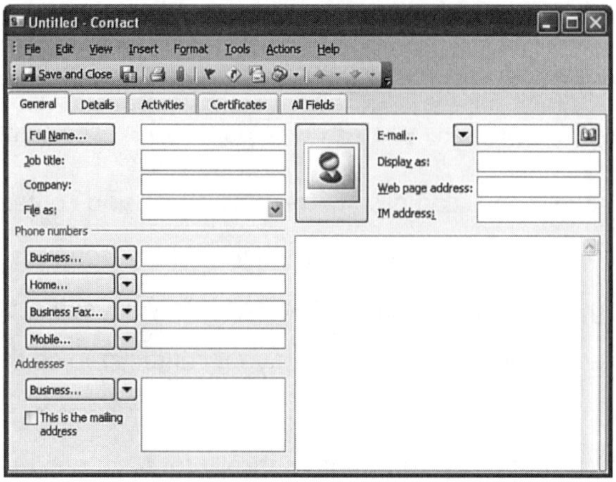

**FIGURE 4.2**

You can use the Contact form to create a new contact.

The Contact form's General tab includes fields for the contact's name, address, phone number, and other common fields. You can click in the Full Name field and enter the name, but I suggest that you click the Full Name button to open the Check Full Name dialog box, which has separate fields for first, middle, and last names, as well as fields for title and suffix. If you just enter the information in the text field on the General tab, Outlook tries to separate the information into fields for you. It often guesses right, but not always. To be safe, you should use the Check Full Name dialog box to add a name.

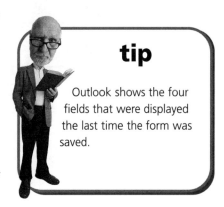

**tip**

You can modify an existing contact in almost the same way that you create a new one. You just open the Contacts folder and double-click a contact to open the Contact form, as described in this section.

Some of the fields on the Contact form—such as Web Page Address and IM Address—are just text fields without associated buttons. You can click in these fields and enter the appropriate text.

Other fields in the form have buttons beside them. The fields in the Phone Numbers group are a good example. Outlook actually supports 19 different phone number fields, but it displays only 4 phone numbers in the form. It provides 3 physical address fields and 3 email fields, but it shows only 1 of each.

You can click the arrow beside a field, as shown in Figure 4.3, to select the field in which you want to enter information. Then you click in the text box and type the information. You can click the arrow again to select a different field in which to add information.

The option This Is the Mailing Address, just below the Addresses fields, lets you specify which of the three address fields is the main mailing address for the contact. Outlook uses this address for mail-merge letters, automatically inserting the correct mailing address based on this option.

The Display As field on the Contacts form shows how the address will be listed in the To field of an email message. This field also appears as the Display Name field when you view the address book. You can click in the field to change the way the name is displayed.

**tip**

Outlook shows the four fields that were displayed the last time the form was saved.

⇨   See the section "Controlling How Outlook Saves and Displays Contact Names" in Chapter 8, "Outlook Settings to Change," to learn how to change the default Display As format.

Click here

Finally, you can use the notes field on the General page to add notes about the contact. You just click in the field and type any notes you like.

## Setting Other Contact Properties

The Details tab of the Contact form (see Figure 4.4) is where you add other information about a contact, such as his or her assistant's or manager's name, profession,
spouse's name, and so on.

**FIGURE 4.4**
You can use the
Details tab of
the Contact
form to add
extra informa-
tion about a
person.

Most of the fields on this tab are easy to figure out. You might not be familiar with these, however:

- **Directory Server**—This is the contact's NetMeeting directory server. NetMeeting is included with both Windows 2000 and Windows XP, but in Windows XP its functions are replaced by MSN Messenger. Microsoft no longer provides a NetMeeting server, but you can use this field to specify the address of a third-party NetMeeting server that the person uses to handle NetMeeting requests.

- **E-mail Alias**—You use this field to enter an email alias, which is usually the user's email account. NetMeeting uses the email alias to locate the user on the NetMeeting directory server.

- **Call Now**—You click this button to start a NetMeeting conversation with the contact.

- **Internet Free-Busy Address**—Outlook can publish schedule availability information (called *free/busy information*) to a Web site or a File Transfer Protocol (FTP) site. You enter the address of the user's free/busy server and page (or file) in this field.

> **tip**
>
> You can use the Microsoft Office Internet Free/Busy Service to publish your own free/busy information. In Outlook, you click Tools, Options, Calendar Options, Free/Busy Options to configure this service. If you are using group scheduling on Exchange Server, you don't need to publish your free/busy information— Exchange Server makes free/busy information for users on the Exchange Server available to other users. However, you can also publish your free/busy information to an external server to allow people who are not part of your Exchange Server organization see your free/busy times.

The Activities tab of the Contact form gives you a means to locate items associated with the selected contact.

➪   The Activities tab and other search methods are discussed in the section "Finding Email or Other Items Associated with a Contact," later in this chapter.

The Certificates tab of the Contact form lists the certificates Outlook should use to send encrypted email messages to the contact. You don't need to add a certificate specifically for a contact because Outlook uses your default certificate. You need to add one for a contact only if you need to use a different certificate for that particular contact.

You use the All Fields tab of the Contact form when you need to set or view properties that are not displayed on the other tabs.

## Saving a Contact

When you create a new contact or make changes to an existing contact, those changes are not saved automatically. To save the changes, you click Save and Close in the Contact form's toolbar. To close a contact without saving any changes, you click the Close button in the form's title bar and then click No when you're prompted to save the changes.

# Importing Addresses from Outlook Express

If you're moving from Outlook Express to Outlook, it's likely that you have at least some addresses in your Outlook Express address book that you want to add to your Contacts folder in Outlook. You can import the addresses into Outlook as contacts, and then you can modify the contacts to add other information that is not supported by the Outlook Express address book. Here's how you import addresses from Outlook Express into Outlook:

1. Open Outlook and select File, Import and Export. The Import and Export Wizard appears.

2. Choose Import Internet Mail and Addresses and then click Next. The Outlook Import Tool dialog box (see Figure 4.5) appears.

**FIGURE 4.5**

You can select Outlook Express from the Outlook Import Tool dialog box.

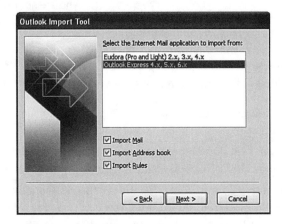

3. Select the Outlook Express option from the list of mail services.

4. If you want to import only addresses and not existing mail messages, clear the Import Mail check box. Clear the Import Rules check box if you don't want to import mail rules from Outlook Express. Then click Next.

5. The wizard prompts you to select one of the following options (see Figure 4.6):

- **Replace Duplicates with Items Imported**—When you select this option, existing contacts in Outlook will be replaced if they have the same information as those in Outlook Express.

- **Allow Duplicates to Be Created**—If you select this option, Outlook will create a new contact for each Outlook Express address, even if it duplicates an existing contact.

- **Do Not Import Duplicate Items**— If you select this option, Outlook will not import addresses that duplicate those already in the Contacts folder.

6. Click Finish.

**tip**

If you decide to import messages from Outlook Express, you should take the time to weed out old messages you don't need, including those in the Sent Items folder. You should also clear out the Deleted Items folder before you import messages. The fewer messages Outlook has to import, the quicker the process will be and the smaller the resulting set of Outlook personal folders will be.

**FIGURE 4.6**

You need to decide how Outlook should handle duplicate addresses.

# Viewing the Contacts Folder in Different Ways

By default, Outlook uses the Address Cards view, shown in Figure 4.1, to display the Contacts folder. The Address Cards view shows the name, email address, address, and phone numbers for the contact, but that might not be the information you really want to see. For example, maybe you need to see the Company, Job Title, or other fields.

Outlook gives you several ways to view the Contacts folder. To choose one, you can open the Contacts folder and choose View, Arrange By, Current View, and then select one of the predefined views. Figure 4.7 shows the Phone List view.

**FIGURE 4.7**

A customized Phone List view can show phone number fields.

Here's a list of the predefined Contact form views, with suggestions for how you might use them:

- **Address Cards**—This default view shows name, address, phone numbers, and email address.

- **Detailed Address Cards**—This view adds other fields to the Address Cards view, such as Job Title and Company. You should use this view when you need to see those extra fields.

- **Phone List**—This view shows the contact's name and phone numbers, along with a couple other fields. You should use this view when you need to quickly find a phone number or print a phone directory.

- **By Category**—You can use this view to organize contacts by their categories. For example, you might assign a category named Personal to nonbusiness contacts and a category named Business to business-related contacts. This view would help you quickly find all the personal addresses, for example.

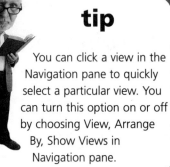

**tip**

You can click a view in the Navigation pane to quickly select a particular view. You can turn this option on or off by choosing View, Arrange By, Show Views in Navigation pane.

■ **By Company**—You can use this view to organize the Contacts folder by the company for which each contact works. This view organizes the view based on the Company field.

■ **By Location**—You can use this view to organize the Contacts folder by the contacts' countries or regions.

■ **By Follow-up Flag**—You can use this view to organize the Contacts folder according to whether the contacts are flagged for follow-up.

> **tip**
>
> Simplifying your Contacts folder view can go a long way toward helping you find contacts. You should create a custom view that shows only the name and one or two other useful fields (depending on how you use the contacts). If you don't use a field regularly, it probably doesn't need to be in your default view.

*Table views*, such as the Phone List and By Category views, display information in a table, with column headings at the top of each column. You can click a column heading to sort or organize the view based on that column. For example, you might click the Business Phone column in the Phone List view to sort the list by area code. Or you might click the State column in the By Location view to sort by state.

⇨   You have probably guessed that you can create your own views to suit your needs. That topic applies to all Outlook folders, so I don't cover it here. See the section "Creating Custom Views," in Chapter 8 for details.

# Finding a Contact

If you look at the Address Cards and Detailed Address Cards views of the Contacts folder, you'll see a navigation tab at the right edge of the view. You can click a letter on this tab to jump to the section of the folder that contains contacts that start with that letter.

You also have another way to locate contacts. You can click in the Find a Contact text box in the toolbar (see Figure 4.8), type some or all of the contact's name, and press Enter. If there is only one match, Outlook opens the contact's form. If there are multiple matches, Outlook displays the Choose Contact dialog box, from which you select a contact and click OK to open its form.

Find a Contact text box

**FIGURE 4.8**

You can use the Find a Contact text box to quickly locate a contact.

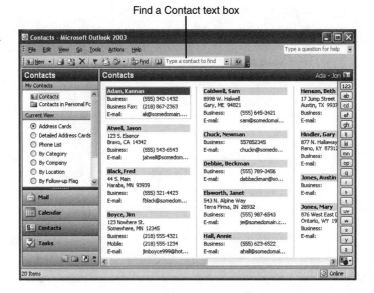

# Finding Email Messages and Other Items Associated with a Contact

Sooner or later you need to locate an email message or another item associated with a contact. You could search through the Inbox, for example, to locate messages you've received from a particular contact. Sometimes it's easier to do your searching from the Contacts folder, however. That's particularly true if you need to find more than one kind of Outlook item (such as messages and appointments) associated with a contact.

Here's how you search for multiple items for a contact:

1. Open Outlook and then open the Contacts folder.
2. Double-click the contact to open its form.
3. Click the Activities tab (see Figure 4.9). Outlook starts searching for all items associated with the contact and displays them in the list.
4. To search for a specific type of item, click Stop and then select an item type from the Show drop-down list box.
5. You can open an item of interest simply by double-clicking it.
6. Close the contact form when you're finished reviewing items.

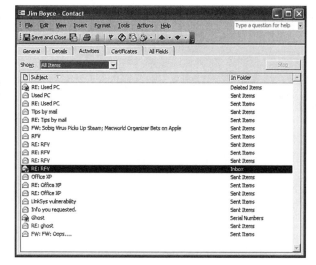

# Calling or Emailing a Contact

It's a good bet that you will frequently want to send email to and call your contacts. Outlook makes it easy to do both by providing quick access to those features from the Contacts folder.

## Sending Email to a Contact

When you need to send an email message to a contact, you click To (or Cc or Bcc) in the new message form and then select the contact from your Outlook Address Book. The Select Names dialog appears, and you can use it to quickly address the email message (see Figure 4.10).

You don't have to type the address manually. If you do start typing an email address that you've used before, however, Outlook automatically tries to complete the address for you. Outlook stores addresses in a *nickname cache* and checks the cache as you type to try to find a matching email address. If Outlook finds the correct match, you can simply press Tab to accept the address.

You can start a new message just as easily when you are working in the Contacts folder. To do so, you right-click a contact and choose New Message to Contact to open a message form that has the contact's address already filled in. Unfortunately, Outlook isn't very discriminating when it fills in the address. If the contact has more than one address, Outlook includes all of them in the address field. This can result in up to three copies of the message going to the person unless you delete the extra addresses.

**FIGURE 4.10**

You can use the Select Names dialog box to choose a contact when addressing an email message.

## Calling a Contact

You can have Outlook dial the phone number of a contact for you if you have a modem connected to your computer and it is on the same line as your phone. Or you could use a voice modem on a different line because voice modems include the capability to connect a headset and use the modem as a phone.

You need to make sure to add the phone number in the contact form and then right-click the contact and choose Call Contact to open the New Call dialog box (see Figure 4.11).

**FIGURE 4.11**

You use the New Call dialog box to start a phone call to a contact.

The contact's name appears in the Contact drop-down list box. You can choose a different contact from the list, if needed. If the phone number shown in the Number drop-down list box isn't the right one, you just select the correct number from the list. You click Start Call when you're ready to start the call.

You should select the Create New Journal Entry When Starting New Call check box on the New Call dialog box if you want to keep track of the call in your Journal folder (which is explained in Chapter 6, "Keeping Track of Appointments and Other Big [or Small] Events"). Outlook opens a new journal entry form and starts the timer when you click Start Call. You can add notes about the call and keep track of the time spent on it.

# Sorting and Organizing Contacts

The section "Viewing the Contacts Folder in Different Ways," earlier in this chapter, explains how to use the different predefined views for the Contacts folder. By using those views, you can organize your contacts and change the way Outlook displays them.

When you're using a table type view such as the Phone List view, for example, you can click a column head to change the sort order for contacts. You could click the Business Phone field to sort the list by area code, for example.

One of the most powerful tools for organizing the Contacts folder is *grouping*, which you can change when you customize a view. For example, you might want to organize a view by company, business phone number, department, or even mailing address. Whatever the case, it's easy to make the change. Here's what you do:

1. Open the Contacts folder and choose a view that shows the type of information you need.

2. Click Customize Current View in the Navigation pane or choose View, Arrange By, Current View, Customize Current View. Either action displays the Customize View dialog box (see Figure 4.12).

**FIGURE 4.12**

You can use the Customize View dialog box to change the way Outlook shows your contacts.

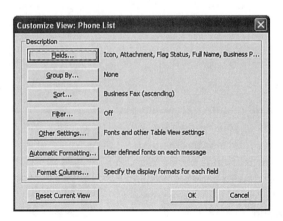

3. Click Group By to open the Group By dialog box (see Figure 4.13).

**FIGURE 4.13**

You can group
your contacts
by more than
one field.

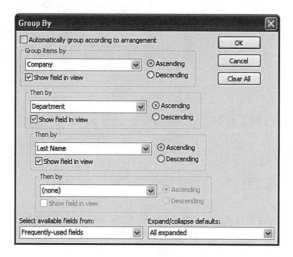

4. Clear the option Automatically Group According to Arrangement.

5. Select the first item by which to group the contacts from the Group Items By drop-down list box.

6. Select other grouping levels with the three other drop-down list boxes. For example, you might choose Company as the first field, Department as the second, and Last Name as the third.

7. Click OK and then click OK again to organize the view.

If you made the selection suggested in the example in step 6, Outlook would organize the contacts by company. Within each of those groups, contacts would be organized by department, and within each department they would be organized by their last name.

# Sharing Contacts

You might spend several months—or even years— accumulating contacts in your contact list. You can easily share your contacts with others who have accounts on your Exchange Server. You can also share your contacts with people who do not use your Exchange Server by exporting your contacts to a set of personal folders. The following sections describe how to do these things.

**tip**

You can reset a view back to its original settings after you change it. To do so, you open the Customize View dialog box and click Reset Current View.

## Sharing Contacts with Users of Your Exchange Server

Exchange Server creates a Global Address List that contains the addresses for all users in the Exchange Server site. Exchange Server administrators can also create external contacts and distribution lists, as well as custom address lists.

Addresses that you store in your Contacts folder reside in your mailbox and are not automatically available to other Outlook users, even if they have mailboxes on the same Exchange server as you. However, you can share your Contacts folder so others can view and optionally modify them. Here's how:

1. In Outlook, open the Contacts folder.

2. Right-click the Contacts folder where it appears under My Contacts in the Navigation pane and then choose Properties. The Contacts Properties dialog box appears.

3. Select the Permissions tab (see Figure 4.14).

**FIGURE 4.14**

You use the Permissions tab to enable others to see your contacts.

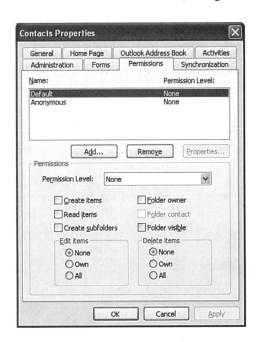

4. Click Add. The Add Users dialog box appears. Select a user from the Global Address List and click Add. Repeat this step to add others to the list and then click OK.

**tip**

You can also open the Contacts folder and then choose File, Properties to open the folder's Contacts Properties dialog box.

5. On the Permissions tab, select a user and then select a permission level from the Permission Level drop-down list box.

6. Review the list of permissions granted by the permission level and select one or more of the following options:

- **Create Items**—When this option is set, the selected user can create new contacts in the folder.

- **Read Items**—When this option is set, the selected user can read contacts in the folder.

- **Create Subfolders**—When this option is set, the selected user can create subfolders in your Contacts folder.

- **Folder Owner**—When this option is set, the selected user owns your Contacts folder.

- **Folder Contact**—When this option is set, the selected user is the designated contact for the folder.

- **Folder Visible**—When this option is set, the selected user can view the Contacts folder.

- **Edit Items**—This option sets the types of items the selected user can change.

- **Delete Items**—This option sets the types of items the selected user can delete from the Contacts folder.

7. When you have the permissions the way you need them for each user, click OK.

You don't automatically see another user's folder even if you have been given permission to view it. To open another user's Contacts folder, you choose File, Open, Other User's Folder. The Open Other User's Folder dialog box appears (see Figure 4.15).

**FIGURE 4.15**
You can choose the user whose Contacts folder you want to view.

You can either type the user's name in the Name text box or click Name and select the appropriate name from the Select Names dialog box. You then select Contacts from the Folder Type drop-down list box and click OK. Outlook opens the other user's Contacts folder in a separate window.

## Sharing Contacts from a Personal Folders File

You can share your Contacts folder with non–Exchange Server users by exporting the folder to a PST file, or Personal Folders file:

1. Open the Contacts folder and choose File, Import and Export.

2. Choose Export to a File and click Next.

3. Choose Personal Folder File (PST) and click Next.

4. Click Contacts in the folder list. If you have subfolders under your Contacts folder, select the Include Subfolders option. Then click Next.

5. Enter a filename for the PST file and click Finish.

6. Put the PST file on a shared network folder or send it to others by email, on disk, or via another medium.

> **tip**
>
> Only one person can use a PST file at one time. If you need to share a PST file with more than one other person, you should put the PST file in a shared network folder and have each other user copy the PST file to his or her Windows Briefcase. Then you need to have each other user open the PST file from the Briefcase. The users can update the shared copy of the PST file by synchronizing the Briefcase. If you're not familiar with the Briefcase, you can search Windows Help on the keyword *briefcase*.

To open a PST file in Outlook, choose File, Open, Outlook Data File. Select the PST file in the Open Outlook Data File dialog box and click OK.

# The Absolute Minimum

This chapter explores the Contacts folder and explains how to add and work with contacts, such as how to use contacts to send email or start a phone call. In this chapter you also learned how to sort and organize the Contacts folder with different views, locate messages from a specific contact, and share your contacts with others.

If you use Exchange Server, your contacts are stored in your Exchange Server mailbox. You can share your Contacts folder with others and set permissions on the folder to determine the tasks that others can perform within the folder.

One task you're likely to want to accomplish with Outlook is send and receive email. The following chapter will help you get started.

5

# ALL YOUR EMAIL IN ONE HANDY SPOT

Email isn't the only thing that Outlook can do, but it's certainly one of the most common uses most people have for Outlook. Outlook 2002 in Office XP included some new features that made Outlook a much better program for email, and Outlook 2003 expands on those features and adds some new ones to make it even better.

This chapter explains how to work with the Inbox, create other mail folders, and send and receive messages. It also explains how to use some of the more advanced features, such as filtering out all that dreaded junk mail, using the Bcc field for blind carbon copies, and processing messages automatically with rules. That's a lot to cover, so let's get on with it!

# A Quick Tour of the Inbox

The first time you run Outlook, a wizard steps you through the process of adding an email account, so at this point I assume you already have one set up. If you do not, you should see the section "Setting Up an Email Account," later in this chapter, and then come back here.

## Working in the Inbox

Learning about the Inbox is the first stop in learning about email in Outlook. Figure 5.1 shows the Inbox folder.

You can click the Mail button on the Navigation pane to show the Inbox folder. The folder pane shows the *message headers* for the messages in the Inbox folder. These headers show the subject, sender, and date of each message. By default, the headers are organized by date, but as you'll learn a bit later in this section, you can change the way Outlook organizes messages.

The right pane in the Inbox view is the *Reading pane*, called the *Preview pane* in previous versions. The Reading pane shows as much of the selected message as possible. You can use scrollbars to view the recipient list and the message body. You just click a message header to view its contents in the Reading pane.

**note**

The Navigation pane—the left pane in the Outlook window—is a common feature for all Outlook folders. You can move between Outlook folders and perform other common tasks by using the Navigation pane. See the section "Working with the Navigation Pane," in Chapter 2, "Office Basics," for details on using this Outlook feature. When you understand how the Navigation pane works, you'll be ready to start using the Inbox and other Outlook folders.

### Sorting Messages

The mail folders, including the Inbox, show certain message fields, including From, Subject, Received, and Size. By default, Outlook sorts messages based on the Received column, which helps you quickly find the newest messages. If you're looking for a message from a particular sender or with a specific subject, you can easily resort the view. You just click the column header of the field you want to use as the sort field. For example, you can click From to sort the message headers by sender.

**tip**

If you work with the Inbox most of the time, you might want to hide the Navigation pane in order to gain more room for headers and the Reading pane. You choose View, Navigation pane to turn on or off the Navigation pane.

Navigation pane          Message headers          Reading pane

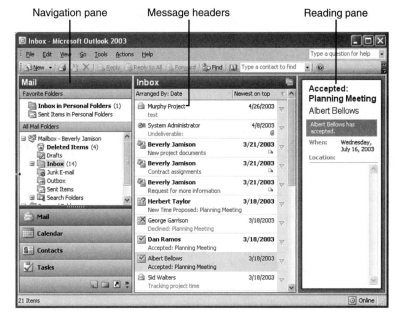

**FIGURE 5.1**

Outlook delivers
new email to the
Inbox.

As Figure 5.2 shows, the current sort field includes an up or down arrow beside the
column name. The arrow indicates ascending or descending sort order. You just click
a column header a second time to reverse the sort order.

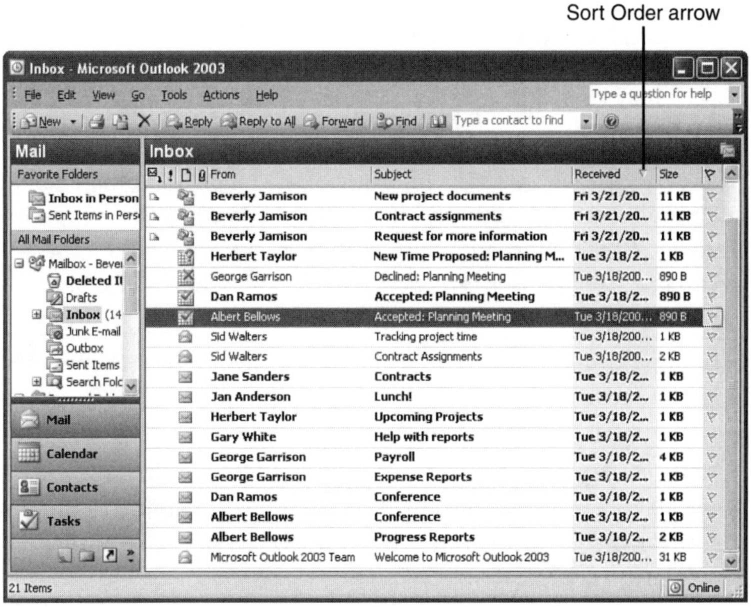

Sort Order arrow

**FIGURE 5.2**

You can click a
column header
to change the
sort field or sort
order.

## Moving or Hiding the Reading Pane

You can change the Reading pane's location or turn it off if you prefer to open each message to read it. For example, you can choose View, Reading pane, Bottom to move the Reading pane to the bottom of the window, as shown in Figure 5.3.

**FIGURE 5.3**

You can move the Reading pane to the bottom of the window.

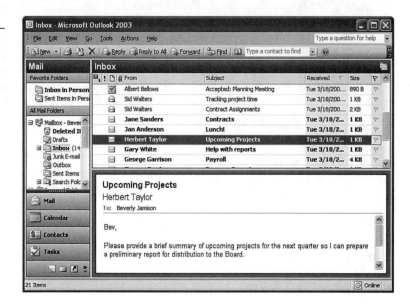

If you want to turn off the Reading pane, you choose View, Reading pane, Off.

## Working with Different Views

Outlook includes several predefined views that show the contents of each Outlook folder in different ways. The Inbox, for example, offers 13 different views. Using a different view lets you view information not shown in other views or organize the information in different ways. For example, let's say you have three email accounts, and all of them place messages in your Inbox. You can use the E-mail Account view to organize the messages by account. In this example, the Inbox would show three groups—one for each account.

Choosing a different view is easy. You just choose View, Arrange By and then select a view from the menu.

## Expanding and Collapsing Message Groups

Outlook groups message headers in the Inbox according to the current view. For example, if you use the Date view (the default Inbox view), Outlook groups messages as Today, Last Week, Older, and so on. If you are used to Outlook Express or a previous version of Outlook, you might want to turn off grouping. You choose View, Arrange By, Show in Groups to turn it on or off.

Outlook uses the current view, which specifies a particular sort field, to group headers. If you use the From view, for example, Outlook groups the headers based on the sender.

You can expand or collapse a particular group to either view more information or simplify the view. You click the plus or minus button beside a group name to expand or collapse it, respectively. Or you can choose View, Expand/Collapse Groups and then select the action you want from the menu (such as Collapse All).

**tip**

You can customize a view to add other fields or change the way the information appears. See the section "Creating Custom Views" in Chapter 8, "Outlook Settings to Change," for details. You can also add the views to the Navigation pane, which is handy if you change views often. You choose View, Arrange By, Show Views in Navigation pane to turn on or off this feature.

## Reading Messages

What good is the Inbox if you can't read your email messages with it? None, of course! Fortunately, Outlook makes it easy to read messages.

When you click a message header, Outlook shows the message in the Reading pane—at least, it shows as much of the message as it can. To read a message that doesn't fit in the Reading pane, or if you have the Reading pane turned off, you just double-click the message to open it in its own form (see Figure 5.4).

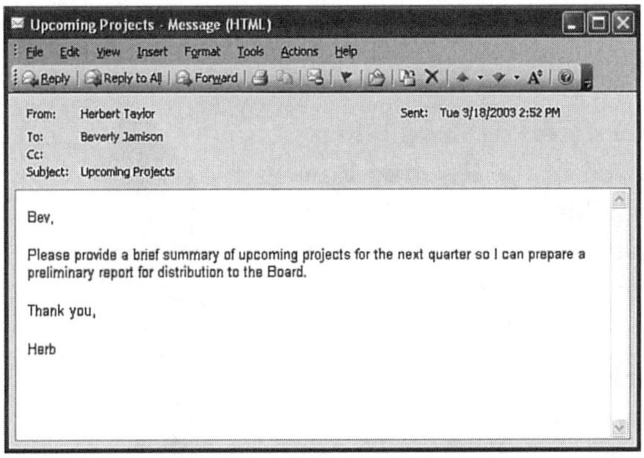

**FIGURE 5.4**

Outlook can show a message in its own form.

You can also use AutoPreview to view the first few lines of each message below its header (see Figure 5.5). AutoPreview just wastes space if you use the Reading pane, however. You choose View, AutoPreview to turn AutoPreview on or off.

**FIGURE 5.5**

AutoPreview shows the first few lines of each message.

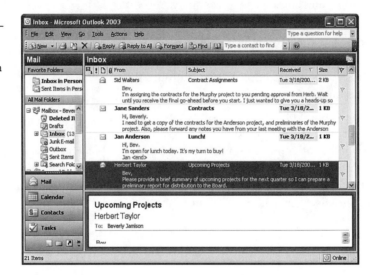

As you work with the Inbox, you'll soon discover that some headers appear in bold. Those are messages that haven't been read. When you double-click a message to open it, Outlook marks the message as read and removes the bold from the header. You can also have Outlook mark a message as read in a couple other ways. Follow these steps to set options that control these other ways:

1. Choose Tools, Options. The Options dialog box appears. Select the Other tab.

2. Click Reading Pane.

3. Set these options:

   ■ **Mark Items as Read When Viewed in the Reading Pane**—When this option is enabled, Outlook marks a message as read when you leave it selected for more than the specified number of seconds.

   ■ **Mark Item as Read When Selection Changes**—When this option is enabled, Outlook marks a message as read when you select another header.

**tip**

You can right-click a message header and choose either Mark as Unread or Mark as Read to change the message's read/unread status.

■ **Single Key Reading Using Spacebar**—When this option is enabled, you can press the spacebar to move from one message header to the next.

# Sending and Receiving Messages

Outlook makes it easy to send and receive messages. Let's take these tasks one at a time.

## Sending Messages

Sending a message is easy. In most cases, you just compose a message, add the address and subject, and click Send. Follow these steps to send a message:

1. Open Outlook and open the Inbox folder.

2. Click New on the toolbar or choose File, New, Mail Message.

3. Outlook opens a message form similar to the one shown in Figure 5.6 if you set up Outlook to use Word as the message editor. Outlook opens the form shown in Figure 5.7 if Outlook is the message editor.

**FIGURE 5.6**

Outlook can use Word as the message editor.

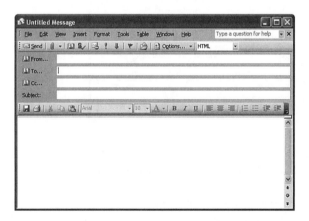

4. Click the To button to open the Select Names dialog box, which is shown in Figure 5.8.

5. Select a name and click To.

6. If you need to send a "carbon" copy of the message to another person, select the name and click Cc.

7. To send a blind carbon copy to another person, select the name and click Bcc.

8. Add any other names as needed and click OK.

**FIGURE 5.7**

Outlook includes its own form for editing messages.

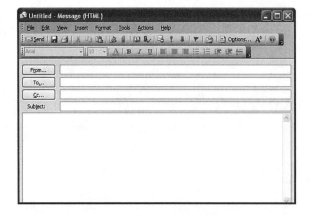

**FIGURE 5.8**

You select recipients from the Select Names dialog box.

9. Press Tab to get to the Subject field, or click in that field with the mouse. Type a short subject for the message.

10. Press Tab or click in the text area of the message. Type the message and then click Send.

Outlook places the message in your Outbox folder. Whether it sends the message right away

**tip**

You can click in the To, Cc, or Bcc field and then double-click a name to add it to that field.

depends on how Outlook is configured and whether it is currently connected to the server by a dial-up or network connection.

If Outlook doesn't deliver messages right away, you can click the Send/Receive button on the toolbar to send and receive for all accounts. Or you can choose Tools, Send/Receive and select an account from the menu if you want to process only one account.

⇨   See the section "Controlling When and How Outlook Checks Your Mail" in Chapter 8 to learn more how to control how Outlook processes mail accounts.

## Receiving Messages

Earlier in this chapter you learned about the Inbox and message headers. When you receive new messages, those messages appear in the Inbox, with bold headers to indicate that they haven't been read.

You can retrieve messages from all accounts or just from one account. In either case, Outlook always sends your outgoing messages when it checks an account for new messages.

To retrieve all messages, you click the Send/Receive button on the toolbar. You can also choose Tools, Send/Receive, Send/Receive All.

To retrieve messages from a specific account, you choose Tools, Send/Receive and select the account from the menu.

⇨   Outlook can check for new mail automatically at a time interval that you specify. See the section "Controlling When and How Outlook Checks Your Mail," in Chapter 8 to learn more.

# Working with Attachments

An *attachment* is a file that you attach to an email message. For example, maybe you want to send a digital picture file to family members or friends. You create a new message just as you would for a text-only message, and then you attach the file to it and send the message.

Here's how you attach a file to a message:

1. Open Outlook and start a new message, as explained in the section "Sending Messages," earlier in this chapter.

2. With the message form open, add the addresses, subject, and body text for the message.

3. Click the Insert File button (which shows a paper clip icon) on the toolbar. Or choose Insert, File. In either case, Outlook shows the Insert File dialog box (see Figure 5.9).

**FIGURE 5.9**

You can select a file from the Insert File dialog box.

4. Browse for and select the file you want to attach and then click Insert.

5. Outlook adds an attachment field, with the file listed in it, and it also adds an Attachment Options button and Attachment Options pane (see Figure 5.10).

**FIGURE 5.10**

You use the Attachment Options pane to perform special tasks on the attachment before sending.

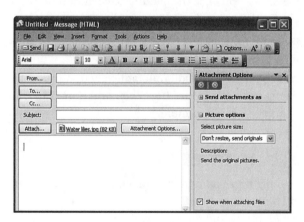

6. You can use the options in the Attachment Options pane to compress pictures, if you want. Compressing pictures makes the file size smaller but decreases the quality of the image.

7. Click Send to send the message.

You should check the file size of attachments before you send them to decide whether they should be compressed, either directly in Outlook or via a program such as WinZip (www.winzip.com). You should avoid sending large attachments to people who have dial-up connections because a large file takes a long time to download over a dial-up connection. Also, most mailboxes are limited to a certain capacity by the mail server administrator. Sending lots of large attachments to someone can quickly fill up his or her mailbox.

note

If you are using Word as your email editor, start the new message and click the arrow beside the Options button, then choose Bcc to display the Bcc field. If Outlook is your email editor, choose View, Bcc to display the Bcc field.

# Using Bcc and Other Message Options

Outlook doesn't show the Bcc field on its message form, but you can add it easily. With the message form open, you choose View, Bcc Field. People listed in the Bcc field receive the message, but their addresses are not seen by other recipients. You should use Bcc when you want to send a message to multiple recipients but you don't want them to know who else is receiving the message or you don't want them to see each others' addresses.

You can set several other options for a message before you send it. Because this is a beginner's guide, this book doesn't cover them in detail. However, I'll tell you where to find them so you can experiment on your own.

To set message options, you open the message form and click the Options button on the form's toolbar. You should see the Message Options dialog box shown in Figure 5.11.

Here's a quick rundown of what you'll find on the Message Options dialog box:

- **Importance**—You can choose from High, Normal, or Low importance. Outlook shows a different icon for each importance level, but the recipient's email program, if different from yours, might not make any distinction for importance.

- **Sensitivity**—You can choose from Personal, Private, or Confidential. As with Importance, the recipient's email program might not make any distinction between these sensitivity levels.

**FIGURE 5.11**

You can use the
Message
Options dialog
box to set sev-
eral options for
a message.

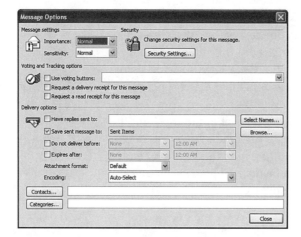

- **Security**—You can click the Security Settings button to add a digital signature or encrypt the message. You need to obtain a digital certificate from a security provider such as VeriSign before you can add a digital signature or encrypt messages.

- **Use Voting Buttons**—You can add voting buttons and vote choices to the message. This option is available only for Exchange Server accounts.

- **Request a Delivery Receipt for This Message**—You can request to receive a receipt (that is, a short message) when the message has been delivered.

- **Request a Read Receipt for This Message**—You can request to receive a receipt when the recipient reads the message.

- **Have Replies Sent To**—You can specify a different reply address from the one in your account settings. You use this option to redirect the reply to a different address.

- **Save Sent Message To**—You can save a copy of the message to the specified Outlook folder. By default, outgoing messages are stored in the Sent Items folder.

- **Do Not Deliver Before**—You can keep the message in the Outbox until the specified time arrives.

- **Expires After**—You can mark the message as unavailable when the specified time arrives.

- **Attachment Format**—You can choose the type of attachment encoding to use.

■ **Encoding**—You can specify language encoding.

■ **Contacts**—You can associate contacts with the message. This option does not attach contacts to the message.

■ **Categories**—You can associate categories with the message.

# Setting Up an Email Account

At some point you will need to add an email account to Outlook, whether it is the first time you run Outlook or because you have more than one account. Outlook supports four types of email accounts as well as additional server types:

■ **Microsoft Exchange Server**—You use this account type if you have an Exchange Server mailbox and want to take full advantage of your Exchange Server account's features, such as message recall and group scheduling.

■ **POP3**—This is perhaps the most common account type for business and home users (except those who use Hotmail or Yahoo!). With Post Office Protocol 3 (POP3), your mail stays on the server until you download it to your computer, and then it is deleted from the server.

■ **IMAP**—This type of account is growing in popularity because the mail stays on the server until you delete it. This makes it easy to access your mail from more than one computer without worrying about synchronizing different copies of your Inbox. IMAP stands for Internet Mail Access Protocol.

■ **HTTP**—Currently, Outlook includes only canned support for Hotmail and MSN. But there is nothing to prevent a Hypertext Transfer Protocol (HTTP) mail service from supporting Outlook. You should check with your mail provider to find out more about Outlook support.

■ **Additional Server Types**—This option enables you to add the Fax Mail Transport, which makes it possible for Outlook to send outgoing faxes. Outlook doesn't ship with built-in support for any other mail server types.

---

**WHICH TYPE OF EMAIL ACCOUNT IS RIGHT FOR YOU?**

With all these types of email accounts, which one should you use? Each has certain advantages. For example, even though you can access an Exchange Server mailbox by using POP3, IMAP, or even HTTP (through Outlook Web Access [OWA], which is built into Exchange Server), you won't be able to use all of Outlook's features when you do. For example, you can perform group scheduling, voting, and message recall only if you use the Exchange Server account type in Outlook.

POP3 is very common and is supported by almost every mail server. The main drawback of it is that the messages get copied to your local computer. If you don't access your mailbox from more than one computer, that's not a problem, and POP3 is the choice I recommend for non–Exchange Server accounts. If you need to read your mail from more than one computer, however, I recommend IMAP, which leaves the messages on the server, eliminating the problem of synchronizing multiple copies of your Inbox on different computers. Most POP3 mail servers also support IMAP.

If you have an Exchange Server account and want to use it from different computers, you should ask your system administrator whether OWA is installed and enabled on your server. OWA lets you get to your mailbox from a Web browser such as Internet Explorer. You can use most, but not all, Outlook features with OWA.

## Adding an Account

When you've decide what type of account you want to add, it's time to add it. Outlook includes a wizard that steps you through the process. Here's how you use it:

1. In Outlook, choose Tools, E-mail Accounts to open the E-mail Accounts Wizard.

2. Select Add a New E-mail Account in the wizard and click Next.

3. Choose the type of account to add (see Figure 5.12) and click Next.

**FIGURE 5.12**
You need to choose the type of account to add.

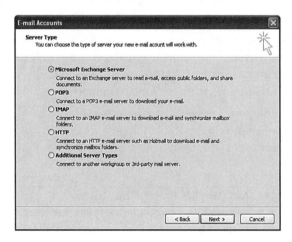

Outlook presents different options, depending on the type of account you've selected. The following sections describe the account-specific settings.

## Setting Up an Exchange Server Account

Outlook shows the Exchange Server Settings dialog box (see Figure 5.13) when you add an Exchange Server account. The dialog box includes the following settings:

- **Microsoft Exchange Server**—You enter the name or IP address of your Exchange server. You should check with your Exchange Server administrator if you're not sure of the server name.

- **User Name**—You enter the name of your mailbox on the server. Usually, this is your logon account name. You can click Check Name to make sure you have the right account. You should ask your system administrator what to enter if you're not sure.

- **Use Cached Exchange Mode**—You can select this option to have Outlook keep a copy of your mailbox on your local computer. Outlook then automatically synchronizes the local copy with the server copy. This is handy if you need to disconnect from the network (such when you take your notebook home) but still want to continue to use Outlook. Unless you don't have much space left on your hard disk, I recommend that you use this option.

**FIGURE 5.13**

You enter your account and server information in the Exchange Server Settings dialog box.

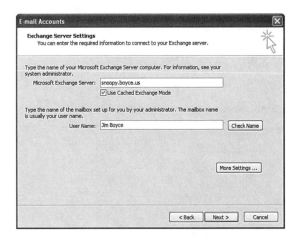

You can click More Settings to open a dialog box that contains several additional Outlook settings for an Exchange Server account. You can leave these settings as they are in most cases, so I don't discuss them here.

After you enter the server and account name, click Next and then click Finish to add the account.

## Setting Up a POP3 or IMAP Account

POP3 and IMAP accounts are very similar to one another as far as setup is concerned. You run the E-mail Accounts Wizard and choose either POP3 or IMAP, and then you click Next. Figure 5.14 shows the settings for a POP3 account. Figure 5.15 shows the settings for an IMAP account.

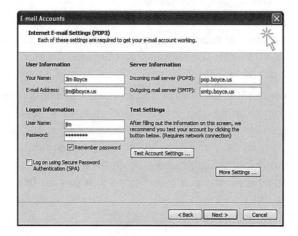

**FIGURE 5.14**

Outlook settings for a POP3 account include server, account name, and other information.

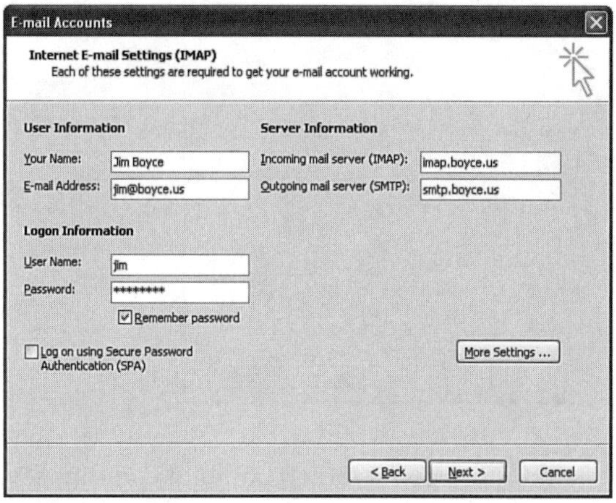

**FIGURE 5.15**

Outlook settings for an IMAP account are similar to those for a POP3 account.

You need to enter these settings for either type of account:

- **Your Name**—You enter your name as you want it to appear in the From field when others read messages you send to them.

- **E-mail Address**—You enter your email address in the form `mailbox@server`, where `mailbox` is your mailbox name and `server` is your mail server name. For example, my email address is `jim@boyce.us`.

- **Incoming Mail Server**—You enter the name or IP address of the server where your mailbox resides.

- **Outgoing Mail Server**—You enter the name or IP address of the server that accepts your outgoing messages. Often this is the same as the incoming mail server, but it might not be.

- **User Name**—You enter the name of your mailbox on the server. Usually this is the part of your email address that comes before the `@`.

- **Password**—You enter the password for your mailbox.

- **Remember Password**—You should enable this option if you want Outlook to automatically enter your password for you to receive mail. You should clear this option if you want Outlook to prompt you each time it connects to your mail server; this offers better security, and you should use it if you're concerned about other people checking your mail from your computer.

- **Log On Using Secure Password Authentication (SPA)**—You should enable this option if your mail server requires that Outlook use SPA to connect. Most servers do not. One exception is CompuServe Classic, which supports SPA. However, even with CompuServe Classic, you don't have to use SPA if you configure your account with a POP3-only password. In your CompuServe Classic software, you use the command `GO POPMAIL` to set your POP3 password.

- **Test Account Settings**—You can click this button with a POP3 account to check your settings. Outlook logs on to your POP3 server and sends a test message through your outgoing mail server. This helps you identify potential problems with your settings.

- **More Settings**—You can click this button to open a tabbed dialog box with additional settings for the account.

You can click More Settings to set other options for the account, but you shouldn't have to do so in most cases. If you do, the Internet E-mail Settings dialog box appears, and it contains the following tabs:

**tip**

If you use SPA with CompuServe Classic, you must also install CompuServe's Virtual Key software. See `www.compuserve.com/rpa/default.asp` for more information.

■ **General**—You can use this tab to change the account name as it appears in your profile or set a reply address if you want it to be different from the email address entered for the account (that is, you can redirect replies to outgoing mail to a different mailbox).

■ **Outgoing Server**—You can use this tab to configure settings if your outgoing mail server requires that you provide a username and password to send mail.

■ **Connection**—You can use this tab to specify how Outlook should connect to your mail server, whether over a dial-up or local area network (LAN) connection.

■ **Advanced**—You can use this tab to change server ports (which is rarely required), use Secure Sockets Layer (SSL), set server timeout for slow connections or busy servers, leave a copy of your POP3 messages on the server, or specify the root folder for an IMAP mailbox.

## Setting Up an HTTP Account

Outlook includes built-in support for HTTP-based Hotmail and MSN mail accounts, which is no surprise because Microsoft owns both of those services.

In the E-mail Accounts Wizard, select HTTP and click Next. Outlook displays the dialog box shown in Figure 5.16.

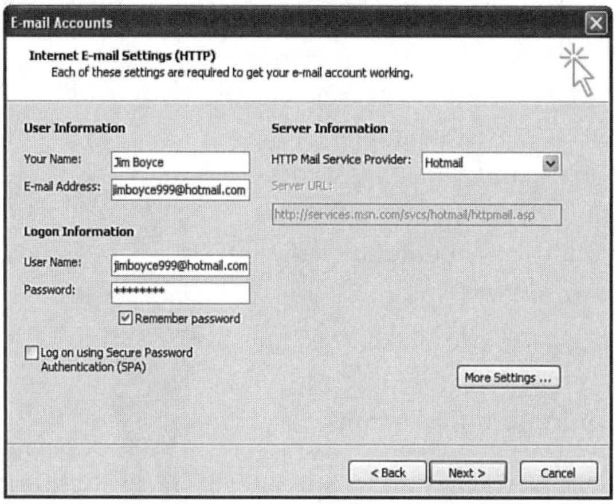

**FIGURE 5.16**

HTTP account setup is much like POP3 and IMAP account setup.

The settings you enter for an HTTP account are the same as those for a POP3 or IMAP account (explained in the previous section), with one main exception: You don't specify the incoming and outgoing mail servers. Instead, you select the mail service from the HTTP Mail Service Provider drop-down list box. Outlook automatically enters the correct URL for Hotmail or MSN.

If you find an HTTP service other than Hotmail or MSN that supports Outlook, you can select Other from the drop-down list box and then enter the complete URL for the mail server in the Server URL text box.

## Specifying Where Outlook Should Deliver New Messages

When you have more than one email account, you have some control over where Outlook delivers new messages. For example, if you have an Exchange Server account and a POP3 account, Outlook can deliver new messages to either your Exchange Server mailbox or to a set of personal folders (that is, a PST file). There is one exception: Each HTTP and IMAP account always has its own PST file, created automatically by Outlook when you add the account. Even if you specify an Exchange Server mailbox or a separate PST file as the destination for incoming mail, the HTTP and IMAP accounts deliver messages to their own PST files.

> **note**
>
> The Internet E-mail Settings dialog box for HTTP accounts, which appears when you click More Settings, includes only the General and Connection tabs discussed earlier in this chapter, in the section "Setting Up a POP3 or IMAP Account."

You follow these steps to set the incoming mailbox location:

1. In Outlook choose Tools, E-mail Accounts to start the E-mail Accounts Wizard.
2. Select View or Change Existing E-mail Accounts and click Next.
3. Choose a destination for new mail by using the Deliver New E-mail to the Following Location drop-down list box. When you're done, click Finish.

➪   You can store Outlook settings in more than one profile. See the section "Adding or Changing an Outlook Profile," later in this chapter, for details on changing the incoming mail location for a profile.

# Adding More Sets of Folders

Outlook can store messages and other Outlook items (appointments, tasks, and so on) in one of two places: an Exchange Server mailbox or a Personal Folders (PST) file. Outlook adds a PST file for you automatically if you add an account that requires one.

In some situations, you might want to add another PST file. For example, you might create a PST file to store old messages that you don't want to delete but don't want in your Inbox, either.

You follow these steps to add a PST file to a profile:

1. Close Outlook and open the Mail applet from the Windows Control Panel.

2. Click Show Profiles.

3. Select the profile in which you want to add or change data files and then click Properties.

4. Click Data Files. The Outlook Data Files dialog box appears (see Figure 5.17).

**FIGURE 5.17**

You can change data file settings by using the Outlook Data Files dialog box.

5. Click Add. The New Outlook Data File dialog box appears.

6. Choose the type of PST file to create. Choose Microsoft Outlook Personal Folders File if you don't use a version of Outlook prior to 2003. Choose Microsoft Outlook 97–2002 Personal Folders File if you need to use the PST with an older version of Outlook.

7. Click OK. Specify a name and location for the new PST file and click OK. Outlook opens the Create Microsoft Personal Folders dialog box (see Figure 5.18).

8. Choose the following settings for the options in this dialog box:

   ■ **Name**—This is the name that will appear in the folder list in Outlook. You should use a descriptive name, such as Backup Folders, that will help you identify the PST file's purpose.

   ■ **Encryption Setting**—You can encrypt a PST file for better security. When you select the Best Encryption option, Outlook does not compress the PST file to save space.

■ **Password**—You can protect a PST file with a password, which can prevent others from opening the PST file from their own computers.

When you're done making selections, click OK.

**FIGURE 5.18**

You can add a
PST file by using
the Create
Microsoft
Personal Folders
dialog box.

**Create Microsoft Personal Folders** ☒

| | |
|---|---|
| File: | C:\Documents and Settings\bjamison\Local S |
| Name: | Personal Folders |
| Format: | Personal Folders File |

Encryption Setting

○ No Encryption
◉ Compressible Encryption
○ High Encryption

Password

Password: [          ]
Verify Password: [          ]

☐ Save this password in your password list

[ OK ]   [ Cancel ]

9. Click Close, click Close again, and click OK to close all the remaining dialog boxes.

## Changing Account Settings

Hopefully, when you added a new account, you got the settings right and will never have to change them. But if you did make mistakes or need to change settings for some other reason, it's easy enough to make changes:

1. In Outlook, choose Tools, E-mail Accounts to start the E-mail Accounts Wizard.

2. Select View or Change Existing E-mail Accounts and click Next.

3. Select a mail account and click Change. Outlook opens the E-mail Accounts dialog box you used to set up the account (covered in previous sections).

4. Click Finish to save the changes.

**tip**

If you have an existing PST file, you don't have to add it to a profile before you can use it. To open an existing PST file, in Outlook, you choose File, Open, Outlook Data File. Then you select the PST file and click OK. To close the PST file and remove it from the folder list, you right-click the PST file's branch in the folder list and choose Close <name>, where <name> is the name assigned to the PST file.

# Adding or Changing an Outlook Profile

Outlook stores mail accounts and related settings in an Outlook *profile*. Outlook uses only one profile at a time. You can change a profile by adding multiple email accounts to it, which means that you can access all your accounts at one time.

In some cases you might want to use more than one profile. For example, maybe you want to separate your business mail from your personal mail. Or maybe you need to connect to two different Exchange Servers (Outlook supports only one per profile).

## Adding a Profile

Here's how you add a profile in Outlook:

1. Open the Mail applet from the Windows Control Panel.

2. Click Show Profiles in the Mail Setup dialog box to open the Mail dialog box shown in Figure 5.19.

3. Click Add, enter a name for the profile, and click OK. Outlook starts the E-mail Accounts Wizard, which enables you to add accounts to the new profile.

**FIGURE 5.19**

You can use the Mail dialog box to set up mail accounts, data files, and profiles.

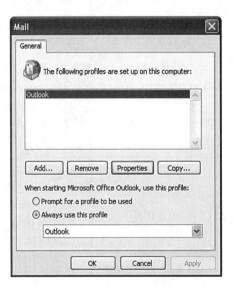

## Changing Settings in a Profile

When you choose Tools, E-mail Accounts in Outlook, you can modify the default profile. You need to use the Mail applet in the Control Panel to add or change settings in a profile other than the default profile:

1. Open the Mail applet from the Windows Control Panel.
2. Click Show Profiles in the Mail Setup dialog box to open the Mail dialog box.
3. Click a profile and click Properties.
4. Click E-mail Accounts to add or change an email account, or click Data Files to add or change a data file (PST file).

⇨   See the section "Adding an Account," earlier in this chapter, to learn how to add an email account. See the section "Adding More Sets of Folders," earlier in this chapter, to learn how to manage data files.

## Switching Between Profiles

Outlook can use only one profile at a time. If you have more than one profile, you need to either configure Outlook to prompt you for a profile each time Outlook starts or manually change the profile.

You follow these steps to set the profile that Outlook uses by default:

1. Close Outlook and open the Mail applet from the Windows Control Panel.
2. Click Show Profiles to open the Mail dialog box.
3. From the drop-down list below the Always Use This Profile option, select the profile you want to use by default.
4. Choose one of the following options:

   - **Prompt for a Profile to Be Used**—When you select this option, Outlook prompts you at startup to choose a profile. Outlook automatically selects the profile you specify in step 3, but you can select a different one from the list at startup.

   - **Always Use This Profile**—When you select this option, Outlook uses the profile specified in the drop-down list.

5. Click OK and then restart Outlook.

# Deleting, Archiving, and Recovering Messages

Your mail folders would quickly fill up if you never deleted any messages. Sometimes you want to throw away a message; other times you want to move it out of the Inbox but keep it in case you need it again. This section covers both situations.

## Deleting a Message

Deleting a message is easy. You just click the message header in the Inbox or other mail folder and click the Delete button on the toolbar or press Delete on the keyboard. Outlook moves the message to your Deleted Items folder.

Outlook does not empty the Deleted Items folder automatically. Deleted messages continue to pile up in the Deleted Items folder until you empty the folder. Here are a few ways to get rid of the messages there permanently:

- Right-click the Deleted Items folder in the folder list and choose Empty Deleted Items Folder.

- Open the Deleted Items folder (by clicking it in the folder list) and then select one or more messages and click the Delete button or press Delete on the keyboard. Outlook asks if you really want to delete the messages. Select Yes if you do.

- Choose Tools, Options and click Other. Enable the option Empty the Deleted Items Folder Upon Exiting and click OK. Outlook then empties the Deleted Items folder each time you close Outlook.

## Recovering and Archiving Messages

Sometimes you might delete a message and later want it back. As long as the message is still in the Deleted Items folder, you can easily bring it back. To do so, you open the Deleted Items folder, find the message, and drag it to the Inbox on the folder list. Or you can right-click a message, choose Move to Folder, and then choose a destination folder.

You can leave messages in your Inbox or move them to other folders when you want to keep them in case you need them later. However, there's a better alternative: You can archive messages.

One way to archive messages is to simply move them to a different PST file. You add the PST file as explained earlier in this chapter, in the section "Adding More Sets of Folders," and then you simply drag the message to the folder in the PST file that you want to use for old messages.

**note**

If you deleted a message and it's no longer in the Deleted Items folder, the message is usually unrecoverable. If you use an Exchange Server account and the server administrator has configured a retention policy, your deleted Outlook items will be available for a certain period of time, as defined by the administrator. Choose Tools, Recover Deleted Items to open the Recover Deleted Items From – Deleted Items dialog box and recover the items.

You can also use Outlook's AutoArchive feature, which enables Outlook to automatically move messages to a set of archive folders after they've been sitting in your Inbox for a certain number of days.

To configure AutoArchive settings, including the location for the archive PST file, you choose Tools, Options to open the Options dialog box, and then click Other. Then you click AutoArchive to open the AutoArchive dialog box (see Figure 5.20).

**FIGURE 5.20**

You can set archive options by using the AutoArchive dialog box.

You set the message age for archival by using the Run AutoArchive Every option. You set the archive PST file location by using the Move Old Items To option. After you select the appropriate options, you click OK and then click OK again to close the Options dialog box.

To archive messages, you can simply let Outlook handle it according to your AutoArchive settings or you can choose File, Archive to open the Archive dialog box (see Figure 5.21) and archive messages at any time.

**note**

Your archive PST file doesn't have to be open in Outlook or included in your profile in order for Outlook to move messages to it.

# Managing Mail Folders

Outlook creates a small number of mail folders to help you manage your mail.
These include the Inbox, Outbox, Sent Items, Deleted Items, and Drafts folders.
However, you might want some additional folders for organizing message. For
example, you might create a couple additional mail folders to hold your personal
mail or messages from a discussion group. You might also want to share a folder so
others can use it.

## Creating a Folder and Moving or Copying Items

Creating Outlook folders is easy:

1. In Outlook, choose File, New, Folder. The Create New Folder dialog box
   appears (see Figure 5.22).

2. Enter a name for your new folder.

3. Select Mail and Post Items from the Folder Contains drop-down list box.

4. Click the folder in which you want the new one created. To create the folder
   at the same level as the Inbox, Drafts, and other folders, select the Mailbox or
   Personal Folders branch.

5. Click OK to create the folder.

You can easily move messages to another folder. You right-click a message and
choose Move to Folder to open the Move Items dialog box. Then you select the destination folder and click OK. You can also drag messages from one folder to another.

**FIGURE 5.22**

You can add folders by using the Create New Folder dialog box.

You can also copy a message to a different folder, leaving the original alone:

1. Open the folder where the message is located.

2. Scroll in the folder list until you can see the destination folder.

3. Hold down the Ctrl key and drag the message header to the destination folder in the folder list. Release the mouse button to copy the message.

## Sharing a Folder (with Exchange Server Only)

If you use Exchange Server, you can share one or more folders in your mailbox to allow others to read their contents or even add items to them. For example, you might want to share your Contacts folder so others can use them. Follow these steps to share a folder in your Exchange Server mailbox:

1. Open Outlook, open the folder list, right-click the folder you want to share, and click Sharing to open the Permissions tab of the Calendar Properties dialog box (see Figure 5.23).

2. Click Add on the Permissions tab to open the Add Users dialog box (see Figure 5.24).

3. Select one or more names and click Add. Then click OK.

4. Back in the Permissions tab, place a check mark beside the permissions you want to assign to the selected user(s). The following list provides suggestions:

   ■ **Create Items**—When you select this option, a person can create new items—such as new contacts—in the folder.

**FIGURE 5.23**

You can use the Permissions tab to share a folder.

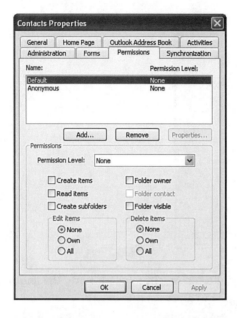

**FIGURE 5.24**

You use the Add Users dialog box to select the user(s) who needs access to your folder.

- **Read Items**—When you select this option, a person can view (that is, read) items in the folder.
- **Create Subfolders**—When you select this option, a person can create other folders in this folder.

- **Edit Items**—With this option, you can determine whether a person can modify existing items in the folder. You can choose None to prevent a person from making changes, Own to allow the person to change items that he or she creates, or All to allow the person to change all, regardless of whether he or she created them.

- **Delete Items**—With this option, you can determine whether a person can delete items from the folder. You can choose None to prevent the person from deleting items, Own to allow the person to delete items he or she creates, or All to allow the person to delete any item.

5. Click OK.

# Filtering Out Junk Mail

Unwanted messages (known as *spam*) are the scourge of the Internet. In my opinion, the people who send them (known as *spammers*) should be strung up by their thumbs in the hot sun and poked with sharp sticks.

Although it's tough to keep out all the junk and adult-content mail, Outlook at least helps you make a big dent in the problem. Outlook provides several features to help you block junk mail. If you have any experience with a previous version of Outlook, you'll find that Outlook 2003 radically changes the options you have for managing junk mail, and for the better. The following lists summarizes these features:

- **Automatic protection levels**—You can choose one of four predefined protection levels to control which types of messages Outlook will block. Outlook uses a set of built-in filters to determine the likelihood that a message is spam.

- **Safe Senders list**—You can create a list of senders whose messages should always be received and not treated as spam, regardless of the content. You can also specify that mail from anyone in your Contacts folder not be treated as spam.

- **Safe Recipients list**—You can use this list to allow mail sent to a specific recipient, even if Outlook would otherwise consider the message spam. This feature is useful for receiving mailing list messages sent to a list address rather than your own email address.

- **Blocked Senders list**—You can create a list of senders whose messages should always be treated as spam and blocked.

The following section explains how to configure each of these features in Outlook.

## Choosing a Junk Mail Protection Level

It's easy to set the level of protection you want against junk mail in Outlook. Follow these steps to configure your own junk mail settings:

1. Choose Tools, Options to open the Options dialog box and then click Junk E-mail on the Preferences tab to open the Junk E-mail Options dialog box (see Figure 5.25).

**FIGURE 5.25**

You choose a protection level from the Options tab.

2. On the Options tab, choose the general level of protection you want, using the following list as a guide:

   - **No Protection**—Outlook will not block an incoming message unless the sender is included on the Blocked Senders list. This option provides very little protection against junk mail.

   - **Low**—Outlook blocks the most obvious junk mail, based on its internal filters.

   - **High**—Outlook aggressively blocks messages it considers junk mail, but some wanted messages might be blocked as well.

   - **Safe List Only**—Outlook blocks everything except messages from people on your Safe Senders list, recipients on your Safe Recipients list, and (optionally) people in your Contacts folder.

   - **Permanently Delete Suspected Junk E-mail Instead of Moving It to the Junk E-mail Folder**—Outlook moves messages to the Junk

E-mail folder by default. You can choose this option to have Outlook delete junk mail, instead. However, you should not use this option until you have a chance to monitor how Outlook handles your junk mail for several weeks to make sure it isn't deleting wanted messages.

3. Click OK to close the Junk E-mail Options dialog box.

## Managing the Safe Senders, Safe Recipients, and Blocked Senders Lists

The Safe Senders list lets you specify the addresses or domains of people whose mail you want delivered to your Inbox and not treated as junk, regardless of the content. If you specify a domain, any mail from any address in that domain is treated as regular mail (not junk). For example, if you add boyce.us to the list, messages from jim@boyce.us, junk@boyce.us, and all other senders would be treated as valid senders.

You can use the Safe Recipients list to enter the email addresses at which you receive certain types of email, such as messages from a mailing list. For example, maybe you receive regular messages from office-list@boyce.us that provide information about Office. If you don't add that address to the Safe Recipients list, it's likely that Outlook will think the message is junk because it isn't addressed directly to you. As with the Safe Senders list, you can specify an email address or a domain in the Safe Recipients list. You specify a domain if you want all messages sent to a specific domain to be accepted (such as when you receive messages sent to different addresses in the same domain).

The Blocked Senders list lets you specify the email addresses or domains of senders whose messages you want Outlook to always block, regardless of content, recipient, or sender.

Follow these steps to configure your junk mail lists and other options:

1. Choose Tools, Options to open the Options dialog box and then click Junk E-mail on the Preferences tab to open the Junk E-mail Options dialog box.

2. Select the Safe Senders tab (see Figure 5.26) and click Add.

3. In the Add Address or Domain dialog box, type the email address or Internet domain that you want to add to the list and then click OK. Repeat this step to add other addresses or domains as needed.

4. If you want Outlook to always accept mail from people in your Contacts folder, select the option Also Trust E-mail from My Contacts.

5. Select the Safe Recipients tab.

**FIGURE 5.26**

You add
addresses or
domains of
trusted senders
by using the
Safe Senders
tab.

6. Click Add and type an address at which you receive list or other messages not sent directly to your regular address, or type the name of a domain at which you receive these types of messages. Repeat this step to add other addresses or domains to your Trusted Recipients list.

7. Select the Blocked Senders tab.

8. Click Add and type an address or domain for a sender whose messages you want Outlook to always block and then click OK. Repeat this step to add other addresses or domains as needed.

9. Click OK to close the Junk E-mail Options dialog box and then click OK to close the Options dialog box.

Outlook by default moves junk mail to the Junk E-mail folder. You should browse through this folder regularly to make sure the messages are all really junk.

## Marking Messages as Junk or Not Junk

If Outlook doesn't catch a particular message, you can easily mark that message as junk, which places the sender's email address in the Blocked Senders list for you. You can also easily add an address to the other filter lists.

You just right-click the message and choose Junk E-mail and then choose the list to which you want the address or domain added. If you are reviewing messages in the Junk E-mail folder and want to move a message back to the Inbox, choose Mark as Not Junk from the pop-up menu.

# Controlling Messages by Using Rules

In this chapter you have learned how to block spam by using Outlook's Junk E-mail features. You can also use *messaging rules* in Outlook to process messages automatically in other ways. For example, maybe you want to move messages you receive from certain people to a special folder. Or maybe you want to have Outlook play a unique sound when you receive a message from a particular person. The following sections describe how to create and run rules.

You can apply a message rule either when messages arrive in your Inbox or when you send a message.

## Creating a Rule

You follow these steps to create a rule:

1. In Outlook, open the Inbox and choose Tools, Rules and Alerts. The Rules and Alerts dialog box appears (see Figure 5.27).

**FIGURE 5.27**

You can manage rules in the Rules and Alerts dialog box.

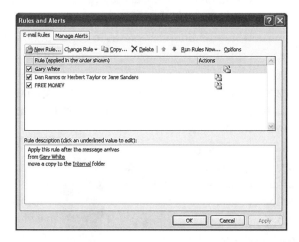

2. Click New Rule to start the Rules Wizard (see Figure 5.28).
3. Select Start from a Blank Rule and click Next.

**FIGURE 5.28**

You can add a
rule by using
the Rules
Wizard.

4. Choose Check Messages When They Arrive if you want to process the message when it arrives in your Inbox. Choose Check Messages After Sending to process outgoing messages with the rule.

5. Click Next to show the condition list shown in Figure 5.29. Place a check mark beside each condition the message must meet for the rule to operate on it.

6. In the Step 2: Edit the Rule Description list in the Rules Wizard dialog box, click each underlined link and specify the condition (for example, sender's address or words in the subject).

7. Click Next to show the action list (see Figure 5.30). Select the action(s) you want Outlook to take if a message matches the rule's conditions.

8. In the Step 2: Edit the Rule Description list, click each underlined link and specify the action.

9. Click Next, set up any exceptions for the rule, and click Next.

10. Specify a name for the rule and click Finish.

**tip**

You can use one of a handful of templates offered by Outlook to quickly create rules for specific tasks. You just select the template from the Step 1: Select a Template list in the Rules Wizard.

**FIGURE 5.29**

You need to choose the conditions for a rule.

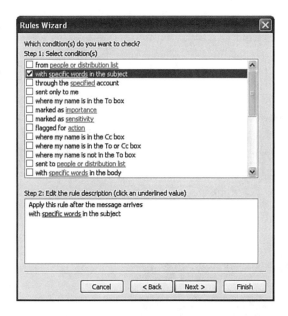

**FIGURE 5.30**

You need to choose the action Outlook should take if a message matches the rule's conditions.

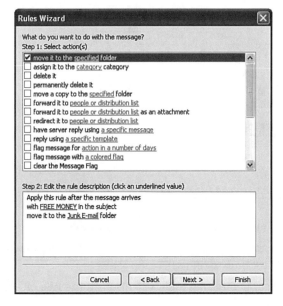

You can add as many rules as you like. Outlook processes the rules in the order in which they appear in the Rules and Alerts dialog box. You can use the up arrow and down arrow buttons to change their order. Keep in mind that one rule might prevent another from operating on a message. For example, if a rule moves a message out of the Inbox, a following rule would not find the message and therefore couldn't take any action on the rule.

## Running a Rule Manually

Most of the time you'll want rules to fire automatically when messages arrive or depart. In some cases, however, you might want to run rules manually. For example, maybe you've created a rule to move lots of existing messages from your Inbox to a different folder, and now you want to run the rule to move those messages.

Here's how you run a rule manually:

1. In Outlook, choose Tools, Rules and Alerts.

2. Click Run Rules Now. The Run Rules Now dialog box appears (see Figure 5.31).

**FIGURE 5.31**

You can run rules manually by using the Run Rules Now dialog box.

3. Place a check mark beside each rule you want to run.

4. If you need to run rules on a folder other than the one shown in the Run in Folder field, click Browse and select the folder.

5. Select the option Include Subfolders to also run the rule on any subfolders in the selected folder.

6. Select from the Apply Rules To drop-down list box the types of messages on which to apply the rule (read, unread, or all) and then click Run Now.

# Opening Another Person's Mailbox with Your Own

If you have an Exchange Server account, you can open other people's folders if they have set permissions on them to allow you access. You can also open other mailboxes, whether they belong to you or someone else, as long as you've been given access permissions to them. For example, you might need to open your boss's mailbox so you can manage his schedule and wade through his email before you forward it to a private mailbox.

You follow these steps to add another mailbox to your own profile:

1. In Outlook, choose Tools, E-mail Accounts to start the E-mail Accounts Wizard.

2. Choose View or Change Existing E-mail Accounts and click Next.

3. Select the Exchange Server account and click Change.

4. Click More Settings and then click the Advanced tab (see Figure 5.32).

**FIGURE 5.32**

You can use the Advanced tab to add other mailboxes to a profile.

5. Click Add, enter the mailbox name, and click OK.

6. Click OK, click Next, and then click Finish.

7. Restart Outlook. The other mailbox appears under its own branch in the folder list.

Opening a single folder from another person's mailbox is even easier than adding another mailbox to your own profile. Here's what you do:

1. Choose File, Open, Other User's Folder.

2. Click Name and browse for the user's name. Select the name and click OK.

3. From the Folder Type drop-down list box, select the folder you want to open and then click OK. The folder appears under its own branch in the folder list.

⇨ See the section "Sharing a Folder (with Exchange Server Only)," earlier in this chapter, to learn how to give someone else permission to use one of your folders.

# THE ABSOLUTE MINIMUM

Working with email is one of the most common tasks most people perform with Outlook. In this chapter you took a tour of the Inbox and learned how to add email accounts, send and receive email messages, and add attachments. This chapter also explains how to back up and recover messages, use features such as the Bcc field, and set other message options.

If you receive a lot of messages, you'll appreciate the Junk E-mail features in Outlook 2003 that help you block unwanted messages. This chapter covers these features in detail and also explains how to create and use rules to process messages automatically.

In the next chapter you'll learn how to work with the Calendar folder to manage your appointments, events, and other items for your schedule.

**6**

# KEEPING TRACK OF APPOINTMENTS AND OTHER BIG (OR SMALL) EVENTS

Many people use Outlook to manage their schedule, to keep track of appointments, birthdays, holidays, meetings, and other events. Outlook includes holidays for many countries, and you can easily add your own. You can also add your own meetings and appointments, and you can have Outlook remind you about them ahead of time. When you use Outlook with Exchange Server, you can easily see others' schedules and organize group meetings.

This chapter explains how to use the Calendar folder in Outlook to manage your schedule.

# A Quick Tour of the Calendar Folder

You use Outlook's Calendar folder (see Figure 6.1) to manage appointments and other events. When you open the Calendar folder, the Navigation pane shows the *date navigator*, which is just a small calendar that you can use to select a month or day.

**FIGURE 6.1**

The Calendar folder's Day view shows a single day.

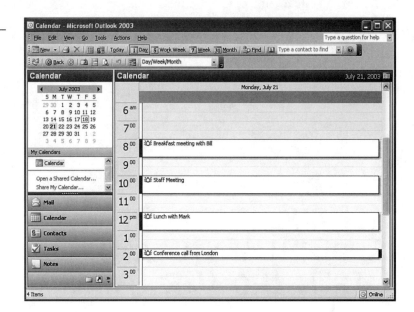

Like the other Outlook folders, the Calendar folder includes several predefined views, and you can also create your own. Figure 6.1 shows the Day view, and Figure 6.2 shows the Month view. You choose View, Arrange By, Current View to select a different view. You can also click the Today, Day, Work Week, Week, or Month buttons on the toolbar to open views.

The appointments and other events that you have added to your schedule appear in the Calendar folder on their assigned days. Events that span more than one day (such as conferences or vacations) span the appropriate days on the calendar. The Calendar folder also shows events that it has added, such as holidays.

⇨ See the section "Creating Custom Views" in Chapter 8, "Outlook Settings to Change," to learn how to create your own views of the Calendar.

The next section explains how to use the Calendar folder to add and work with appointments.

**FIGURE 6.2**

The Calendar folder's Month view shows an entire month.

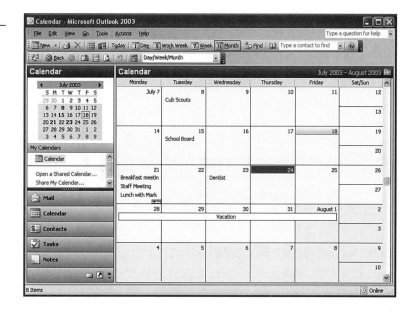

# Adding and Working with Events in the Calendar Folder

You can create *events* in the Calendar folder. Outlook treats all events the same, but you can use them for different purposes. For example, you might add an event for a meeting, an appointment, a project you need to complete, and so on.

## Adding an Event

Adding an event appointment in Outlook is easy:

1. Click Calendar on the Navigation pane to open the Calendar folder.

2. If you are viewing the Calendar folder in the Day or Work Week view, click the time slot for the beginning of the event. If you're working in the Week or Month view, click the day.

3. Type a name for the event, such as **Meeting with Joe**, and then press Enter. The event should now show up in the Calendar.

**tip**

You can highlight a range of slots, such as 9:00 a.m. to 11:30 a.m., to enter an event that spans that time.

Outlook treats the event a little differently, depending on what view is being used when you add it. In the Day and Work Week views, Outlook creates an appointment (that is, an event) within the time slot you selected when you started typing. In the Week and Month views, Outlook creates an all-day event on the selected date.

⇨ See the section "Working with Reminders," later in this chapter, for details on changing the default reminder time or the reminder for a specific appointment.

## Viewing and Changing an Event

Outlook events are much more than just a bit of text on the Calendar. You can add all sorts of information to an event. Double-click an appointment to open its form, as shown in Figure 6.3.

**FIGURE 6.3**

You can add lots of information to an event.

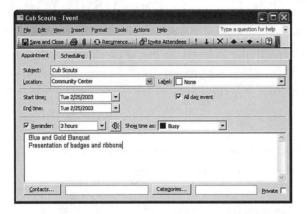

The subject of the event is what appears in the Calendar folder. You can also enter a location, start time, end time, and notes. Although the times in the drop-down list boxes on the event form are in half-hour increments, you can enter your own values if needed. For example, you might start an appointment at 9:05 a.m. and end it at 10:20.

You can set several other properties for an event. You click the Contacts button to select one or more contacts in order to associate them with the event. For example, if you're setting up an event for a conference call, you might add the contacts for the people involved in the call so you have quick access to their phone numbers.

You can also click Categories to associate one or more categories with the event. For example, if the event is a meeting for a particular project, you can associate the project's category with the event. You can then sort the Calendar folder by categories and quickly find all items associated with a specific category.

## Group Scheduling

When you open an event, you find a Scheduling tab on the event form (see Figure 6.4). You can use this tab to set a tentative meeting time and invite others to attend the meeting. You can also see if the other invitees' schedules are open to choose an appropriate time for the meeting. However, this requires at least one of the following:

**FIGURE 6.4**

You use the Scheduling tab to invite others to a meeting.

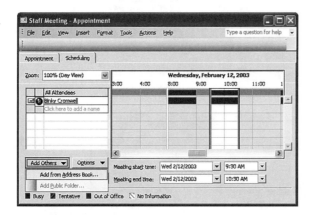

- **You need to share the same Exchange Server site**—If this is the case, you can view the schedules of others in your Exchange Server organization.
- **Each participant must publish free/busy information to a server**—If this is the case, you can view schedules published to a free/busy service such as the Microsoft Internet Free/Busy Service.

Outlook 2003 gives you two ways to view group schedules. First, you can view schedules when you create a meeting request. Second, you can create a named group schedule. Follow these steps to create a meeting request:

1. In Outlook, open the Calendar folder and click New to create a new event.

2. Fill in the subject and other information on the Appointment tab of the event form.

3. Select the Scheduling tab.

4. Click the Add Others drop-down list and then select Add from Address Book (refer to Figure 6.4).

5. Select the others whose schedules you want to view and click Required or Optional.

6. Click OK.

**tip**

Select a resource such as a meeting room or piece of equipment and click Resources in the Select Attendees and Resources dialog box to add that resource to the meeting request.

At this point Outlook checks the free/busy server you've specified in your calendar options or in each contact and display the free/busy times in the Scheduling tab, as shown in Figure 6.5.

**FIGURE 6.5**

The Scheduling tab shows free/busy times for each attendee.

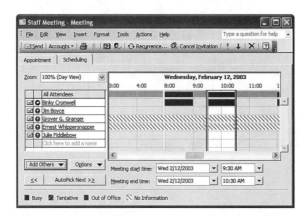

Use the free/busy times shown in the Scheduling tab to find a meeting time that enables everyone (or as many people as possible) to attend. Outlook automatically tries to pick a time that supports all users and at least one resource. You can choose a different AutoPick strategy from the Options button. Click AutoPick Next to automatically locate the next available time that matches your current AutoPick option.

Finally, set the meeting start and end time by using the combo boxes on the Scheduling tab, and then click Send when you're satisfied with the meeting request.

The second method that Outlook 2003 offers for creating and viewing group schedules doesn't require you to create an event. You can create multiple group schedules and save them by name for use any time. The main reason to use this method is to create schedules that you use primarily to manage resources or personnel rather than to create meeting requests. Here's how you use this method to create and view a schedule:

1. In Outlook, open the Calendar folder and choose Actions, View Group Schedules. The Group Schedules dialog box appears. This dialog box lists the schedules you've previously created and lets you create and delete schedules.

2. Click New, type a name for the group schedule, and click OK. Outlook opens a scheduling dialog box similar to the one shown in Figure 6.6, which is very similar to the one shown in Figure 6.5.

**FIGURE 6.6**

You can create a group schedule without creating an event.

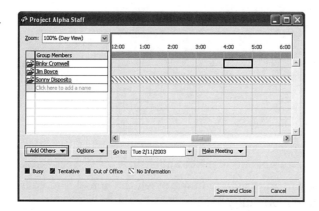

3. Add attendees and resources, as explained earlier in this section for an event. Then click Save and click Close to save the schedule.

## Publishing Free/Busy Information

If you want to do group scheduling with others who don't share your Exchange Server organization, you need to publish your free/busy times to a server that is accessible to those other people, and other people need to publish their free/busy information to a server that you can access.

Microsoft maintains a service called the Microsoft Internet Free/Busy Service that you can

**tip**

The group schedule dialog box includes a Make Meeting button that you can click to create a meeting request or send an email message to one or more of the people included in the schedule.

use to share schedules. With it, you have control over who can view your published schedule.

Follow these steps to specify the location for publishing your free/busy information:

1. In Outlook, choose Tools, Options and then click Calendar Options.

2. Click Free/Busy Options. The Free/Busy Options dialog box appears (see Figure 6.7)

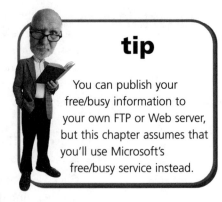

**tip**

You can publish your free/busy information to your own FTP or Web server, but this chapter assumes that you'll use Microsoft's free/busy service instead.

**FIGURE 6.7**

Set your free/busy server location by using the Free/Busy Options dialog box.

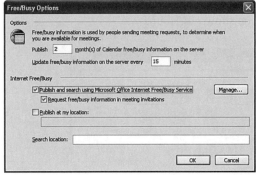

3. Enter the number of months to publish.

4. Enter the frequency, in minutes, at which Outlook should update your free/busy information.

5. Choose Publish and Search Using Microsoft Internet Free/Busy Service.

6. Select Request Free/Busy Information in Meeting Invitations.

7. Click Manage.

At this point, your Web browser opens and takes you to the Microsoft Internet Free/Busy Web site. If your computer isn't configured to automatically log on with your Microsoft Passport, you need to log on. If you don't have a Microsoft Passport, you have to sign up for one.

After you log in with your Passport, the Microsoft Internet Free/Busy Web site steps you through the process of setting up your free/busy information and specifying who can view it.

# Working with Reminders

When you create an event such as an appointment in your Outlook Calendar folder, Outlook automatically adds a *reminder* to the event and sets it to fire (that is, go off) 15 minutes before the event's start time. When the reminder fires, Outlook plays a reminder sound and displays a dialog box that contains the reminder and any other triggered reminders, as shown in Figure 6.8.

**FIGURE 6.8**

The Reminders dialog box shows Outlook reminders for events.

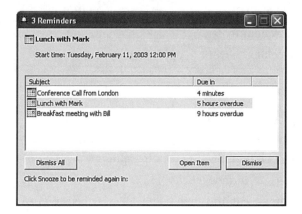

You can postpone a reminder so that it fires again later. For example, you might not be ready to make a phone call, but you might want to be reminded about the call again in 10 minutes. In this case, just click the appropriate reminder in the Reminders dialog box, select a time from the drop-down list box, and click Snooze.

You can also dismiss one or more reminders. To do so, select the reminder(s) you want to dismiss and click Dismiss. Or click Dismiss All to dismiss all the reminders that are set.

➪ See the section "Changing the Reminder Sound and Default Time" in Chapter 8 to learn how to assign a different sound to reminders.

You don't have to snooze or dismiss reminders. Instead, you can simply minimize the Reminders dialog box and restore it again when you want to work with the reminders. Or you can click the Close button to close the dialog box. Choose View, Reminders Window when you want to open the Reminders dialog box again.

# Coloring Certain Types of Events

The calendar provides at-a-glance access to your appointments and other events by displaying them in the calendar. Wouldn't it be great if you could make certain types of events appear in a particular color to make them stand out? Well, you can! Even better, it's easy to do. You just have to apply a label to the event. You can also change label color or even use automatic formatting to color items automatically.

## Applying Labels to Events

A *label* is a combination of a color and a description that identifies a particular type of event. Outlook provides 10 different labels that you can use as they are or change to suit your needs. Follow these steps to color an event in the Calendar folder:

1. Open the Calendar folder, right-click an event, and choose Label.

2. Choose the color you want to apply to the event.

## Customizing Labels

Each of Outlook's 10 different labels has its own combination of color and text (for example, the Personal label is green). But you can change the text associated with a color. For example, you might want green to represent pending projects.

You follow these steps to change label:

1. Right-click any event and choose Label, Edit Labels to open the Edit Calendar Labels dialog box (see Figure 6.9).

**FIGURE 6.9**

Change labels by using the Edit Calendar Labels dialog box.

Edit Calendar Labels

- Important
- Business
- Personal
- Vacation
- Must Attend
- Travel Required
- Needs Preparation
- Birthday
- Anniversary
- Phone Call

OK    Cancel

2. For any label, highlight the text you want to change and type the new text.

3. When you are done changing the labels, click OK.

You can't add new colors or change the existing colors, but you can change any or all of the text descriptions for your labels.

## Coloring Events Automatically by Using Formatting

Wouldn't it be great if you could have Outlook automatically color certain types of events? For example, maybe you want all holidays to appear in blue in the Calendar folder or all events that contain a certain text string in the subject to appear in red.

Outlook 2003 includes an automatic formatting feature that lets you specify rule conditions to color events automatically. With automatic formatting, you don't need to apply a label manually to color the event. Instead, Outlook checks the conditions you've specified for automatic formatting and applies a label for you as soon as you create the event.

Follow these steps to use automatic formatting to color events in the Calendar folder:

1. Open the Calendar folder and choose Edit, Automatic Formatting to open the Automatic Formatting dialog box (see Figure 6.10).

**FIGURE 6.10**

Use the Automatic Formatting dialog box to color Calendar events automatically.

2. Click Add, click in the Name field, and enter a name for the rule, such as **Birthdays**.

3. Select a label from the drop-down list box.

4. Click Condition to display the Filter dialog box (see Figure 6.11).

**FIGURE 6.11**

You can specify complex filter conditions for automatic formatting.

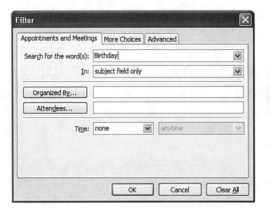

**tip**

Use the Advanced tab to choose fields that do not appear on the other two tabs in the Filter dialog box.

5. Use the controls on the Filter dialog box to specify the conditions for which you want Outlook to check.

6. Click OK and then click OK again to close the Automatic Formatting dialog box. Outlook applies the changes immediately.

# Keeping Track of Holidays, Birthdays, and Other Special Events

You might have already guessed that you can enter any kind of event in the Calendar folder. You're not limited to just keeping track of business meetings or work-related tasks. You can keep track of holidays, birthdays, and other special events.

## Adding Holidays

Outlook doesn't automatically add holidays to your Calendar folder because it has no way of knowing what country you are in. It does, however, include holidays for most countries. You can add them to your Calendar folder easily. Here's how:

1. In Outlook, choose Tools, Options. The Options dialog box appears. Click Calendar Options.

2. Click Add Holidays on the Calendar Options dialog box. The Add Holidays to Calendar dialog box appears (see Figure 6.12).

3. Place a check mark beside the countries whose holidays you want to add to your Calendar folder and then click OK.

**FIGURE 6.12**

Select countries from the Add Holidays to Calendar dialog box.

4. Click Cancel and then click Cancel in the Options dialog box. At this point, Outlook usually opens the Reminders dialog box and beeps like crazy because by default it adds a reminder to each holiday.

5. In the Reminders dialog box, make sure you don't have any important reminders and then click Dismiss All.

## Adding Birthdays and Other Special Events

A birthday or another special event is significant to you, but to Outlook it is no different from a business meeting or holiday. Adding these types of events is easy:

1. In Outlook, click the date (and time, if you're using a view that shows time slots) where you want to add the special event.

2. Type the subject for the event, such as `Mary's Birthday`, and press Enter.

3. Right-click the event you just added and choose Label. Then, optionally, select a label.

Instead of manually adding a label, I recommend that you set up automatic formatting, as described earlier in this chapter, in the section "Coloring Events Automatically by Using Formatting." For example, you can add a Birthday rule that looks for the text *birthday* in the subject. Then, when you enter the birthday, you need to make sure to include the word *birthday* in the subject so Outlook will color it automatically, using the label you've assigned to the automatic formatting rule.

**note**

If you already have holidays for a particular country in your Calendar folder, Outlook warns you and gives you a chance to cancel the holiday addition.

# Printing a Calendar

You probably don't often print email messages or contacts, but you might print your Calendar folder fairly frequently, particularly if you use a paper day planner.

It's as easy to print the Calendar folder as it is to print any other document. You specify which range of dates to print, the type of printout format you want, and other options. You have the ability to create a variety of different views of the same information. For example, you might print a month's worth of the Calendar folder to use as a wall or planning calendar.

To print a range of events, open the Calendar folder and choose File, Print to open the Print dialog box, which is shown in Figure 6.13.

**FIGURE 6.13**

You can choose the print style from the Print dialog box.

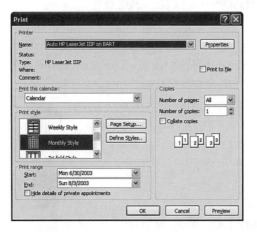

The Print Style list includes five different print styles. Each print style produces a unique output. For example, you would use the Monthly style to print a wall calendar. Each of these styles has certain properties you can change. For example, on the Monthly style, you can turn off weekends so the printout includes only work days.

To set properties for a style, first select the style from the list and then click Page Setup. The Page Setup dialog box appears. Figure 6.14 shows the Page Setup dialog box for the Monthly style.

**FIGURE 6.14**

You can use the Page Setup dialog box to set options for the selected style.

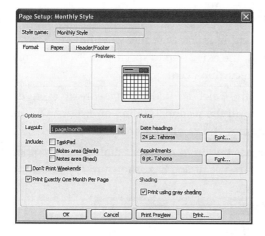

After you select the options you want, click the Print Preview button to view a sample printout. Then click the Page Setup button in the preview toolbar to return to the Page Setup dialog box to make layout changes, or click the Print button to return to the Print dialog box to change options there, such as the start and end times for the printout.

If the existing print styles and options don't give you quite the results you need, or if you don't like having to change them each time, you can create a custom print style. I don't go into detail on custom print styles here because that's a rather advanced topic, but here's a quick overview:

1. Choose File, Print to open the Print dialog box.
2. Click Define Styles to open the Define Print Styles dialog box.
3. Select an existing style and click Copy to open the Page Setup dialog box.
4. Edit the name and settings and then click OK.

You can then choose your custom print style when you need to print your Calendar folder.

# Creating a Recurring Appointment or Event

Almost everyone has some events that recur. For example, I write tips for distribution by email, and those tips are always due on the first Wednesday of the month. Likewise, I have a school board meeting the third Tuesday of each month. These are good examples of *recurring events*. As you might expect, Outlook does a good job of managing these events.

## Creating a Recurring Event

You create a recurring event in much the same way that you create a one-time event. You just need to go the extra step to specify the event's recurrence pattern. Here's how you create a recurring event:

1. In Outlook, open the Calendar folder and create an event as explained earlier in this chapter, in the section "Adding an Event." Or simply double-click a one-time event that you've already created.

2. Click the Recurrence button in the event dialog box's toolbar. The Appointment Recurrence dialog box, shown in Figure 6.15, appears.

**FIGURE 6.15**

Specify an event's recurrence pattern in the Appointment Recurrence dialog box.

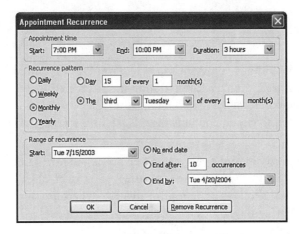

3. Choose the start time, end time, and duration in the Appointment Time group box.

4. Choose Daily, Weekly, Monthly, or Yearly. The rest of the options in the Recurrence Pattern group box change accordingly.

5. Choose options in Recurrence Pattern group box to specify how often and when the event reoccurs.

6. In the Range of Recurrence group, choose the first date for the event. Choose End After if you want to stop the recurring event after the specified number of occurrences. Choose End By to end the event by the specified time.

7. Click OK and then click Save and click Close to save the event.

### Changing a Recurring Event

As with one-time events, you can make changes to recurring events. You can change a single occurrence of an event, or change the entire series of occurrences.

To change a recurring event, double-click the event in the Calendar folder. Outlook displays the Open Recurring Item dialog box, which is shown in Figure 6.16.

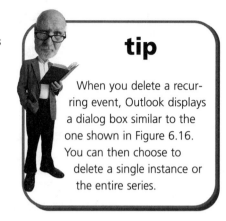

**tip**

When you delete a recurring event, Outlook displays a dialog box similar to the one shown in Figure 6.16. You can then choose to delete a single instance or the entire series.

**FIGURE 6.16**

Choose whether to change one occurrence or an entire series.

Choose Open This Occurrence if you want to make changes to only one instance of the recurring event. Choose Open the Series to make a global change to the series. Click OK to open the event, make the changes, and click Save and Close to save the changes.

## Tracking Documents and Events by Using the Journal

The Journal folder in Outlook lets you keep track of lots of different types of events that don't really fit into the other Outlook folders. For example, you can use the Journal folder to keep notes, to track duration of phone calls, to track the time you spend working on particular documents, and to note other events. In fact, Outlook can automatically track your document usage in the Journal folder if you direct it to do so.

Outlook doesn't show the Journal folder on the Navigation pane by default. You can open the Journal folder from the folder list. Or click Configure Buttons on the bottom right of the Navigation pane and then choose Navigation Pane Options. Place a check mark beside the Journal folder and click OK. The Journal folder then appears on the Navigation pane.

The first time you open the Journal folder, Outlook asks if you want it to automatically keep track of your documents (see Figure 6.17).

**FIGURE 6.17**

**FIGURE 6.17**

Outlook asks if
you want it to
automatically
track documents
and other items.

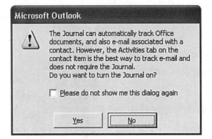

In general, I don't suggest that you turn on automatic journaling of all items in
Outlook because it can bloat the Journal folder. However, selectively journaling
items from specific contacts helps you limit the amount of information Outlook adds
to the Journal folder.

To turn on automatic journaling, you click Yes when prompted, as shown in Figure
6.17. Outlook then displays the Journal Options dialog box, shown in Figure 6.18.

**FIGURE 6.18**

Set up journal-
ing by using the
Journal Options
dialog box.

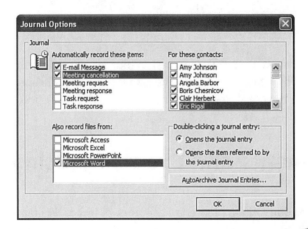

Follow these steps to set up journaling:

1. In the Automatically Record These Items
   list, place a check mark beside each item
   you want Outlook to add to the Journal
   folder.

2. Place a check mark beside each contact
   for whom you want to track the selected
   items.

3. In the Also Record Files From list
   box, place a check mark beside the

**tip**

You can open the Journal
Options dialog box by
choosing Tools, Options and
then clicking Journal Options.
This method lets you configure the Journal folder
options without enabling
automatic journaling.

applications whose documents you want the Journal folder to track automatically.

4. In the Double-Clicking a Journal Entry group box, choose one of the following options:

   ■ **Opens the Journal Entry**—With this option selected, when you double-click an item in the Journal folder, Outlook opens the item itself.

   ■ **Opens the Item Referred to by the Journal Entry**—With this option selected, when you double-click an item in the Journal folder, Outlook opens the document or other item associated with the entry.

5. Click OK to close the Journal Options dialog box.

Unfortunately, you can't track different items for each contact. Outlook tracks the specified items for all selected contacts.

## Using the Journal

Figure 6.19 shows the Journal folder with a few items added to it. The default view shows a linear time line with items organized by type. For example, all phone calls are grouped together, all email messages are together, and all Word documents are grouped together.

**FIGURE 6.19**

The Journal folder holds your journal items.

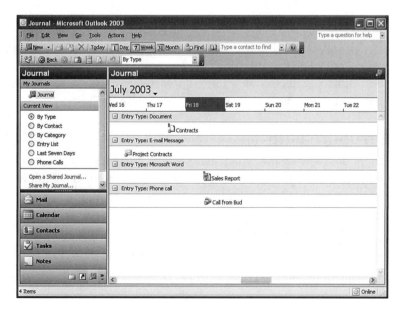

You can open a Journal folder entry by double-clicking it in the Journal folder. Figure 6.20 shows an example of a Journal folder entry—in this case, an entry for a phone call.

**FIGURE 6.20**
Add Journal items to track phone calls and over events.

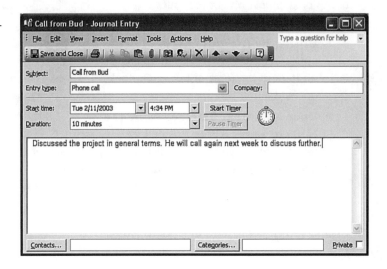

A Journal folder entry is relatively simple. You can specify a subject, choose an entry type, set time and duration, and assign categories or contacts to the item. Note that you can also mark Journal folder entries as private, which prevents your delegated assistant and others from seeing them unless you explicitly give them permission (through folder permissions) to view your private items.

## Creating a Journal Entry Manually

You create a Journal folder entry yourself in much the same way that you create other Outlook items. First, open the Journal folder, and then click New in the toolbar. Outlook displays a new Journal folder item form. Choose the entry type, fill in the other fields as needed, and then click Save and Close.

## Turning Off Journaling

Journaling takes some system overhead, so it can have an impact on your system's performance. If you decide that journaling is having too big an impact on your system's performance, or if you just want to switch to manual journaling, you can turn off automatic journaling.

Outlook doesn't give you a one-click method to turn off automatic journaling. Instead, you need to follow these steps to turn it off:

1. Open Outlook and choose Tools, Options. The Options dialog box appears.
2. Click Journal Options.
3. Remove all the check marks from the Automatically Record These Items and the Also Record Files From lists.
4. Click OK and then click OK to close the Options dialog box.

# The Absolute Minimum

The Outlook Calendar folder helps you keep track of your appointments, meetings, and other events by providing an at-a-glance look at your day, week, or month. You can set reminders to notify you prior to an appointment, a meeting, or an event to help you keep on schedule. You can also use color to help differentiate one type of Calendar item from another, such as personal items from business ones. Using recurring appointments and events eliminates the need for you to set up multiple individual items for items that recur.

The Calendar folder is also useful for tracking holidays and other special occasions, such as birthdays, weddings, and vacations.

Outlook gives you the capability to view the Calendar folder in several ways, and you can also print calendars and individual items.

Finally, in this chapter you learned how you can use the Journal folder to track phone calls, conversations, time spent on a document, and other events.

The following chapter explores another of Outlook's default folders—the Tasks folder. You can use the Tasks folder to create and manage your own to-do list, as well as assign tasks to others.

## IN THIS CHAPTER

- Creating and working with tasks
- Assigning a task to someone else
- Viewing and changing tasks
- Assigning documents and other items to tasks

7

# MANAGING A TO-DO LIST

Outlook isn't just about email, contacts, and appointments. The program also provides some tools to help manage your tasks. You can set due dates for tasks, keep track of tasks' progress and status, and even assign tasks to other people and keep track of their progress.

In this chapter you'll learn about Outlook tasks and how to create your own, and you'll also learn how to assign tasks to others.

# About Tasks and the Tasks Folder

The Tasks folder in Outlook is the main location where you work with tasks. Figure 7.1 shows the Tasks folder with a few tasks in it.

**FIGURE 7.1**

Create and view tasks with the Tasks folder.

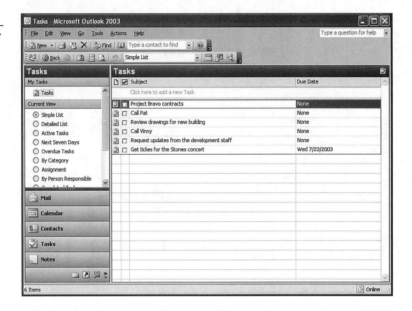

The default Tasks folder view shows your tasks as a list. The list includes the task's name (in the Subject column), completion status, and due date. There are several other views, including a Detailed List view that shows the percentage complete and categories, an Overdue Tasks view that shows the tasks that are overdue, and others.

You can create tasks for yourself, and you can create and assign tasks to other people. Later in this chapter, in the section "Viewing and Changing Task Status," you'll learn about some of the different ways you can have Outlook remind you about your pending tasks. The section "Assigning a Task to Someone Else" explains how to delegate a task to someone else.

Now let's create a few tasks!

# Creating Tasks

You create a task much the same way you create other Outlook items. Click Tasks on the Navigation pane or choose Go, Tasks to open the Tasks folder. Then you click the New button on the toolbar to open the task form shown in Figure 7.2.

**FIGURE 7.2**

A task form is very similar to an appointment form.

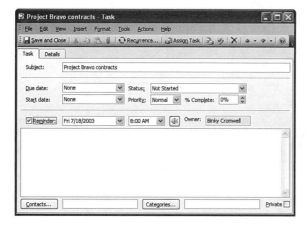

As with other Outlook items, the subject for a task identifies the task. You can specify a due date, priority, status, notes, and other information for the task. You can also set a reminder for the task, just as you can for an appointment or another event.

You can also use the Categories button to associate a task with specific categories. For example, let's say you've created a category for an important project. You should associate each task for that project with the project category. This then helps you search for and quickly locate all items—including tasks—that relate to that project.

Use the Contacts button to associate one or more contacts with a task. For example, let's say you need to prepare some contracts and submit them to someone in another company for approval. When you create the contract creation task, you should associate with it the contact information for the person at the other company who will need to approve the contract. Later, when you work on the task, you'll have this contact information right at hand, making it easier for you to send email messages and letters and to find the contact's phone number when needed.

The Details tab of the task form (see Figure 7.3) includes some additional fields to track extra information for the task. For example, you can enter an estimate of the time required to complete the task, the actual amount of time spent, mileage, and other useful information.

## Creating a Recurring Task

You can create recurring tasks in much the same way that you create recurring appointments or other events. Maybe you won't create a recurring task to remind you to take out the garbage, but I'll bet there are lots of other tasks you need to accomplish on a regular basis that would be handy to track in Outlook.

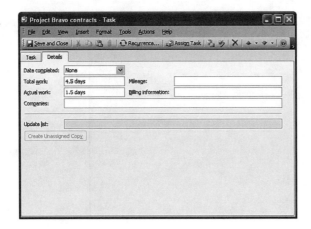

Creating a recurring task is easy. Here's what you do:

1. Open the Tasks folder and start a new task.

2. Enter the subject and other information for the task in the Task and Details tabs.

3. Click Recurrence on the task form's toolbar. The Task Recurrence dialog box appears.

4. Specify the frequency and other options that define the task's recurrence and then click OK.

5. Click Save and then click Close to save the task.

You can set up a task to recur daily, weekly, monthly, or yearly.

⇨ See the section "Creating a Recurring Appointment or Event" in Chapter 6, "Keeping Track of Appointments and Other Big (or Small) Events," for details on specifying the recurrence pattern. The options are the same for a task as for an appointment.

## Assigning a Task to Someone Else

If you manage others, it's likely that you often assign tasks to them. You can use Outlook to assign those tasks if your staff also uses Outlook.

When you assign a task, Outlook sends a message to the other person. The person can either accept or decline the task. When you open the task after you send it, the task form shows the status of the pending task request (see Figure 7.4). The status appears as, Waiting for Response from Recipient until the recipient either accepts or declines. The status message changes to Accepted or Declined after the recipient either accepts or declines the task.

**FIGURE 7.4**

A task's status appears in the task form.

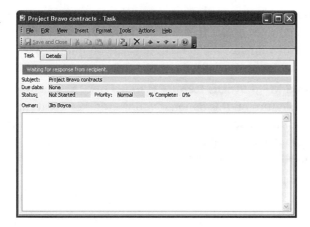

## Assigning a Task

It's easy to assign a task to someone else. You follow these steps to create and assign a task:

1. Open the Tasks folder and click New on the toolbar to start a new task.

2. Enter the subject and other fields on the Task and Details tabs as necessary.

3. Associate categories and contacts with the task, if needed.

4. Click Assign Task on the toolbar to change the form so that it looks as shown in Figure 7.5.

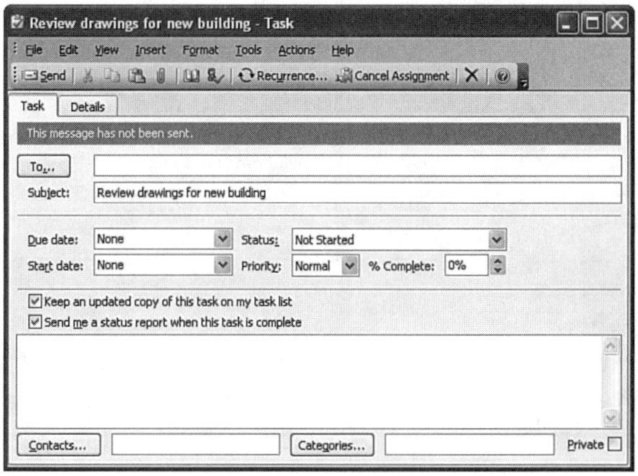

**FIGURE 7.5**

Outlook adds an address field to a task form.

5. Click To and choose the person to whom you want to assign the task.

6. Select the following options, as appropriate:

■ **Keep an Updated Copy of This Task on My Task List**—You should turn on this option if you want Outlook to place a copy of the task in your Tasks folder and to keep you informed with status updates as the other person works on the task.

■ **Send Me a Status Report When This Task Is Complete**—You should turn on this option if you want to receive a status report when the other person completes the task. Outlook, on the other person's computer, automatically generates a status email message to you when the other person marks the task as being completed.

7. Click Send to send the task request.

## Accepting or Declining an Assigned Task

Outlook sends task requests as special email messages. When you receive a task request in your Inbox, Outlook includes Accept and Decline buttons in the Reading pane, as shown in Figure 7.6. Outlook also shows Accept and Decline buttons in the message form if you open the message.

**FIGURE 7.6**

You can simply click Accept or Decline to process a task request.

Just click either Accept or Decline to accept or decline a task. When you do, Outlook displays a dialog box that asks if you want to send the response right away or edit it. You should choose Send the Response Now if you don't want to add any information to the outgoing response. But if you need to add an excuse as to why you can't take on the task, or if you need to add other information to the response, choose

Edit the Response Before Sending. Then click OK. Outlook opens the task form, and you can add notes and make other changes as needed before you click Send to send the response.

Outlook adds the assigned task to your Tasks folder if you accept the task request. If the person who assigned the task requested task updates, Outlook sends those updates (such as percent complete or completion status) automatically whenever you make changes to the task's properties.

**tip**

When you reply to a task request, Outlook places a copy of the response in your Sent Items folder. By default, it also deletes the task request from your Inbox, whether you accept or decline.

# Viewing and Changing Task Status

As explained earlier in this chapter, tasks appear in your Tasks folder. You can see task status at a glance simply by opening your Tasks folder. The following sections explain how to view and change task status in a handful of ways.

## Viewing Task Status

The default Tasks folder view doesn't show task status, although it does show the task's due date. You can change the view to show task status. For example, choose the Detailed List view to see Status and % Complete fields (see Figure 7.7). Use the Active Tasks view to see a list of all incomplete tasks.

**FIGURE 7.7**

The Detailed List view shows task status fields.

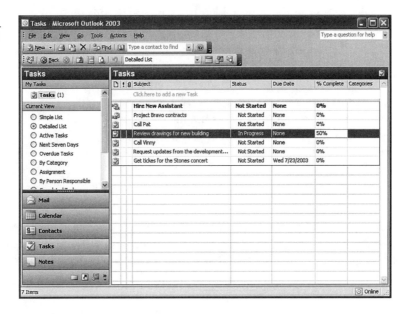

The Tasks folder isn't the only place you can view tasks. Your tasks also show up in the Outlook Today view (see Figure 7.8). You can mark a task as completed in the Outlook Today view, or click a task to open the task form to view or change its properties.

**FIGURE 7.8**

Manage tasks in the Outlook Today view as well as the Tasks folder.

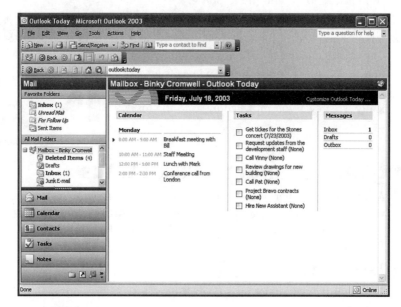

## Changing Task Status

To mark a task as completed, simply place a check mark beside it in the Outlook Today view or in the Tasks folder. You can also do this by right-clicking a task and choosing Mark Complete.

You can change task status in other ways. For example, as you make progress on a task, you might want to change the % Complete entry for the task. If the task has been assigned to you by someone else, Outlook generates a status update to the person who assigned the task when you change the % Complete value (assuming that the person requested updates when he or she assigned it).

The easiest way to change task status is to open the task form and make the changes there. Use the % Complete field on the Task tab (see Figure 7.9) to enter the percentage of a task that is complete and use the Total Work and Actual Work fields on the Details tab to specify changes to the amount of time estimated and actually spent on the task.

**note**

Changing the Total Work and Actual Work fields doesn't change the % Complete value for a task. You have to change that value separately.

**FIGURE 7.9**

You can change the % Complete field on the Task tab of the task form.

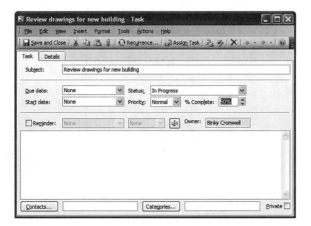

# Assigning Other Outlook Items (Such as Documents) to a Task

Earlier in this chapter, I explained that you can assign categories and contacts to a task. You can also assign documents to a task. For example, let's say you assign someone the task of reviewing a contract. When you send the task request, you want it to either include the contract document or a shortcut to the document in its location on a server.

You can insert documents in a task, or you can insert shortcuts to the document. If you insert the document, it is embedded in the task. This is the option you should use if you need to send the document to someone who doesn't share your access to a network server. You should use a shortcut (that is, a hyperlink) if you just want to point to the document but don't want to actually embed it in the task. You might use this method, for example, when the person to whom you are assigning a task has access to the shared folder where the document resides. You can also use this method for local documents in your own tasks to avoid creating a duplicate copy of the document.

Follow these steps to insert a document or shortcut in a task:

1. Open the task form and click in the notes area of the Task tab.

2. Choose Insert, File or click the Insert File button on the toolbar. The Insert File dialog box appears.

3. In the Insert File dialog box, browse for and select the file (see Figure 7.10). Then click the small arrow beside the Insert button and choose Insert as Attachment to embed the document or choose Insert as Hyperlink to insert a shortcut to the document.

**FIGURE 7.10**

Use the Insert
File dialog box
to insert a docu-
ment or shortcut
in a task.

4. The notes area shows an icon for each embedded document or a hyperlink
   for each shortcut (see Figure 7.11).

**FIGURE 7.11**

Documents and
shortcuts
appear in the
notes area of
the Task tab.

Hyperlinks that you insert locally work just fine for your own tasks. However, you
can't insert a hyperlink to one of your local files and have it work for a task that
you assign to someone else. That's because Outlook treats the hyperlink literally and
tries to open on the other person's computer the same path it opens on yours. So if
the link references your drive c:, Outlook will try to open drive c: on the other user's
computer.

Therefore, when you're inserting a hyperlink for another user to use, you should
enter the shortcut manually and point it to a shared network folder or public

Exchange Server folder. For example, you might enter the following in the notes area:

`\\docserver\contracts\Bravo\contractv1.doc`

This link specifies the file `contractv1.doc` in the `contracts\Bravo` folder on a server named `docserver`.

# THE ABSOLUTE MINIMUM

The Tasks folder provides a place for you to manage your to-do list. Your tasks also appear in the Outlook Today view so you can get a quick overview of pending tasks for the day. You can also use several different views in the Tasks folder to organize and view tasks.

In addition to managing your own tasks, you can also assign tasks to others if you use Exchange Server. You receive status updates when assignees update tasks.

This and several previous chapters have explained how to work with Outlook's various folders and common features. In the following chapter, you'll learn how to change many of Outlook's settings to tailor the program to the way you want it to look and work.

**8**

# OUTLOOK SETTINGS TO CHANGE

Outlook provides many, many settings that control the way the program works and looks. You will probably never touch some of those settings, and many you'll change very seldom. This chapter focuses on the most common settings you're likely to want to change. These settings control many different Outlook features, from email to scheduling.

# Controlling When and How Outlook Checks Your Mail

Outlook uses *send/receive groups* to determine which accounts to check and when to check them. Outlook includes a predefined send/receive group named All Accounts that includes all the email accounts in your profile. You can change the settings for this group or create other groups to handle accounts separately, if you want.

It's likely that, at least at first, you will only need one send/receive group. Therefore, this section focuses on how to edit the existing All Accounts group. Here's how you edit send/receive groups:

1. In Outlook, choose Tools, Send/Receive, Send/Receive Settings, Define Send/Receive Groups. The Send/Receive Groups dialog box appears (see Figure 8.1).

**FIGURE 8.1**

Use the Send/Receive Groups dialog box to configure email send/receive settings.

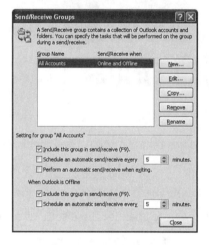

2. Click All Accounts and then click Edit. The Send/Receive Settings - All Accounts dialog box appears (see Figure 8.2).

3. Click an email account in the left pane, select Include the Selected Account in This Group, and then use the remaining options to specify the types of actions to perform (send, receive, and so on).

4. Click the next account and configure its settings. When you're done configuring account settings, click OK.

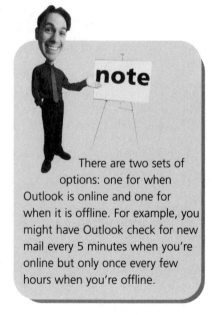

**note**

There are two sets of options: one for when Outlook is online and one for when it is offline. For example, you might have Outlook check for new mail every 5 minutes when you're online but only once every few hours when you're offline.

**FIGURE 8.2**

You can config-
ure each account
with different
settings within a
group.

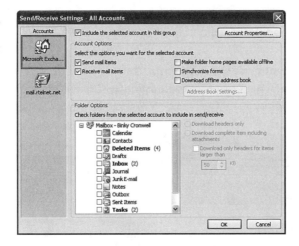

5. Back on the Send/Receive Groups dialog box, choose from the following
   options, as needed:

   - **Include This Group in Send/Receive**—When this option is selected,
     Outlook processes the selected group when you click Send/Receive on
     the toolbar or press F9.

   - **Schedule an Automatic Send/Receive Every**—When this option is
     selected, Outlook automatically sends and checks for new mail every *n*
     minutes.

   - **Perform an Automatic Send/Receive When Exiting**—When this
     option is selected, Outlook sends outgoing mail and checks for new
     mail when you exit Outlook.

6. Click Close to close the Send/Receive
   Groups dialog box.

Outlook processes send/receive groups when you
click Send/Receive on the toolbar. You can also
select Tools, Send/Receive and then choose a specific account to process only that one account.

## Creating Custom Views

You might have already guessed that you can
create your own views to suit your needs. You can
either modify an existing view or define a new

**tip**

Choose Tools, Options and
then click the Mail Setup tab
and turn off the option Send
Immediately When
Connected if you want messages to stay in your
Outbox until the next
send/receive. Otherwise, messages
are delivered immediately.

one. You probably won't need to create custom views right away, so I don't cover that in detail. Instead, I just point you in the right direction so you can experiment on your own.

To change the current view, click Customize Current View in the Navigation pane or choose View, Arrange By, Current View, Customize Current View. The Customize View dialog box that appears (see Figure 8.3) includes several buttons:

**FIGURE 8.3**

You use the
Customize View
dialog box to
create a custom
view.

- **Fields**—You can click this button to choose the fields that will appear in the view and the order in which they appear.

- **Group By**—You can click this button to group items together. For example, you can group contacts by company to create a company-specific phone list.

- **Sort**—You can click this button to change the order by which items are sorted for display in the folder. You can sort by multiple criteria.

- **Filter**—You can click this button to create a filter to view only the items that meet the filter conditions. For example, you can view only contacts with addresses in Colorado.

- **Other Settings**—You can click this button to change the fonts used for column and row labels, choose a grid line style, and make other general settings.

- **Automatic Formatting**—You can click this button to display items in a font you specify if they match a certain condition. For example, you can use a red header for messages from your boss and gray for junk mail.

- **Format Columns**—You can click this button to change the way each column appears, including its name (such as changing From to Sender).

- **Reset Current View**—You can click this button to reset the current view back to its default settings.

# Customizing the Navigation Pane

By default, the Navigation pane includes a button for most of the Outlook folders, and shows the folder list and a few other items that change with the selected folder. You can customize the Navigation pane to add other folders, add shortcuts to Web sites or local file folders, and so on.

**tip**

Right-click any button in the Navigation pane and choose Navigation pane Options to add or remove buttons.

To add or remove standard folder buttons, click Configure Buttons at the bottom right of the Navigation pane, click Add or Remove Buttons, and select the folders you want displayed.

You can also add or remove shortcuts from the Shortcuts section of the Navigation pane. To view the Shortcuts section, click the Shortcuts button on the Navigation pane.

## Adding Outlook Shortcuts

Follow these steps to add your own shortcuts to the Navigation pane:

1. Click the Shortcuts button to display the Shortcuts area of the Navigation pane.

2. Click the Add New Shortcut link to open the Add to Navigation Pane dialog box, shown in Figure 8.4.

**FIGURE 8.4**

Select the folder to which you want to add a shortcut.

3. Select an Outlook folder, a search folder, or a public folder from the list and click OK. Outlook adds the shortcut to the Shortcuts group.

You can also add your own groups to help organize your shortcuts:

1. Click the Add New Group link on the Navigation pane. Outlook adds a new group named New Group and highlights the name.

2. Type a new name for the group and press Enter.

After you create a new group, it's easy to add shortcuts to the new group. You can drag existing shortcuts from another group and drop them on the group name where you want the group to be located. Or you can right-click the group, choose Add New Shortcut from the pop-up menu, and add a shortcut as explained previously. Outlook adds the shortcut to the selected group rather than to the default Shortcuts group.

## Adding Other Types of Shortcuts

Outlook doesn't offer a direct way to add shortcuts to Internet Web sites, local folders or documents, or other non-Outlook folders, but you can use drag-and-drop to add shortcuts to these items. Follow these steps to add shortcuts from the Internet Explorer Favorites folder to Outlook:

1. Open Internet Explorer and click Favorites on the toolbar to open the Favorites folder in the Explorer Bar (or choose View, Explorer Bar, Favorites).

2. Position Internet Explorer and Outlook so that you can see the Favorites folder in Internet Explorer and the Navigation pane in Outlook.

3. Click and drag Internet shortcuts from the Favorites folder to a shortcut group in Outlook.

You can use a similar method to create shortcuts to document folders such as My Documents. Just open Windows Explorer, locate the folder for which you want to create a shortcut, and drag it to a shortcut group in Outlook.

# Setting How Outlook Handles Text for Replies and Forwards

Outlook automatically includes the original message content when you reply to or forward an email message. However, Outlook doesn't apply any special formatting, such as indention, for replies or forwards. You can configure Outlook to omit the original message, attach it, indent it, and so on. You can also have Outlook prefix each line of the original with a character (such as >) and add your name or other text in your replies.

Choose Tools, Options to open the Options dialog box. Then click E-mail Options on the Preferences tab to open the E-mail Options dialog box (see Figure 8.5), where you can change these settings.

**FIGURE 8.5**

Use the E-mail Options dialog box to configure reply and forward options.

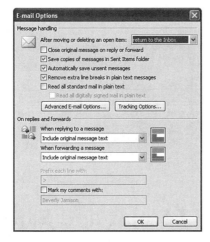

Use the On Replies and Forwards group of controls to change how Outlook handles replies and forwards.

# Changing How Outlook Notifies You of New Messages

Outlook does several things to let you know when a new message comes in, such as play a sound and display a desktop alert.

Choose Tools, Options to open the Options dialog box. Then select E-mail Options on the Preferences tab and Advanced E-mail Options to open the Advanced E-mail Options dialog box (see Figure 8.6).

You can use the four options in the When New Items Arrive in My Inbox group to specify what action(s) Outlook should take when a new message arrives. If you don't like Outlook 2003's new desktop alerts, click Desktop Alert Settings to open the Desktop Alert Settings dialog box to set the length of time and transparency for the alert.

**FIGURE 8.6**

Change new
message alerts
in the Advanced
E-mail Options
dialog box.

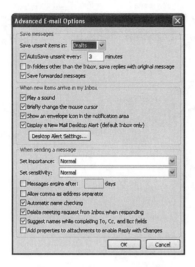

# Setting the Default Mail Format and Editor

The default mail format for new messages is Hypertext Markup Language (HTML),
and Outlook uses Word as the default message editor. I personally don't like either
one. Some of the people I know prefer not to receive HTML messages, and I don't
need the editing features in Word when I compose email.

Whatever your preferences, you can change the default mail format and editor.
Choose Tools, Options to open the Options dialog box, and then select the Mail
Format tab (see Figure 8.7).

**FIGURE 8.7**

Use the Mail
Format tab of
the Options dia-
log box to set
the default mes-
sage format and
editor.

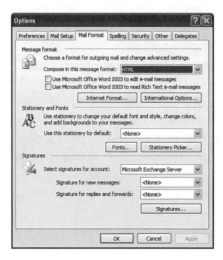

Use the Compose in This Message Format drop-down list box to choose your desired format (HTML, rich text format [RTF], or plain text). Use the two check boxes under this list box to specify whether you want to use Word to compose new messages and read RTF messages. Outlook uses its own forms if you clear these check boxes.

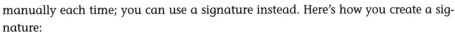

**note**

Keep in mind that a witty saying isn't so witty the 753rd time you see it in a message.

# Adding a Signature Block to Messages

You might want to include your contact information, a disclaimer, or a witty saying at the bottom of each message you send. You don't need to type it manually each time; you can use a signature instead. Here's how you create a signature:

1. Choose Tools, Options. The Options dialog box appears. Select the Mail Format tab.
2. Select an account from the Select the Signatures to Use with the Following Account drop-down list box.
3. Click Signatures and then click New.
4. Enter a name for the signature and click Next.
5. Type the signature text, format it, and click Finish.
6. Add other signatures, as needed, and click OK.
7. Choose a signature from the Signature for New Messages list box, and choose a signature from the Signature for Replies and Forwards drop-down list box.
8. Click OK.

# Changing the Reminder Sound and Default Time

Outlook defaults to a 15-minute reminder and uses the Reminder.wav file for an audible reminder. You can change the default reminder lead time and use a different sound file.

You can set the default reminder time on the Preferences tab of Outlook's Options dialog box (which you access by choosing Tools, Options). To change the sound, click the Other tab in the Options dialog box. Then click Advanced Options and click Reminder Options to open the Reminder Options dialog box. Next, click Browse and select a different sound file. Or you can clear the Play Reminder Sound option if you don't want Outlook to play a reminder sound.

# Turning Instant Messaging On and Off

Outlook 2003 provides some integration with Microsoft Windows Messenger, which is the chat and conferencing program included with Windows 2000 and later versions of Windows. For example, Outlook can show you the online/offline status of your Windows Messenger contacts in the Inbox when you click a message from a contact listed in your Messenger contacts. Outlook can also display a Person Names smart tag in certain forms, which helps you quickly perform certain messaging-related actions for the contact, such as starting a chat session.

You can find the options that enable/disable these two features in the Person Names group on the Other tab of the Options dialog box (which you access by choosing Tools, Options).

# Setting Calendar Week and Weekend Options

Outlook assumes that Monday through Friday is your work week and displays the Calendar folder accordingly (for example, compressing Saturday and Sunday into one column). You can change your work days and set the start of your work week, your work day (which also affects the Calendar folder and appointment default settings), and first week of the year.

To make changes to week and weekend options, choose Tools, Options to open the Options dialog box. Then click Calendar Options on the Preferences tab to open the Calendar Options dialog box (see Figure 8.8).

**FIGURE 8.8**

Set your work week and other calendar options in the Calendar Options dialog box.

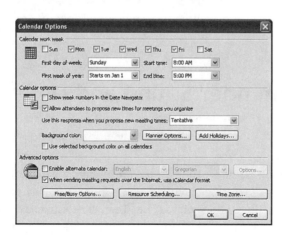

This dialog box includes three option groups:

- **Calendar Work Week**—With this group you can set the work week, daily start and end time, first day of the week, and first week of the year.
- **Calendar Options**—With this group you can set colors and other options for your Calendar folder and options for the Date Navigator (that is, the small calendar).
- **Advanced Options**—With this group you can use a non-Gregorian calendar and/or a different language. You can also set free/busy time, resource scheduling, and time zone options.

# Controlling How Outlook Saves and Displays Contact Names

By default, Outlook shows contacts' full names in the form *First Middle Last*. It files contacts by using the format *Last, First*. You can change these options if you prefer a different way of displaying contacts.

To control how Outlook displays contact names, choose Tools, Options to open the Options dialog box. Then click Contact Options on the Preferences tab (see Figure 8.9) and make any needed changes.

**FIGURE 8.9**

Use the Contact Options dialog box to control how Outlook displays contact names.

You can also choose to show an additional index in a different language.

Follow these steps to change the way Outlook sorts contact names:

1. Choose Tools, E-mail Accounts to start the E-mail Accounts Wizard.
2. Choose View or Change Existing Directories or Address Books and click Next.
3. Select the address book and click Change to open the Microsoft Outlook Address Book dialog box (see Figure 8.10).

**FIGURE 8.10**

Set the sort
method by
using the
Microsoft
Outlook Address
Book dialog
box.

4. Choose First Last (John Smith) to sort names by first name and last name or choose  File As (Smith, John) to sort based on the File As format specified in the Contact Options dialog box.

# The Absolute Minimum

As with all the other Office programs, Outlook provides many settings and options you can use to control the way the program looks and functions. You can access most of these options from the Options dialog box, which you open by choosing Tools, Options.

There are many other settings that you can change that aren't discussed here. Take some time to review the other tabs in the Options dialog box and the options they contain to decide what other settings you might want to change.

This chapter finishes our look at Outlook. In the next part of the book, you'll begin to learn about Microsoft Word, which you can use to create a rich variety of documents.

# PART III

# WRITING WITH WORD

**9**

# CREATING AND EDITING WORD DOCUMENTS

There's no doubt about it: Creating and editing documents in Word is one of the most common tasks for people who use Microsoft Office. Word started out as a DOS program back in the early 1980s. I've been using it since just about day one. I use it at least four hours a day, and usually more. As you begin to use Office, it's a good bet that you'll find yourself using Word a lot.

This chapter provides an introduction to Word, including how to work in Word's interface and how to open, create, and save documents. It also takes a look at some other basic tasks, such as moving text around, selecting text, and dealing with those green and red squiggly lines you see in some documents.

# Starting or Opening a Document

Word is designed primarily to create printed documents such as letters, reports, and newsletters, but you can create other types of documents with it, too. For example, you can even create Web pages with Word. Regardless of the type of document, as with other Office programs, you need to start by either opening an existing document or creating a new one.

> **tip**
>
> Word is okay for occasionally creating Web pages, but you should use a Web development program such as FrontPage it you need to create anything more for the Web. FrontPage is a separate Web page creation tool from Microsoft and is not included with Office 2003.

## Starting a New Document

When you first start Word, it opens a Getting Started task pane (see Figure 9.1). Click the Create a New Document link to open the New Document task pane (see Figure 9.2). This pane shows recently used documents, some links to help you quickly start a new document, and links to online information about Word and the other Office applications.

**FIGURE 9.1**

The Getting Started task pane helps you start a new document or open an existing one.

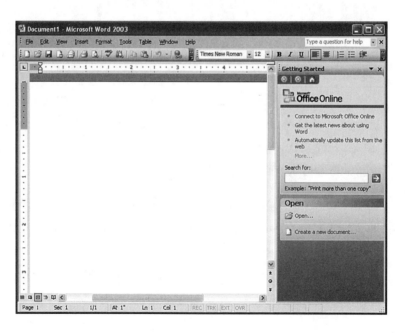

You really don't have to do anything else to create a new document—Word starts one automatically. Just close the task pane by clicking its Close button and then start typing.

If you want to create a new Web page, XML document, or email message, or if you want to create a new document from an existing one, click the Create a New Document link under the Open area. Word offers some new options in the New Document task pane (see Figure 9.2). Just click the type of document you want to create.

**tip**

You can open the New Document task pane by selecting File, New.

**FIGURE 9.2**

Word offers links for different types of documents.

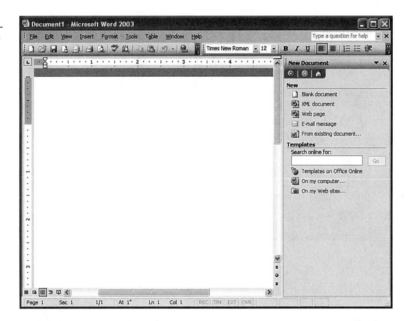

You can also create a new document from an existing one. For example, you might create a new letter from a previous letter you wrote. When you do this, Word starts a new document with all the content of the old one.

⇨ You can also start a new document from a document template. I explain how to use templates in Chapter 10, "Adding Pizzazz with Word."

**tip**

You can just click the New button on the toolbar to start a new document.

## Opening an Existing Document

Opening an existing document is just as easy as starting a new one. If you worked on the document recently, it might appear in the task pane, depending on how recently you worked on it. Just click the document link to open the document.

If you don't see the existing document you want in the task pane, click the More link under the Open area. Word shows the Open dialog box (see Figure 9.3).

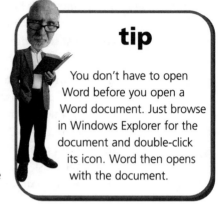

### tip

You don't have to open Word before you open a Word document. Just browse in Windows Explorer for the document and double-click its icon. Word then opens with the document.

Places Bar        Select a folder

**FIGURE 9.3**
Browse for and select a document in the Open dialog box.

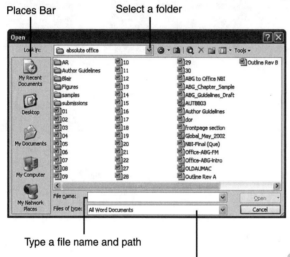

Type a file name and path

Choose the type of file to open

Use the Places Bar on the left side of the Open dialog box and the Look In drop-down list box to choose the location where the document is stored. When you find the document you want, click on it and then click Open (or just double-click the document).

Use the Files of Type drop-down list box in the Open dialog box to choose the types of files you want Word to show in the Open dialog box. Word defaults to All Word Documents, which includes

### note

The Open button in the Open dialog box includes a small arrow you can use to open a document in different ways. For example, you can open the document in read-only mode to make sure you don't change it.

more than just DOC files (such as documents and Web pages). You should choose Word Documents if you only want to see DOC files listed.

## Adding Text Where You Want It

When you work in Word, you use the cursor to determine where the text you type will be entered in the document. The *cursor* is the flashing vertical bar that you see just to the right of the text you type. You can think of the cursor as the *insertion point* for text—in other words, the place in the document where text will be entered when you type or insert text from the Clipboard.

Positioning the cursor is easy: Just use the arrow keys and the Page Up and Page Down keys on the keyboard to move the cursor into position. Or you can use the scrollbars at the edges of Word's window to find the place where you want the text inserted. Then just put the pointer over the location and click to place the cursor there.

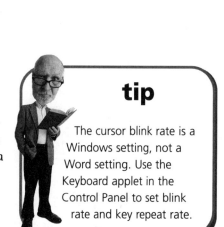

**tip**

As shown in Figure 9.3, the Open dialog box includes a toolbar you can use to delete documents, create folders, change the way documents appear in the dialog box, and perform other tasks.

## Moving Around in a Document and Between Documents

As mentioned in the previous section, you can use the Page Up, Page Down, and arrow keys to move through a document and position the cursor. Use the End key to move to the end of a line and the Home key to move to the beginning of a line. You can also use the mouse and scrollbars to scroll through the document and place the cursor in the document.

**tip**

The cursor blink rate is a Windows setting, not a Word setting. Use the Keyboard applet in the Control Panel to set blink rate and key repeat rate.

You can work with more than one document at a time in Word. For example, you might open a cover letter in one window and a resume in another. Each Word document appears in its own program window, as shown in Figure 9.4.

The easiest way to switch between Word documents is to press Alt+Tab on the keyboard. Or you can simply click a window to select it. You can also choose Window and then select a document from the Window menu to switch to that window.

**tip**

Hold down the Ctrl key and press the up or down arrow keys to move up or down a paragraph. Press Ctrl+Page Up to go to the top of a document or Ctrl+Page Down to go to the end of a document. Press Ctrl+G to move to a specific page.

**FIGURE 9.4**

Word documents appear in their own windows.

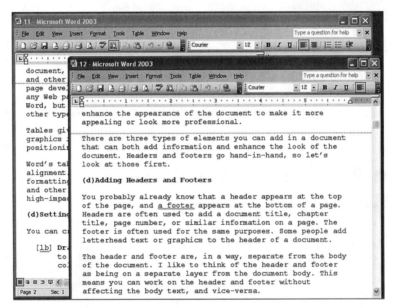

# Becoming Familiar with Word

Word has a user interface that is a lot like those of many other Windows programs. The title bar shows the name of the current document, the menu bar and toolbars give you access to commands, and the status bar shows information about the document. Figure 9.5 shows the Word window with many of its components labeled.

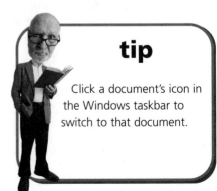

**tip**

Click a document's icon in the Windows taskbar to switch to that document.

Title bar with document title  Toolbars  Menu bar  Type a question here for help

**FIGURE 9.5**

Word includes lots of tools for editing a document.

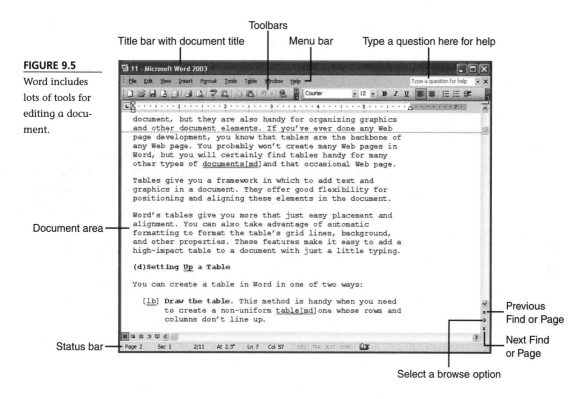

Document area

Status bar

Previous Find or Page

Next Find or Page

Select a browse option

The following sections explain many of the things you will see and use in the Word window.

## The Menu and Toolbars

As with other Windows applications, the menu bar in Word gives you access to Word's commands. You can also use Word's toolbars to access frequently used commands. You can hold the mouse over a toolbar button for a few seconds to see a brief description (called a *ScreenTip*) of the command associated with the button.

The Word toolbars are *dockable*, which means you can stick them at the edges of the Word window rather than let them float on the desktop. Just click a toolbar's handle and drag it to either float or dock it. (The handle is the vertical dashed line at the left edge of the toolbar.)

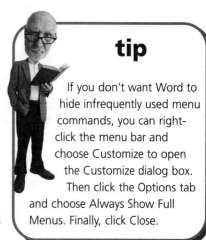

**tip**

If you don't want Word to hide infrequently used menu commands, you can right-click the menu bar and choose Customize to open the Customize dialog box. Then click the Options tab and choose Always Show Full Menus. Finally, click Close.

To remove or add toolbars, choose View, Toolbars and select the toolbar to add or remove.

## Scrollbars

Word adds horizontal and vertical scrollbars to the window to help you navigate through a document. You'll find three buttons at the bottom of the vertical scrollbar. Click the top button to search up through the document based on your previous Find or Go To action. Use the bottom button to search through the document based on the previous Find or Go To action. Click the middle button (the one with the circle on it) to open a menu that lets you browse through the document, using one of several methods, such as Find, Go To, Browse by Heading, and so on (see Figure 9.6).

**FIGURE 9.6**

Use the Select Browse Object button to choose a method for browsing the document.

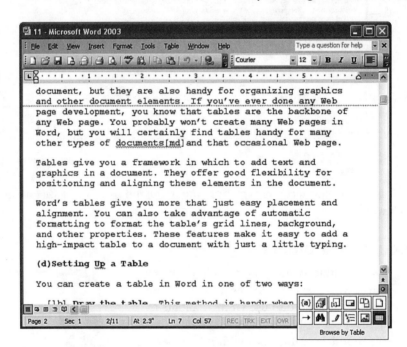

## Red Squiggly Underline

As you type in a document, you're sure to see words underlined with red squiggly lines. These are words that Word thinks are misspelled but for which it can't find a correction in its dictionary.

⇨ Word's spell-checking features and options are explained in Chapter 13, "Checking Spelling and Grammar."

## Green Squiggly Underline

In addition to red squiggly lines in a document, you're sure to see green squiggly lines. These indicate phrases that Word thinks have grammatical errors. If you turn off grammar checking, the lines go away.

⇨ Grammar-checking options are explained in Chapter 13.

# Working with Different Word Views

Word gives you a handful of view types to let you view a document in different ways. Choose View and then select the view type to switch to a particular view.

Normal view doesn't show how the document will look when it's printed, but it does show character formatting and is often best for entering and editing text.

Use Web view when you are working on a page that will be viewed in a Web browser or mainly within Word. Web view shows backgrounds, graphics, and other elements as they will appear when viewed in a browser or in Word.

Print Layout view is best when you need to see how a document will look when it's printed and when you need to edit headers, footers, and other elements that are not easily edited in the other views. Figure 9.7 shows a document in Print Layout view.

**FIGURE 9.7**

Use Print Layout view to see how a document will look when it is printed.

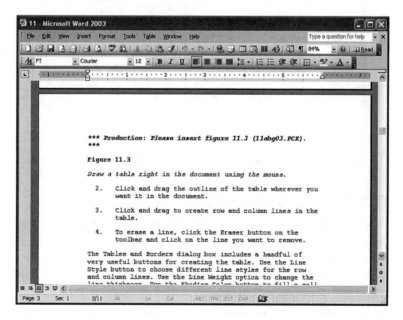

Word's Outline view lets you view a document's outline structure. The section "Working with an Outline," later in this chapter, provides details on outlines and Outline view.

Finally, you can use the Reading view (see Figure 9.8) when you are reading a long document onscreen. Reading Layout view hides unused toolbars, displays the Document Map for easy navigation, and lets you easily add comments to a document.

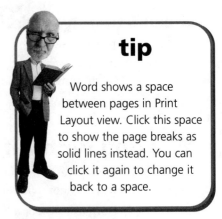

**tip**

Word shows a space between pages in Print Layout view. Click this space to show the page breaks as solid lines instead. You can click it again to change it back to a space.

**FIGURE 9.8**

Use Reading Layout view when reading and commenting on a document.

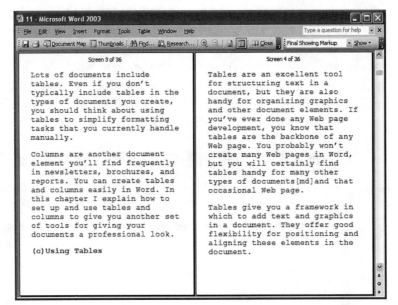

# Selecting and Deselecting Text

Earlier in this chapter you learned how to use the arrow keys and mouse to move around in a document. As you work in a document, you will often need to select and deselect text. For example, you might need to select a phrase to delete it or to make it bold or italic. You need to select a word or selection of text before you can copy it to the Clipboard. Before you perform any action on existing text, you need to select that text. Here are some ways to select text with the mouse:

- **Select a word or phrase**—Click to the left or right of the text and drag the cursor. Word highlights the selected text. You can also double-click a word to select it.

- **Select a line**—Place the pointer at the left edge of the line and when the pointer changes to a right-facing arrow, click the mouse button.

- **Select a paragraph**—Place the pointer at the left edge of the paragraph and when the pointer changes to a right-facing arrow, double-click the mouse button. Or triple-click a paragraph.

**tip**

Hold down the Ctrl key and use the arrow keys to select text up or down to the previous or next paragraph.

You can also select text by using the keyboard. Place the cursor to the right or left of the text, hold down the Shift key, and use the arrow keys to select the text. You can also use the Page Up, Page Down, Home, and End keys to select text.

# Cutting, Copying, and Moving Text

One of the biggest advantages of using a word processing program is its capability to reuse and move text around in a document. The main tool you use to accomplish that is the Clipboard. As with other Windows programs, with Word you can cut, copy, and paste text and other data within or between Word documents. You can also cut, copy, and paste between Word and other programs through the Clipboard.

First, select the text you want to cut, copy, or move. Then choose Edit, Cut or Edit, Copy to cut or copy the text to the Clipboard. To insert data from the Clipboard, place the cursor at the insertion point and choose Edit, Paste or Edit, Paste Special.

You can also move text around in a Word document easily without cutting and pasting. Just select the text to move and drag it with the mouse to the desired location.

# Adding New Lines and Page Breaks

**tip**

You can click the Show/Hide button on the Standard toolbar to turn on or off the display of non-printing characters.

When you press Enter in a Word document, Word inserts a *paragraph mark*, which by default is hidden. The paragraph mark starts a new paragraph on the next line.

In some cases >you might want to start a new line without starting a paragraph. For example, maybe you're adding a bulleted list. If you press Enter, Words adds a new bullet. But what if you want to start a new line without a bullet? You insert a new line. To do this, hold down the Shift key and press Enter to insert a new line character.

Word automatically creates page breaks based on your margin and page settings. However, sometimes you need to force Word to start a new page. To do this, hold down the Ctrl key and press Enter to insert a page break and start a new page.

Figure 9.9 shows a document with paragraph marks, new line characters, automatic page breaks, and manual page breaks.

**FIGURE 9.9**

A Word document can show paragraph marks, new line characters, automatic page breaks, and manual page breaks.

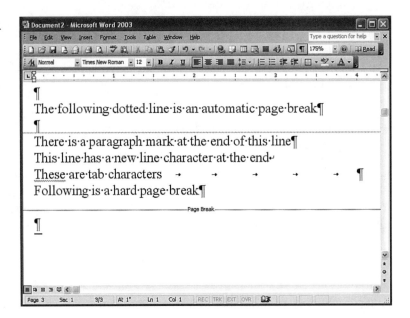

# Using Zoom In and Zoom Out

I work in front of a computer several hours a day, and much of that time is spent in Word. When I hit 40, I suddenly needed glasses. Age is a big factor, but part of the problem I'm sure is the time I spent squinting at the computer screen. Well, you can stop squinting! Just zoom the display.

The Standard toolbar includes a Zoom combo box that lets you either select or type a zoom percentage. If the text onscreen is too small for you to read comfortably, just select a larger zoom factor. You can also choose View, Zoom to open the Zoom dialog box, which is shown in Figure 9.10.

**FIGURE 9.10**

Use the Zoom dialog box to zoom in or out.

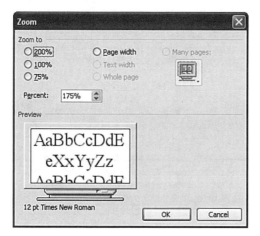

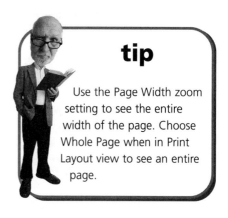

**tip**

Use the Page Width zoom setting to see the entire width of the page. Choose Whole Page when in Print Layout view to see an entire page.

Figure 9.11 shows a document at 100%, and Figure 9.12 shows a document zoomed to 150%.

**FIGURE 9.11**

This document is shown at 100%.

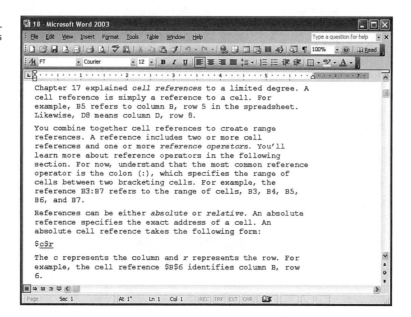

**FIGURE 9.12**

This document
is zoomed to
150%.

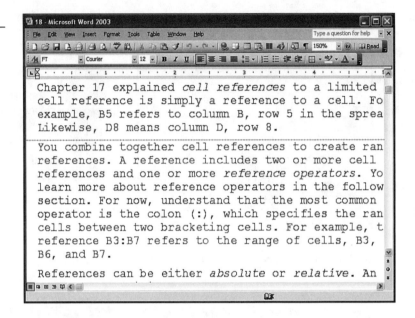

# Finding and Replacing Text

A task you'll likely need to accomplish quite often in Word is to find and possibly replace text. For example, say you want to replace every occurrence of the word *lie* with the phrase *embellish the truth*. Word makes it easy to do that (change text, not lie).

## Finding Text

To locate text in a document, press Ctrl+F or choose Edit, Find to open the Find and Replace dialog box (see Figure 9.13).

**FIGURE 9.13**

Use the Find
and Replace
dialog box to
locate text in a
document.

On the Find tab, type the text you want to find and then click Find Next. You can select the Highlight All Items Found In option to have Word highlight (that is, select) all occurrences of the text.

Click the More button to expand the Find and Replace dialog box as shown in Figure 9.14. These additional options let you refine a search by choosing the search direction, case, and so on.

**tip**

After you locate the first occurrence of the word or phrase you're searching for, you can close the Find and Replace dialog box and click the Previous Find and Next Find buttons in the vertical scrollbar to locate other occurrences.

**FIGURE 9.14**

You can expand the Find dialog box to set other search options.

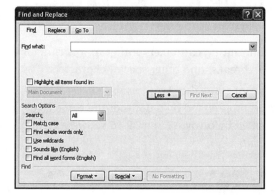

## Replacing Text

Many times you need to replace text rather than just locate it. The Replace tab of the Find and Replace dialog box lets you do just that. Figure 9.15 shows the expanded Replace tab. (As on the Find tab, you can click More to view these additional options.)

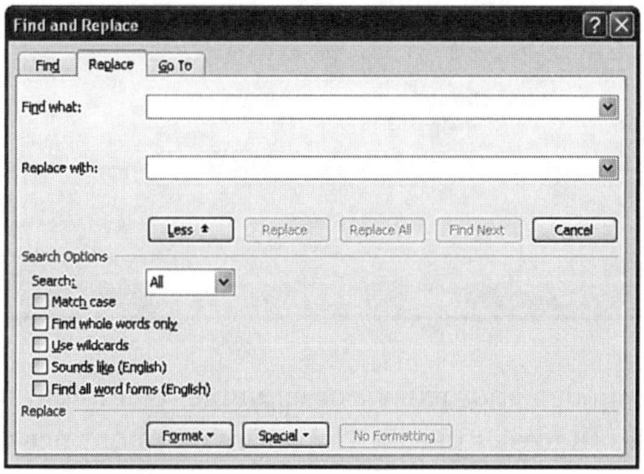

**FIGURE 9.15**

You can use the Replace tab to replace text throughout a document.

In the Find What text box, enter the text you want to replace. Enter the new text in the Replace With text box. Click Find Next to locate the next occurrence without replacing it. Click Replace to replace the current selection. Click Replace All to replace all occurrences of the text without being prompted to approve each change.

**tip**

Oops! You didn't want to make that last global replacement? Just press Ctrl+Z to undo the change.

# Showing/Hiding Hidden Characters

I touched briefly on nonprinting characters earlier in this chapter when I explained page breaks, paragraph breaks, and other special characters.

There are lots of other characters that Word usually hides. For example, a space is a unique character that is represented by a dot (not the same as a period) in a document. Tabs are represented by arrows. Figure 9.16 shows several types of hidden characters in a document.

**FIGURE 9.16**

You can show nonprinting characters in a document.

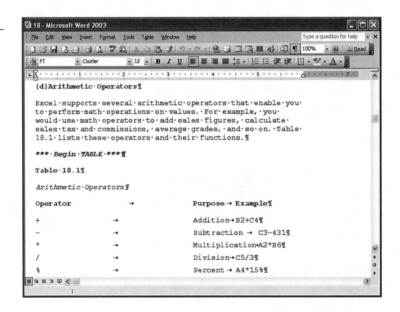

It's often useful to see hidden characters. For example, you might need to know where a document uses spaces in place of tabs. Or you might need to know which paragraphs use new line characters instead of paragraph marks.

You can turn on or off nonprinting character display in Word. To do so, just click the Show/Hide button on the Standard toolbar.

You can also turn on certain nonprinting characters. For example, maybe you want to see tab characters but not paragraph marks. In this case, you can choose Tools, Options to open the Options dialog box and then click the View tab. In the Formatting Marks group box, place a check mark beside each item you want to see in the document. The items you select here appear in the document, regardless of whether you have directed Word to show nonprinting characters by clicking Show/Hide.

# Working with an Outline

It's easy to navigate through short documents such as letters. When you're working with a long document such as a contract, a report, a term paper, an article, or a chapter in a book, it's best to work from an *outline*. Using an outline not only helps you organize your thoughts and the document's content, but it also makes it easier to navigate through the document by using the Document Map. Word makes it easy to create an outline and to use that outline to create your document.

## Using Outline View

Word provides the Outline view that displays the document's outline. You can expand and collapse headings in Outline view to easily navigate the document, add or change headings, and create the outline.

Choose View, Outline to switch to Outline view. Word shows the outline in expandable/collapsible form (see Figure 9.17). You can click a plus sign beside a heading to expand that heading, and you can click a minus sign to collapse a heading.

When you use Outline view, Word displays the Outlining toolbar, as shown in Figure 9.17. You can use the tools in the toolbar to change a heading's level, expand or collapse the entire outline to a specified level, turn formatting on or off, update the table of contents, and perform other outline-related tasks.

## Adding and Changing Outline Headings

When you work in Outline view, you can easily add headings and change their levels. Type a heading and then press Ctrl+Alt+left arrow to promote (increase) the heading level or Ctrl+Alt+right arrow to demote (decrease) the level. You can also use the Outline Level drop-down list in the Outlining toolbar to choose a specific level for a heading.

The Outlining toolbar

**FIGURE 9.17**

Use Outline
view to create
and view a doc-
ument outline.

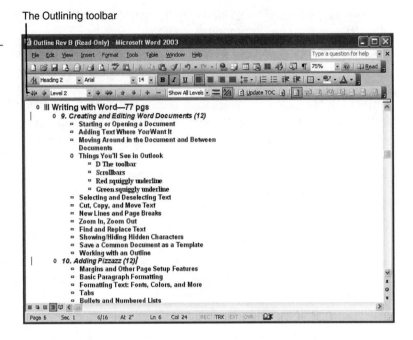

You can easily move headings around in an outline, as well. You can click a heading and press Ctrl+Alt+up arrow to move it up or Ctrl+Alt+down arrow to move it
down. You can also use the Move Up and Move Down buttons on the Outlining toolbar to move a heading.

## Moving Around an Outline

The Document Map gives you an easy way to
work with a lengthy outline and is particularly
handy for moving around a document as you
work on it. You simply choose View, Document
to turn on or off the Document Map. Figure 9.18
shows the Document Map.

Just click a heading level in the Document Map
to move to that point in the document.

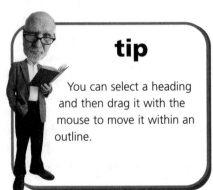

**tip**

You can select a heading
and then drag it with the
mouse to move it within an
outline.

**FIGURE 9.18**

You can use the Document Map to navigate a long document.

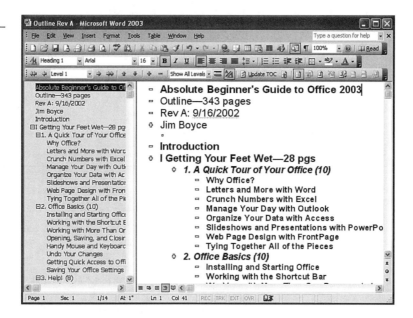

# THE ABSOLUTE MINIMUM

Word makes it easy to create documents of types including letters, reports, brochures, and even simple Web pages. In this chapter you learned how to start a new document, open an existing one, and work within documents in Word.

Most documents you create in Word contain mostly text, and learning how to select, copy, move, and cut text is important in your quest to become proficient with Word. This chapter explains those tasks.

When you work with large documents, an outline can help you organize your thoughts and the document's content, and it can also help you navigate through the document. This chapter explains how to create an outline and add headings to the outline.

The next chapter takes you beyond adding text to a Word document, explaining how to format words, paragraphs, and other items in the document, as well as add bulleted and numbered lists, colors, borders, and more.

## IN THIS CHAPTER

- Setting margins and other page settings
- Working with font and paragraph formatting
- Using bulleted lists, numbered lists, and tabs
- Using sections, templates, and styles
- Using borders and shading

10

# ADDING PIZZAZZ WITH WORD

There is a lot more to creating a professional-looking or visually interesting document than just typing. Word makes it easy to add pizzazz to a document. You can add font and paragraph formatting, color, highlights, bulleted lists, and other document elements to spice up a document.

This chapter explains the most common formatting features in Word and how to create basic document elements such as bulleted and numbered lists and tabbed columns. It also explains how to use templates and styles to simplify common formatting.

# Margins and Other Page Setup Features

Word uses a default set of margins and other settings that determines the look and layout of a document. These settings control a wide range of properties for the document, from margins to headers and footers. The following sections explain how to set and use these settings.

## Setting Margins

You don't need to set a document's margins or other layout settings before you begin typing. In fact, you can experiment with margins and other settings at any time.

To set margins, choose File, Page Setup. When the Page Setup dialog box appears, click the Margins tab (see Figure 10.1).

**FIGURE 10.1**

Use the Margins tab to set page margins, orientation, and other settings.

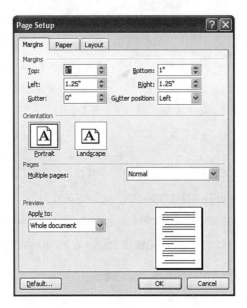

Use the controls in the Margins group box to set the four page margins. The Gutter option sets the size of the document *gutter*, which is a blank area of a page that is separate from (and in addition to) the space for the margin. The gutter is typically used with bound documents such as books to provide space for the binding. You use the Gutter Position option to specify where Word should locate the gutter.

The Orientation group lets you choose between Landscape and Portrait mode for the document. Use the Pages group to select the layout for the document; for example, you can choose Book Fold layout for a folded handout or an event program.

Finally, you can use the options in the Preview area to view the way your changes will affect the document. You can also apply changes to an entire document or to just the rest of the document, beginning at the current cursor location.

## Setting Paper Size and Other Settings

Use the Paper tab (see Figure 10.2) of the Page Setup dialog box to set paper size and other paper options for a document.

**FIGURE 10.2**

Use the Paper tab to set paper size and other paper-related settings.

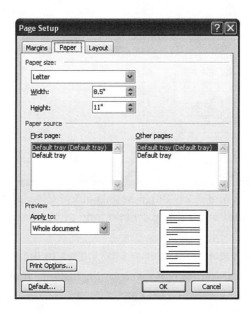

You can choose a predefined paper size from the Paper Size drop-down list box or enter a custom size, if needed. Use the Paper Source list boxes to choose where the paper should come from when you print the document. Use the Preview group box to see how your changes affect the document and whether to apply the changes to the entire document.

## Setting Page Layout Options

Use the Layout tab (see Figure 10.3) of the Page Setup dialog box to set layout options for a document.

**FIGURE 10.3**
Configure headers and footers by using the Layout tab.

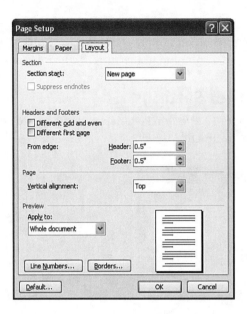

The Section options determine how Word handles sections. You can divide a document into different sections and apply different formatting to each of them. For example, one section might have a single column, and another section might have three columns.

➪ I explain sections in more detail later in this chapter, in the section "Sections."

You can use the Headers and Footers options to set the distance from the top and bottom edges of the page to the header and footer, respectively. You also can set two other options in this section:

- **Different Odd and Even**—You can select this option to use one header/footer combination on even pages, and a different header/footer on odd pages.

- **Different First Page**—You can select this option to use on the first page of a section or document a header or footer that is different from the headers or footers on the rest of the section or document.

Use the Vertical Alignment option in the Page group box to position the text on the page in relationship to the margins. For example, you can choose Bottom to have partial pages align with the bottom margin rather than with the top margin. The Justified option applies only to full pages; partial pages are aligned with the top margin when you select this option.

Use the Apply To drop-down list box to apply page layout settings to the entire document or only to the remainder of the document, beginning at the current point.

## Using Line Numbers

Line numbers in a document can help you structure the document or quickly locate certain sections. You don't need to add the line numbers manually—that would be a real chore! Instead, just turn on line numbers and then turn them off when you no longer need them.

Choose File, Page Setup to display the Page Setup dialog box, and then click the Layout tab. Next, click Line Numbers to open the Line Numbers dialog box (see Figure 10.4). Select Add Line Numbering and then use Start At to specify the starting line number. Use the From Text option to set the distance from the left margin to the line numbers. Use the Count By option to set the line number increment. The Numbering options let you choose how Word applies the numbers throughout the section or document.

**FIGURE 10.4**

Add line numbers by using the Line Numbers dialog box.

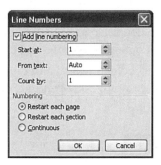

## Using a Page Border

You might want to include a border around the text on a page for some documents. Word makes it easy to do this. Simply choose File, Page Setup to open the Page Setup dialog box, and then click Borders on the Layout tab to open the Borders and Shading dialog box. Then select the Page Border tab, as shown in Figure 10.5.

Choose the border type from the Setting options, and then choose the line style, width, color, and optional pattern for the border. Use the Apply To drop-down list to specify how much of the document should have the border, and then click Options to set the margin and other settings for the border.

⇨  See the section "Borders and Shading," later in this chapter, for information on paragraph borders and shading.

**FIGURE 10.5**

Configure a page border by using the Borders and Shading dialog box.

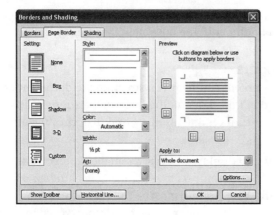

# Basic Paragraph Formatting

Most documents need at least some paragraph formatting. For example, in a letter you might want to set the distance between paragraphs so you don't have to insert a blank line between paragraphs. Or you might want to justify a paragraph against the right margin instead of the left or use double-spacing instead of single-spacing. Whatever the case, Word gives you lots of options for formatting paragraphs.

You can format a paragraph either before you add text to it or after the fact. Just select the paragraph and choose Format, Paragraph to open the Paragraph dialog box (see Figure 10.6).

**FIGURE 10.6**

You can add paragraph formatting by using the Paragraph dialog box.

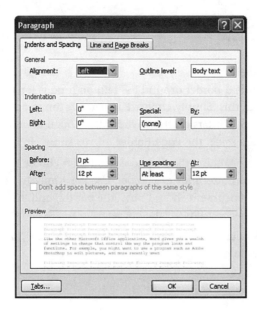

The Indents and Spacing tab contains the options that let you set the indentation, paragraph alignment, spacing between paragraphs (that is, before and after the paragraph), and line spacing. You can also set the outline level for a paragraph by using the Outline Level drop-down list box.

**tip**

You can also right-click a paragraph and choose Paragraph to open the Paragraph dialog box.

Use the Line and Page Breaks tab to control how Word handles breaks between lines and paragraphs. The options on this tab include the following:

- **Widow/Orphan Control**—You can prevent Word from printing the last line of a paragraph at the top of a page. Word moves the entire paragraph to the start of the page instead. This option also prevents Word from putting the first line of a paragraph at the bottom of a page by itself.

- **Keep with Next**—Use this option to make sure Word does not put a page break between one paragraph and the next.

- **Keep Lines Together**—Use this option to make sure Word does not put a page break within a paragraph.

- **Page Break Before**—Use this option to insert a manual page break (that is, start a new page) before a paragraph.

- **Suppress Line Numbers**—Use this option to make sure Word does not include line numbers beside a paragraph.

- **Don't Hyphenate**—Use this option to make sure Word does not use automatic hyphenation in a paragraph.

- **Tabs**—Click this option to set tabs.

You can use styles to automatically format paragraphs. Styles are covered later in this chapter, in the section "Templates and Styles." See the section "Tabs," later in this chapter, for more information on setting and using tabs.

# Text Formatting: Fonts, Colors, and More

Word doesn't limit your format control to just paragraphs. You can apply lots of different formatting options to text, changing fonts, colors, and more. The ability to change these settings gives you a lot of control over how a document appears and can really improve a document's look and impact.

## Using Fonts, Font Styles, and Colors

A *font* is the combination of a *font face* and other characteristics for text. Most people use the word *font* to mean the font face, such as Arial, Times New Roman, Courier, and so on. For simplicity's sake, I use the same convention in this book.

You can choose different fonts and other characteristics to change the way text appears. You can format text as you go along, or you can format it any time after you add it to a document. To format some existing text, first select the text and then choose Format, Font to open the Font dialog box (see Figure 10.7).

**FIGURE 10.7**

Use the Font dialog box to format text.

Almost all the options on the Font tab are self-explanatory. The Underline Style drop-down list box includes several options for underlining text. Choose the Words Only option if you don't want Word to underline spaces between words.

The other option on this tab to understand (and possibly stay away from) is the Default button. You should click this if you want Word to use the current font settings as the default for all documents based on the Normal.dot template. Templates are explained later in this chapter, in the section "Templates and Styles."

Click the Text Effects tab to choose from a small number of special character effects such as blinking text. Naturally, these only affect the way the text appears onscreen. Use the Character Spacing tab to set spacing, scale, kerning, and other settings that change the spacing and proportions of the text.

# Tabs

Tabs are particularly handy when you need to align columns in a document or section of a document. You can also use tabs to create a simple table of contents for a document.

Word defaults to a tab spacing of .5 inches, but you can set tabs at any spacing to suit your needs. The tabs affect the current paragraph or selection of paragraphs and any that you add after setting the tabs. Changing tab stops doesn't affect paragraphs that are not selected, so you can easily localize tab changes.

**note**

Word can automatically create tables of contents, indexes, and other document elements. To learn more, you can choose Insert, Reference, Index and Tables.

## Setting Tabs

Setting tabs is really easy. Just click in the paragraph where you want to set the tabs or select multiple paragraphs. Then choose Format, Tabs to open the Tabs dialog box (see Figure 10.8).

**FIGURE 10.8**

You can set and clear tabs by using the Tabs dialog box.

Enter a spacing value in the Tab Stop Position field and click Set. Enter another value and click Set again. The values you enter are measured from the left margin.

## Aligning Tabs and Using Leaders

Use the Alignment group of options in the Tabs dialog box to control how text is aligned with the tab. The Left, Center, and Right options align text at the left, center, and right of the tab stop, respectively. In other words, if you use a right-aligned tab stop, text will be inserted to the left of the tab as you type (that is, it will be right-aligned with the tab stop).

The Leader option determines whether Word adds a leader character with the tab. For example, a table of contents typically includes a leader character that fills the space between each heading and its page number. Just select the desired leader before you click Set to set the tab leader.

## Clearing Tabs

You can clear one or more tabs in a paragraph or a selection of paragraphs. When you clear a tab, Word defaults back to its default .5-inch spacing for the cleared tab. For example, assume that you set tabs at 1 inch, 4 inches, and 5 inches. You type a line and use three tabs, placing text at the 1-inch, 4-inches, and 5-inches spacing. You then clear the 4-inches tab. The result is tabs at 1 inch, 1.5 inches, and 5 inches.

To clear one or more tabs, select one or more paragraphs and choose Format, Tabs. In the Tabs dialog box, select the tab you want to clear and click Clear. You can click Clear All to clear all tabs.

# Bulleted and Numbered Lists

Bulleted and numbered lists are common in many types of documents. This book includes lots of bulleted lists to identify and explain program features and options. It uses numbered lists for step-by-step procedures.

Word gives you lots of options for creating automatic bulleted and numbered lists as you type so you don't have to set up lists manually. What's more, you can use different formats and characters for the lists.

## Using Bulleted Lists

The easiest way to add a bulleted list to a document is to click the Bullets button on the Formatting toolbar. This adds a bullet to the selected paragraph(s), using Word's default bullet settings and character.

To change bullet character or other aspects of a bulleted list, highlight the paragraphs and choose Format, Bullets and Numbering to open the Bullets and Numbering dialog box (see Figure 10.9).

**tip**

You can just click the Bullets button a second time to turn off bulleting.

**FIGURE 10.9**
You can choose
a bullet charac-
ter on the
Bulleted tab.

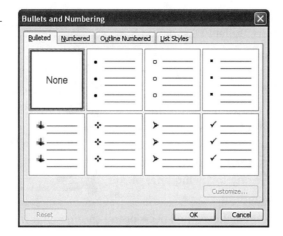

You can click an example on the Bulleted tab to use the bullet character in the
example. If you don't like any of the default options, click Customize to open the
Customize Bulleted List dialog box (see Figure 10.10).

**FIGURE 10.10**
Choose a differ-
ent bullet char-
acter from the
Customize
Bulleted List dia-
log box.

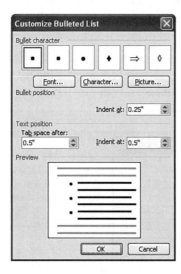

Click Character to choose a symbol character to use for a bullet. Or if you really
want to get fancy, click Picture to choose from a broad selection of small graphics.
You can also import your own graphics if Word's collection doesn't include one that
suits you.

Here's a bulleted list that explains the other options in the Customize Bulleted List dialog box:

- **Bullet Position**—You can use this drop-down list to set the indent from the margin to the bullet character.

- **Text Position**—You can use the Tab Space After option to set the distance from the bullet to the start of text on the first line. You can use the Indent At option to set the indent for any following lines of the bulleted paragraph.

- **Preview**—This area shows the effects of the changes you make to the bullet settings.

## Using Numbered Lists

You can use numbered lists for step-by-step explanations, procedures, or any other list for which you want Word to automatically number each paragraph in the list. Word gives you lots of options to control number format, starting number, and so on.

To quickly create a numbered list, select one or more paragraphs and click the Numbering button on the Formatting toolbar. To fine-tune the list, choose Format, Bullets and Numbering to open the Bullets and Numbering dialog box, and then click the Numbered tab (see Figure 10.11).

**FIGURE 10.11**
Choose a numbering style from the Numbered tab.

If the options on this tab don't suit you, you can click Customize to open the Customize Numbered List dialog box. These options perform essentially the same functions for numbered lists that the options in the Customize Bulleted List dialog box perform for bulleted lists. See the previous section for an explanation of these settings, or just experiment and observe the effect they have in the Preview area of the dialog box.

## Continuing Numbering from a Previous List

In some cases you might have unnumbered paragraphs in the middle of a numbered list. You type the list, format it as a numbered list, and then add unnumbered paragraphs after it. Now you're ready to add some more numbered paragraphs.

When you click the Numbering button, however, Word starts numbering at 1 again. This is easy to fix. Just choose Format, Bullets and Numbering to open the Bullets and Numbering dialog box, and then select the Numbered tab. Then choose Continue Previous List and click OK.

## Restarting Numbering a List at a Specific Number

Say you've created a numbered list, but now you decide you need to start the list at a different number. To do this, you select the paragraph in the list where you want to start renumbering and choose Format, Bullets and Numbering. When the Bullets and Numbering dialog box appears, click Customize, choose a number from the Start At drop-down list box, and click OK.

# Sections

A *section* in a Worddocument is pretty much what it sounds like—a section of the document that has different properties from other sections. For example, you might want to have one section of single-column paragraphs, followed by a section of two-column text, followed by a section of graphs and charts. Each section needs to have different margins or other page layout settings. Figure 10.12 shows a document with different sections.

Sections vary the layout of a document within a page or from one page to another. You start a new section by inserting a *section break*. You can insert a handful of different section breaks by choosing Insert, Break:

- **Next Page**—This type of section break starts the section on a new page.
- **Continuous**—This type of section break starts the section on the same page.
- **Odd Page or Even Page**—These types of section breaks start a new section on the next odd or even page, respectively.

**FIGURE 10.12**

You can use sections to vary formatting in a document.

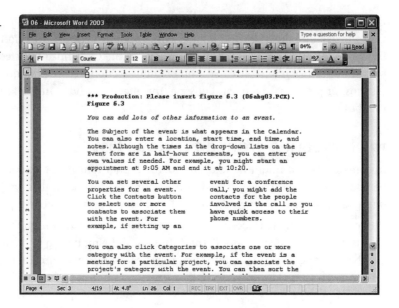

You can set several formatting options for a section:

- Margins, paper size, paper source, and orientation
- Page borders and vertical alignment
- Headers, footers, footnotes, and endnotes
- Page numbering and line numbering
- Columns

A section break holds the formatting of the section that precedes it. If you delete a section break, the preceding text takes on the formatting of the following section.

## Inserting a Section Break

To insert a section break, choose Insert, Break to open the Break dialog box. Then choose the type of break you want to insert from the four options in the Section Break Types list and click OK.

**note**

The last paragraph mark in a document holds the formatting for the last section of the document—or for the entire document, if there are no other sections.

## Formatting a Section

After you insert a section break, it's a snap to format the section. Just click anywhere in the section and use Word's formatting options to format the page layout and other characteristics for the section, as described earlier in this chapter.

# Templates and Styles

Setting up formatting can take a lot of time, particularly if you need to use lots of different formatting across paragraphs or sections. Word provides two features that help you quickly and easily apply formatting for characters, paragraphs, and an entire document: styles and templates.

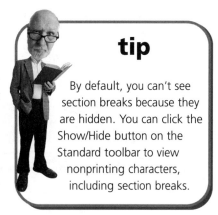

**tip**

By default, you can't see section breaks because they are hidden. You can click the Show/Hide button on the Standard toolbar to view nonprinting characters, including section breaks.

## Using Styles

A *style* is a set of formatting properties that you can apply to text, tables, and lists in a Word document. You can think of a style as a collection of formatting commands that you apply as a whole. Applying formatting with styles simplifies complex formatting. Word includes several predefined styles, and you can create as many of your own as needed.

For example, let's say that you want to apply a certain font face, font size, font style, and paragraph formatting to a document heading. Instead of going through all the motions to accomplish those formatting tasks manually, you can just apply a style to the paragraph and—poof!—it's formatted.

You can create four types of styles:

- **Paragraph**—This type of style sets alignment, line spacing, tabs, borders, and character formatting.

- **Character**—This type of style controls the font face, size, and style of selected text in a paragraph.

- **Table**—This type of style applies borders, shading, alignment, and fonts in a table.

- **List**—This type of style applies alignment, numbering, bulleting, and font characteristics to numbered or bulleted lists.

## Creating a Style

You follow these steps to create a style:

1. In Word, choose Format, Styles and Formatting to open the Styles and Formatting pane (see Figure 10.13).

**FIGURE 10.13**

You can choose a style or create new styles from the Styles and Formatting pane.

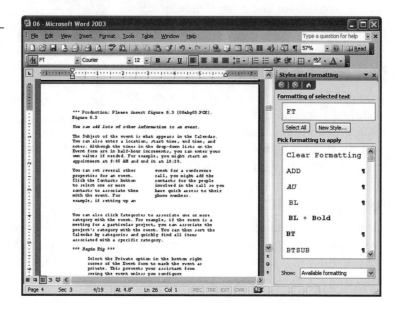

2. Click New Style to open the New Style dialog box (see Figure 10.14).

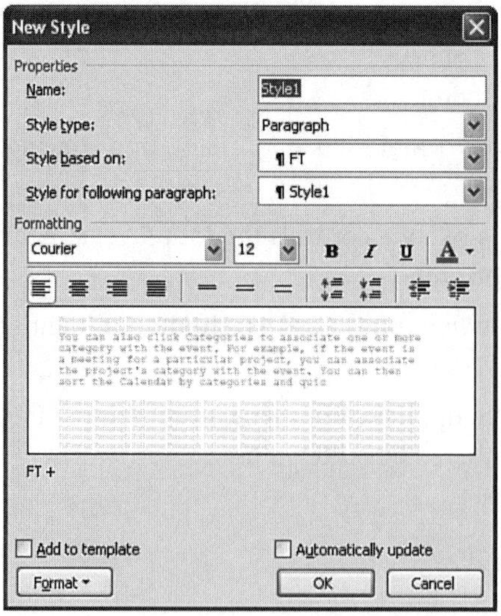

**FIGURE 10.14**

You can create a new style by using the New Style dialog box.

3. Type a name for the style in the Name text box.

4. Choose the style type from the Style Type drop-down list box.

5. Choose an existing style from the Style Based On drop-down list box if you want to base the style on an existing style. Otherwise, choose (no style) from the list to start a new style, using Word's default settings.

**tip**

Choosing the correct style for the following paragraph can really simplify formatting. All you have to do to apply the correct style to the next paragraph is simply press Enter.

6. From the Style for Following Paragraph drop-down list box, choose the style you want to apply to the paragraph that follows the one to which you are applying this style.

7. Click Format, choose the type of item you want to format (such as Paragraph), and then choose the desired formatting options in the resulting dialog box. You can also use the buttons on the New Style dialog box to quickly apply formatting.

8. Repeat step 7 to apply other formatting as needed for the style.

9. Choose the following options, if appropriate, and then click OK to create the style:

   ■ **Add to Template**—You can add the style to the template that is attached to the current document. If this option is not selected, Word adds the style only to the document itself and not to its attached template.

   ■ **Automatically Update**—You can automatically update the style through the document when you make a formatting change where the style is already applied. If this option is not selected, Word applies the change only to the selected text.

**tip**

I prefer to apply styles by using the keyboard because for me, it's quickest. You can press Ctrl+Shift+S to highlight a style in the Style list, and then type the name of the style and press Enter.

## Applying Styles

Using the Formatting toolbar is the easiest way to apply a style. You simply click in a paragraph, select some text or a list, and choose a style from the Style drop-down list box.

You can also apply a style by choosing Format, Styles and Formatting and then selecting a style from the Styles and Formatting pane. Close the pane when you're satisfied with the style.

### Changing a Style

You can easily modify an existing style:

1. Choose Format, Styles and Formatting.

2. Place the cursor over the style in the Pick Formatting to Apply list.

3. Click the down arrow at the right edge of the style name and choose Modify to open the Modify Style dialog box, which is identical to the New Style dialog box.

4. Make the appropriate changes and click OK. The style is modified, and depending on the Automatically Update option, the document changes anywhere the style has already been used.

**tip**

Press Ctrl+Z to undo a style application.

## Using Templates

A *template* is a special type of document that you use to quickly set up another document. For example, let's say you frequently create contracts that are formatted a particular way and even have common text. With a template, you don't have to set up the formatting or enter the common text more than once. You just create a new document based on the template.

### Saving a Document as a Template

Basically, a template is a regular Word document saved as a document template. Templates use a .dot filename extension rather than .doc.

Follow these steps to create a template:

1. Start a new document or open an existing document if you want to base the template on an existing document.

2. Create styles in the document, as needed.

3. Add common text to the document, as needed.

**tip**

Word includes a handful of predefined templates, and you can easily create your own to suit your needs.

4. Add macros to the document, as needed.

5. Choose File, Save As. Enter a name and location for the document template, choose Document Template from the Save As Type drop-down list box, and click Save to save the template and close the dialog box.

## Attaching a Template to a Document

When you apply a template to a document, all the styles and macros in the template become available in the new document. You can direct Word to update the existing styles in a document with the ones from a template when you attach the template.

You follow these steps to attach a template to a document:

1. Open Word and open the document to which you want to attach a template.

2. Choose Tools, Templates and Add-ins. The Templates and Add-ins dialog box appears.

3. On the Templates tab (see Figure 10.15), click Attach and browse for and select the template. Then click Open.

**FIGURE 10.15**

Choose and attach a template from the Templates tab.

4. If you want styles updated automatically with those from the template, click the Automatically Update Document Styles check box.

5. Click OK. Word adds the template's styles to your document. If you selected the Automatically Update Document Styles check box, styles in the document change to reflect the new styles in the template.

### Starting a New Document from a Template

In addition to assigning a template to a document you already have open, you can start a new, blank document from a template. Here's how you do it:

1. Choose File, New to open the New Document task pane.

2. Click the On My Computer link under the Other Templates area.

3. Click a tab, choose a template, and click OK. Word starts a new document based on the template.

# Borders and Shading

Earlier in this chapter I explain that you can add a border and/or shading to an entire page. You can also apply borders and shading to paragraphs. For example, you might want to put a box around a paragraph to set it off.

To add borders and shading, first select the paragraphs to format and choose Format, Borders and Shading to open the Borders and Shading dialog box. Then select the Borders tab (see Figure 10.16).

**FIGURE 10.16**

Use the Borders and Shading dialog box to add borders and shading to a paragraph.

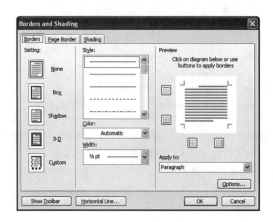

Use the options on the Borders tab to add a border around one or more paragraphs. Use the Shading tab to apply a color or a pattern to the selected paragraphs. Use the Page Border tab to apply a border to the entire page.

# THE ABSOLUTE MINIMUM

Creating an appealing document with Word requires much more than just typing text. In this chapter you learned how to add font and paragraph formatting to a document, add bulleted and numbered lists, and work with tabs. You also learned how sections enable you to format various parts of a document in different ways.

When you need to use the same format several places in a document or from one document to the next, you can rely on styles to apply that formatting. In addition, templates enable you to quickly create documents that contain similar elements or text.

In addition to font and paragraph formatting, you can also apply borders and shading to a document to add further appeal.

Now that you are familiar with some of the ways to add pizzazz to documents, you're ready to learn about a few more advanced topics. The next chapter explains how to add tables and columns to a document.

**11**

# Organizing with Tables and Columns

Lots of documents include tables. Even if you don't typically include tables in the types of documents you create, you should think about using tables to simplify formatting tasks that you currently handle manually.

Columns are another document element you'll find frequently in newsletters, brochures, and reports. You can create tables and columns easily in Word. This chapter explains how to set up and use tables and columns so that you have another set of tools for giving your documents a professional look.

# Using Tables

Tables are excellent tools for structuring text in a document, and they are also handy for organizing graphics and other document elements. If you've ever done any Web page development, you know that tables are the backbone of any Web page. You probably won't create many Web pages in Word, but you will certainly find tables handy for many other types of documents—and occasionally Web pages.

Tables give you a framework in which to add text and graphics in a document. They offer good flexibility for positioning and aligning elements in a document.

Word's tables give you more that just easy placement and alignment. You can also take advantage of automatic formatting to format a table's grid lines, background, and other properties. These features make it easy to add a high-impact table to a document with just a little typing.

## Setting Up a Table

You can create a table in Word in one of two ways:

- **Draw the table**—This method is handy when you need to create a nonuniform table—that is, one whose rows and columns don't line up.

- **Insert a table**—This method works well for uniform tables, where column and row layout is consistent throughout the table.

Figure 11.1 shows two tables. The first one was created using the Draw Table command and the second was created by inserting a uniform table.

**FIGURE 11.1**

You can draw tables by using two different methods.

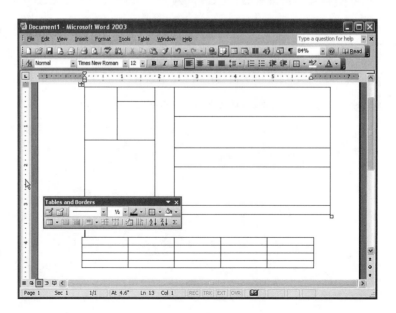

## Inserting a Table

The method you'll likely find easiest for creating tables is to insert them. Follow these steps to insert a uniform table:

1. Place the cursor where you want the table to be inserted.

2. Choose Table, Insert, Table. The Insert Table dialog box appears (see Figure 11.2).

**tip**

Regardless of how you create a table, you can change its layout to make it more or less uniform. See the following section for details.

**FIGURE 11.2**

You can insert a table by using the Insert Table dialog box.

3. Choose the number of rows and columns for the table from the Table Size drop-down list boxes.

4. Choose one of the following options:

   ■ **Fixed Column Width**—With this option you can choose Auto to let Word create equal column widths, or you can select a specific column width.

   ■ **AutoFit to Contents**—When you select this option, Word adjusts the column width according to the amount of text you type in it.

   ■ **AutoFit to Window**—When you select this option, you can create a table that automatically resizes to fit the Web browser window. The table resizes dynamically as the browser window size changes.

**tip**

You can add columns and rows after you create a table, so don't worry about getting the exact number right when you create the table.

5. If you want to use the current settings as the default for future tables, select the Remember Dimensions for New Tables check box.

6. Click OK to create the table.

## Drawing a Table

Drawing a table is handy when you need to rough out a table that doesn't have a uniform number of rows and columns. You follow these steps to draw a table:

1. Choose Table, Draw Table. Word switches to Print Layout view and opens the Tables and Borders toolbox (see Figure 11.3).

**FIGURE 11.3**

You can draw a table right in a document by using the mouse.

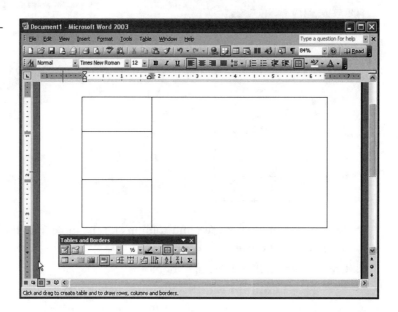

2. Click and drag the outline of the table to wherever you want it in the document.

3. Click and drag to create row and column lines in the table.

4. To erase a line, click the Eraser button on the toolbar and click the line you want to remove.

The Tables and Borders toolbox includes a handful of very useful buttons for creating tables. Use the Line Style button to choose different line styles for the row and column lines. Use the Line Weight option to change the line thickness. Use the Shading Color button to fill a cell with color. You should spend a few minutes experimenting with the other buttons to learn what they do.

# Merging and Splitting Cells

A table *cell* is the box that is formed by the column and row lines, much like the cells in a spreadsheet are formed by rows and columns. You can enter text, graphics, or other objects in cells.

As you work with tables—particularly nonuniform ones—it's likely that you will need to merge cells to create one larger cell or split a cell to create smaller cells within it.

To merge cells, first select the cells to be merged. Then choose Table, Merge Cells.

If you need to split a cell, click in the cell (or select multiple cells) and choose Table, Split Cells. In the Split Cells dialog box that appears, choose the number of columns and rows needed and click OK.

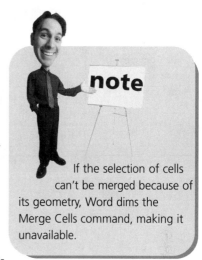

**note**

If the selection of cells can't be merged because of its geometry, Word dims the Merge Cells command, making it unavailable.

# Adding Text to a Table

It doesn't take much effort to add text to a table. You only need to click in the cell where you want the text and start typing. You can press Tab to move to the next cell, press Enter to start a new paragraph within the cell, and press Tab in the last cell to add a new row at the bottom of the table.

Entering text in a table isn't really any different from adding text outside a table. For example, you can use the Clipboard to cut text from a cell and paste it into a different cell. Or you can just highlight the text and drag it to the new location to relocate the text.

# Converting Paragraphs to a Table and Vice Versa

At some point you might have some text in a document that would work better as a table. Or, maybe you decide you don't want a table, but you want to keep the text in the table. Word lets you convert both ways.

## Converting Text to a Table

Follow these steps to convert text to a table:

1. Highlight the text you want to convert (click and drag over the text to select it).

2. Choose Table, Convert, Text to Table. The Convert Text to Table dialog box appears (see Figure 11.4).

**FIGURE 11.4**

You can convert
text by using
the Convert
Text to Table
dialog box.

3. Word scans the text and tries to determine the number of columns based on the text's contents. If needed, change the number of columns by using the Number of Columns drop-down list.

4. Set the column width by using one of the options in the AutoFit Behavior group box.

5. In the Separate Text At group box, choose the character that you want Word to use to identify the table columns.

6. Click OK to create the column. Press Ctrl+Z if it doesn't turn out the way you want.

You might need to adjust your text a bit before converting it to a table. For example, you might need to add separator characters (for example, tabs or commas) so Word will properly convert the text into columns in the table.

## Converting a Table to Text

You created a table and now you've decided it would work better as regular paragraphs. No problem! You just convert it back to text:

1. Click anywhere in the table.

2. Choose Table, Convert, Table to Text. The Convert Table to Text dialog box appears (see Figure 11.5).

3. Choose the character you want Word to insert between columns in the converted text.

4. If the table contains nested tables (that is, tables inside tables) and you want Word to convert those to text, select the Convert Nested Tables check box. Clear this check box to leave the nested tables as tables.

5. Click OK to convert the table to text.

**FIGURE 11.5**

You can convert tables to text by using the Convert Table to Text dialog box.

## Adding Table Captions

You could add a paragraph above or below a table to serve as the table's caption, but that means you would also have to fiddle with formatting to get it into just the right position. You would also have to keep track of which table number to use next. A better method is to let Word place the caption for you. Not only does this simplify formatting, but it means that Word keeps track of the table numbers for you.

Follow these steps to insert a table caption:

1. Click anywhere in the table.

2. Choose Insert, Reference, Caption. The Caption dialog box appears (see Figure 11.6).

**FIGURE 11.6**

Add a caption to a table by using the Caption dialog box.

3. Type the text for the caption in the Caption text box.

4. From the Position drop-down list box, choose the location where you want the caption inserted in relationship to the table.

5. Click Numbering to open the Caption Numbering dialog box (see Figure 11.7).

6. Choose a numbering format from the Format drop-down list box.

7. Optionally, select the Include Chapter Number check box if you want Word to determine a chapter number based on the heading level you choose. To use this option, you must have previously set up the document with an outline and assigned the appropriate heading level to each chapter in the document.

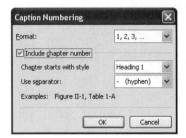

8. Click OK when you're satisfied with the numbering. Click OK to create the caption.

Word positions the caption for you, but you can adjust the formatting to move it away from the table a bit, if needed. Just right-click the caption and choose Paragraph. In the Paragraph dialog box, you change the before or after spacing to add space between the table and caption. You can change the indents to move the caption left or right.

All this easy formatting is nice, but there is another, more important, reason to let Word insert captions for you. Word inserts each caption as a field, which not only enables Word to keep track of table numbers but also helps you navigate the document. For example, you can press Ctrl+G or choose Edit, Go To to open the Go To tab of the Find and Replace dialog box (see Figure 11.8). Choose Table from the Go To What list, enter a table number, and click Go To to navigate right to that table.

The other main advantage of letting Word place captions for you is that you can have Word update the table numbers if you remove a table or insert one. To update the numbering before you print the document, you choose File, Print, to open the Print dialog box, and then you click Options. After you select the Update Links option and click OK, you can print the document.

You can also update fields without printing. To update one field, Select the field and press F9. To update all fields, Choose Edit, Select All and then press F9 to update the fields.

# Sorting Text

We all learned alphabetization in school. In a long table or long stretch of text, spelling *alphabetization* can be easier than actually doing it.

Computers are great at repetitive structured tasks such as sorting, and Word can handle sorting for you. For example, maybe you've entered a long table without worrying about whether the rows are in alphabetical order. Now you realize you'd like to add that order. Here's how to do it:

1. Click anywhere in the table.

2. Choose Table, Sort. The entire table is selected, and the Sort dialog box appears (see Figure 11.9).

**FIGURE 11.9**

Use the Sort dialog box to sort text in or out of a table.

3. From the Sort By drop-down list box, choose the column on which you want to sort. This is often the first column in a table, but it certainly doesn't have to be. Word can sort based on other columns, but it does not change the column order.

4. Choose whether to sort in ascending or descending order.

5. If the table includes a header row that needs to be excluded from the sort so that it remains at the top of the table, choose the option Header Row. Otherwise, choose No Header Row.

6. Click OK to sort the table.

As Figure 11.9 illustrates, there are many other options you can use when sorting text. For example, you can sort based on multiple columns.

You can also sort text outside a table. For example, say you have a series of paragraphs that you've formatted as bulleted text and you want to sort them by the first letter of each paragraph. Just highlight the text you want to sort and choose Table, Sort. Then specify the sort criteria in the Sort dialog box and click OK to sort the text.

# Using Columns

Another useful formatting element is the *column*. By default, Word enters paragraphs in single-column format. In some situations, however, you might need to format text into multiple columns. For example, using columns in a newsletter or brochure can give you very professional-looking results.

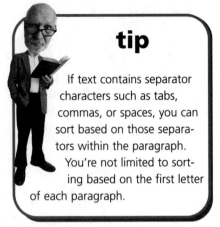

**tip**

If text contains separator characters such as tabs, commas, or spaces, you can sort based on those separators within the paragraph. You're not limited to sorting based on the first letter of each paragraph.

When you format text as columns in Word, you can set the number of columns, spacing between columns, and a handful of other options. The following section explains how to set up and use columns.

You can format text as columns without using sections, but I suggest that you insert section breaks before and after the text you want to format as columns, if possible. This makes formatting easier.

When you format columns, the options available to you vary a bit, depending on the current selection. For example, if you click inside a section without selecting any text, Word lets you choose between formatting the current section or everything from that point forward in the document. If you highlight some text, you can format that selection as columns or use other options offered by Word, depending on the document structure.

Follow these steps to format columns in a document while using sections:

1. Insert section breaks before the first and after the last paragraphs to be formatted as columns.

2. Click in the section and choose Format, Columns. The Columns dialog box appears (see Figure 11.10).

3. In the Presets group box, select the column layout you want.

4. If you selected a column layout with equal column spacing but want to vary the spacing, clear the Equal Column Width check box. Adjust the column spacing by using the options in the Width and Spacing group box.

5. Select the Line Between check box if you want a vertical line added between columns.

**FIGURE 11.10**

Use the Columns dialog box to format text in multiple columns.

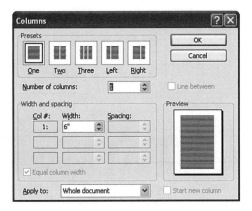

**FIGURE 11.10**

Use the Columns dialog box to format text in multiple columns.

6. Click OK to format the section in columns.

7. Right-click the paragraph after the columns, choose Paragraph, and set the spacing before if needed to add separation between the columns and the following paragraph. Do the same for the paragraph that precedes the columns.

# THE ABSOLUTE MINIMUM

There is much more to creating many documents with Word than simply entering text and formatting fonts and paragraphs. For example, tables are an important part of many documents. Word makes it easy to convert text to tables and vice versa, as well as to sort the text in a table and add headers and captions.

Another useful feature in Word—particularly for reports and brochures—is the capability to format paragraphs in columns. This chapter explains how to set up columns as well as form them and control how the text flows in the columns.

The next chapter explains how to add even more pizzazz to your documents, with graphics, sound, and video clips.

**12**

# MORE THAN JUST WORDS

Many business documents contain nothing but text, although that text might be formatted to make it stand out. Other documents, however, need other elements. For example, you might need to insert headers and footers in a report or term paper. Or maybe you want to add a watermark to the background of a page or add graphics to a document.

This chapter explains how to move beyond text-only documents to create documents that contain graphical and other multimedia elements.

# Adding Headers, Footers, and Watermarks

The text in the body of a document is almost always the most important part of the document. Other elements, however, can add other important information or simply enhance the appearance of the document to make it more appealing or look more professional.

There are three types of elements you can add in a document that can both add information and enhance the look of the document: headers, footers, and watermarks. Headers and footers go hand-in-hand, so let's look at those first.

## Adding Headers and Footers

You probably already know that a *header* appears at the top of the page and a *footer* appears at the bottom of a page. A header is often used to add a document title, chapter title, page number, or similar information on a page. A footer is often used for the same purposes. Some people add letterhead text or graphics to the header of a document.

The header and footer are, in a way, separate from the body of the document. I like to think of the header and footer as being on a separate layer from the document body. This means you can work on the header and footer without affecting the body text and vice versa.

Follow these steps to add to a document header that contains page numbers:

1. Open the document in Word and choose View, Header and Footer.

2. Type in the header area the text that you want included in the header. For example, you could type **Page:** followed by a space.

3. Use the buttons in the Header and Footer toolbar (see Figure 12.1) to insert special elements, such as page numbers. For example, you could click the Insert Page Number button.

4. Press the spacebar, type **of**, and press the spacebar again.

5. Click the Insert Number of Pages button, press the spacebar, and type **pages**.

6. Click Close on the Header and Footer toolbar.

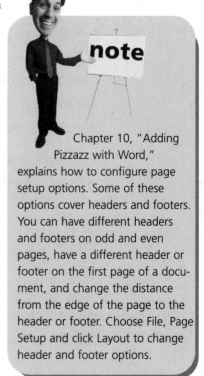

**note**

Chapter 10, "Adding Pizzazz with Word," explains how to configure page setup options. Some of these options cover headers and footers. You can have different headers and footers on odd and even pages, have a different header or footer on the first page of a document, and change the distance from the edge of the page to the header or footer. Choose File, Page Setup and click Layout to change header and footer options.

**FIGURE 12.1**

Type the header text and add special header elements from the Header and Footer toolbar.

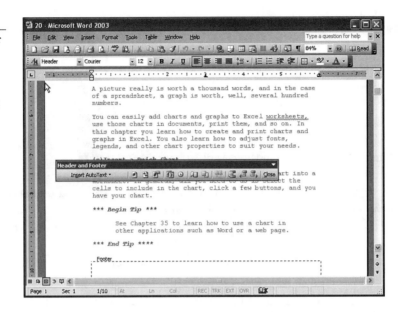

At this point, the document should show a header that contains the text "Page *n* of *nn* pages," where *n* is replaced automatically by the current page number and *nn* is replaced by the total number of pages in the document.

You can add footers in much the same way that you add headers:

1. Choose View, Header and Footer.

2. Click Switch Between Header and Footer on the Header and Footer toolbar or scroll to the bottom of the page and click in the footer area.

3. Type the text for the footer and/or add footer elements by using the Header and Footer toolbar.

4. Click Close on the Header and Footer toolbar.

If you need to change the header or footer size or configure even/odd footers, just click the Page Setup button on the Header and Footer toolbar. Doing so opens the Layout tab of the Page Setup dialog box, where you can configure header and footer options.

**tip**

You can use tabs and/or paragraph justification to position text where you want it in a header or footer.

## Adding Watermarks

As you worked with headers and footers in the previous section, you probably realized that you couldn't change the body text on the page while you are in Header and Footer view. Word dims the body text, and you can't select or modify it in any way.

Remember that I previously described headers and footers as acting as if they are on a different layer from the body text? You can work with one layer or the other, but you can't work with both at the same time. However, even though you can't modify the body text, you can insert other text or graphics within the body area when you work in the Header and Footer view; you aren't limited to just the header or footer areas. This makes it easy to add watermark text or an image to the body area.

Word gives you two ways to add a watermark. For example, let's say you want to add the text "Confidential" vertically in the margin so it appears on every page. Here's how you accomplish that by using the Header and Footer view:

1. Choose View, Header and Footer.

2. Choose Insert, Text Box.

3. Click and drag in the left margin to insert a text box (see Figure 12.2).

**FIGURE 12.2**

You can place watermark text in a text box.

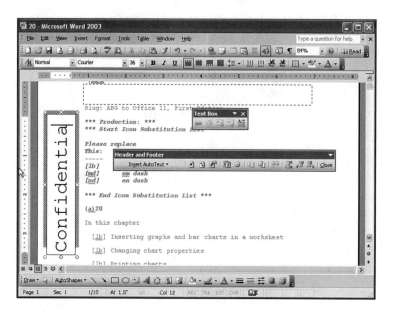

4. Type Confidential in the text box.

5. In the Text Box toolbar, click Change Text Direction twice so that the text reads from bottom to top.

6. Highlight the text and increase the font size.

7. Right-click the text box outline and choose Format Text Box to open the Format Text Box dialog box (see Figure 12.3).

**tip**

If you insert a text box over the body of the document, you should change the text color to gray or another light color so it won't distract from the body text.

**FIGURE 12.3**

Use the Format Text Box dialog box to remove the line around watermark text.

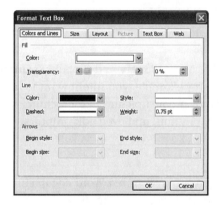

8. Click the Color drop-down list box in the Line option group and choose No Line. Then click OK. Click Close to close the Header and Footer toolbar and return to Normal view.

The method I just described gives you almost infinite control over where the text and graphics are inserted on the page. However, you might prefer a simpler approach. Here it is:

1. Choose Format, Background, Printed Watermark to open the Printed Watermark dialog box (see Figure 12.4).

2. Choose the Text Watermark option.

3. Select the watermark text, font, size, color, layout, and transparency settings and then click OK. You can enter your own text in the Text field—you don't have to use the predefined selections.

You can choose the Picture Watermark option instead of Text Watermark if you want to insert a picture as a watermark. For example, you might have a company logo that you want to use as the background for the document.

# Inserting Graphics

As you become more comfortable using Word, you'll probably want to start adding
nontext elements to documents. For example, you might want to add a picture of
your family in a holiday letter or a product picture in a brochure. Whatever the
case, Word makes it easy to add, position, and even edit graphics.

## Inserting a Picture

You can insert pictures from several sources into a Word document. Word includes a
clip art gallery that contains hundreds of pictures in different categories. You can
also insert a picture from disk, in a variety of graphics formats. The following example assumes that you want to insert a picture that is stored on disk:

1. Place the cursor in the document where you want the picture to be inserted.

2. Choose Insert, Picture, From File to open the Insert Picture dialog box (see
   Figure 12.5).

3. Browse to the folder where the picture is located, select the picture, and click Insert.

You are probably not happy with the position or size of the picture in the document. I explain how to move and resize images in the next section. For now, just use Undo to undo the insertion to remove the picture and consider some other types of graphics you can add.

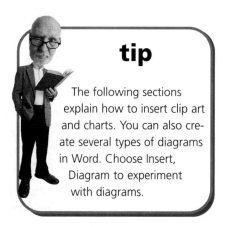

## Inserting Clip Art

Office includes lots of clip art images you can use as-is or modify to suit your needs. Follow these steps to insert a clip art image:

1. Place the cursor in the document where you want the picture to be inserted.

2. Choose Insert, Picture, Clip Art to open the Clip Art pane (see Figure 12.6).

**FIGURE 12.6**

You can search for clip art in the Clip Art pane.

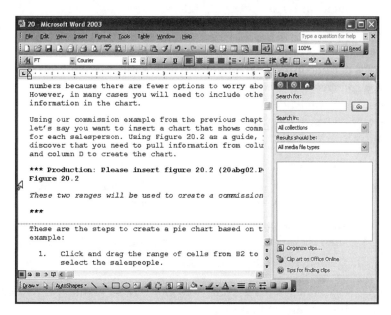

3. If this is the first time you've worked with clip art, Word asks if you want it to organize your clip art. Click Yes and go for a cup of coffee—it's going to take several minutes for Word to identify and categorize all your clip art.

4. Type in the Search Text field a keyword that describes the image you want to find.

5. From the Search In drop-down list box, choose the categories to search.

6. From the Results Should Be drop-down list box, choose the types of clips you want to search.

7. Click Search.

8. Scroll through the results and double-click the picture you want to insert.

9. Close the Insert Clip Art pane.

**tip**

If you didn't install the clip art during Office installation, you can run Setup again to add it.

You can open the Insert Clip Art pane again and look under the See Also group for the clip art you want to use. Click Clip Organizer to open the Microsoft Clip Organizer, a standalone program you can use to browse and preview clip art as well as to add to and create other clip art collections.

## Inserting Charts

Some documents need a chart or two. If you use Excel to create the data for a chart, you can create the chart in Excel, copy the chart to the Clipboard, and simply paste it into a document.

If you need a simple chart, however, you can create the chart right in Word. Here's how:

1. Place the cursor in the document where you want to insert the chart.

2. Choose Insert, Picture, Chart to insert a sample chart in the document and open a simple spreadsheet window (see Figure 12.7).

3. Change the column and row headings to reflect your own chart legends and then click in the cells to change numbers or add numbers as needed.

4. Close the spreadsheet window.

⇨ See Chapter 20, "Pies, Bars, and Other Sweet Additions," for details on creating charts of all kinds in Excel.

**FIGURE 12.7**

You can enter
the data for a
chart right in
Word.

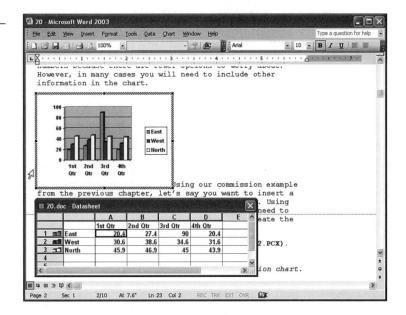

# Moving and Resizing Images

When you insert a picture in a Word document, it's a good bet you'll want to move,
resize, or edit the image. The following sections explain how.

## Moving and Resizing Images

At first, it might seem that pictures are impossible to move. The reason that this task
is seemingly impossible is that Word inserts an image inline with the text. This is
fine if you don't want the text to flow around,
behind, or in front of the picture, but it doesn't
work well if you want to drag the picture to a
different spot on the page.

To move an image, you just need to change the
picture layout:

1. Right-click the picture and choose Format
   Picture to open the Format Picture dialog
   box (see Figure 12.8).

**tip**

If you can't find your pictures, switch to Print Layout
view by choosing View, Print
Layout.

**FIGURE 12.8**

You can change picture layout and other settings by using the Format Picture dialog box.

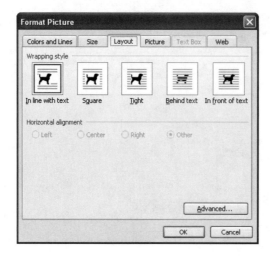

2. Select the Layout tab.

3. Choose a wrapping style from the Wrapping Style group to specify how the text should flow in relationship to the image.

4. Choose an alignment option.

5. Click OK and then click the picture and drag it to a different location on the page.

6. Right-click the picture and choose Format Picture, click the Layout tab, and click Advanced to open the Advanced Layout dialog box (see Figure 12.9).

**FIGURE 12.9**

You can set margins from text to picture in the Advanced Layout dialog box.

7. Use the Wrap Text and Distance from Text options to control how close to the picture the text will flow. Click OK and then click OK again to close the dialog boxes.

Resizing an image is even easier than moving it. When you select an image, Word places control points around the image. The control points are represented by small squares when the picture is inline with text and by small circles when you use other layout options. Just click the image and then click and drag a control point to resize the image.

If you need an image to be a specific size, clicking and dragging probably won't work for you. You should use these steps instead:

1. Right-click the picture and choose Format Picture. The Format Picture dialog box appears. Click the Size tab (see Figure 12.10).

**FIGURE 12.10**

You can set size and proportion with the Size tab.

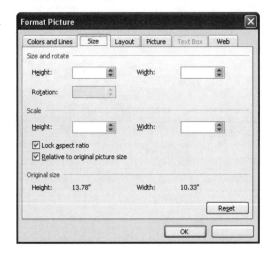

2. Set the picture height, width, and rotation with the options in the Size and Rotate group.

3. Use the options in the Scale group to control the size of the picture. Leave the Lock Aspect Ratio option selected to prevent the image from becoming distorted. Clear this option if you want to stretch the image.

4. Click OK when you're happy with the new settings.

**tip**

See that green control point on a picture when you click the picture? You can use that control point to rotate the picture. Just click the green control point and drag with the mouse to rotate the picture.

# THE ABSOLUTE MINIMUM

When you are creating documents that require headers, footers, or watermarks, you'll find that Word makes creating these items very easy. You simply switch to Header and Footer view and add the items on a separate layer that Word maintains for these items.

Adding, moving, and resizing graphics are relatively easy, as well. This chapter explains how to perform all these tasks.

After you have all the elements you want in a document, whether text or graphics, you will no doubt want to check your spelling and grammar as one of the final steps in preparing a document. The next chapter examines these features.

13

# Checking Spelling and Grammar

Spelling and grammar come naturally to some people but not so naturally to others. Throw in simple typing errors, and I'll bet you might welcome some help with spelling and grammar corrections now and then.

Word offers extensive help for spelling, grammar checking, synonyms, and other features to help you make sure your documents are the best they can be. This chapter explains how to use these features and go beyond them to add your own dictionary entries or use custom dictionaries for special purposes. For example, perhaps you work in a medical field and need to check medical terms. This chapter identifies some resources for custom and special-purpose dictionaries.

# Spell-Checking a Document

As you type, Word checks your spelling by default. Word uses a red squiggly line to underline any words it doesn't find in its dictionary. This doesn't necessarily mean the word is wrong; Word just can't find it.

Word makes some corrections on its own. These corrections are defined in the AutoCorrect entries, which are covered in more detail later in this chapter, in the section "Using Automatic Spell-Checking: AutoCorrect." For now, you just need to understand that Word fixes some of your typos as you go along. For example, if you type `spellling`, Word automatically changes it to *spelling*.

You can easily check spelling of words that are not included in Word's dictionary. To check a single word, click the word and press F7 to open the Spelling and Grammar dialog box, shown in Figure 13.1.

**FIGURE 13.1**

Use the Spelling and Grammar dialog box to check spelling.

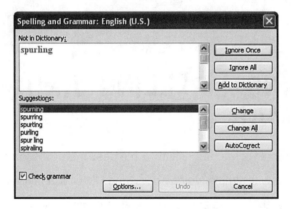

The word in question appears in red in the Not in Dictionary list, and Word offers suggested changes in the Suggestions list. You can use these buttons to accept or reject the change:

- **Ignore Once**—Leave this word alone (that is, reject the correction) and continue to the next misspelled word.
- **Ignore All**—Don't change any occurrence of this word in the document.
- **Add To Dictionary**—Add the unrecognized word to the dictionary so it won't be considered misspelled in the future.
- **Change**—Change the spelling to the selected suggestion.
- **Change All**—Change all occurrences of the word in the document to the selected suggestion.
- **AutoCorrect**—Add the word and its correction to the AutoCorrect list. You should use this option if you frequently misspell or mistype the word in the same way.

If Word doesn't automatically suggest the correct word, you can choose a different word from the Suggestions list. If Word doesn't offer the right suggestion, you can type the correction in the Not in Dictionary box and choose the appropriate action, such as Change or Change All.

You use the same process to check spelling in an entire document. You don't have to start at the top because Word begins where the cursor is placed, searches to the end of the document, and then asks if you want to check starting at the top. To start checking the document, just press F7 to open the Spelling and Grammar dialog box. As you click buttons to select actions, Word cycles through the document.

**tip**

You should clear the Check Grammar check box if you want to check only spelling and not grammar.

# Using Automatic Spell-Checking: AutoCorrect

Word includes a feature called *AutoCorrect* that automatically corrects commonly misspelled words and typographical errors. By default, Word makes these changes without asking you—it just makes the changes as you type. Even though my spelling is usually pretty good, I still like this feature. I type pretty fast, and my brain often gets ahead of my fingers. Word fixes the mistakes as I go along.

To view the AutoCorrect entries, choose Tools, AutoCorrect Options to open the AutoCorrect dialog box (see Figure 13.2).

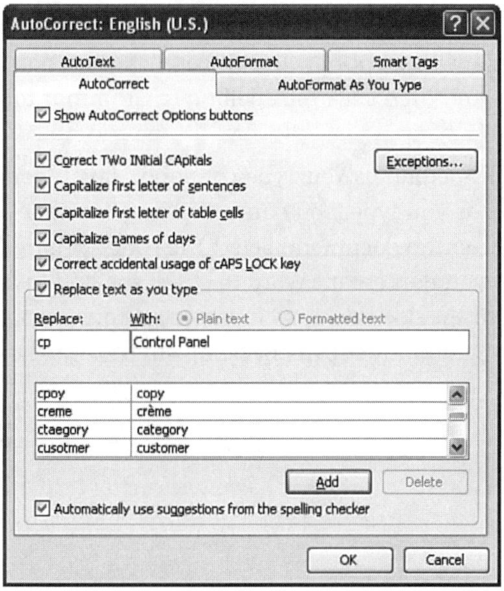

**FIGURE 13.2**

You can review and add or modify entries in the AutoCorrect dialog box.

Several options on the AutoCorrect dialog box control the types of AutoCorrect changes Word will make, and these options are generally self-explanatory.

The list near the bottom of the dialog box shows all the existing AutoCorrect entries. To add a new entry, type the incorrect text in the Replace field and type the correct text in the With field.

You might want Word to make a particular AutoCorrect change in most cases but not in every case. To facilitate this, click Exceptions to open the AutoCorrect Exceptions dialog box (shown in Figure 13.3) to specify exceptions to AutoCorrect's rules.

**tip**

After Word makes an AutoCorrect change, it places a blue line under the first letter of the changed word. You can let the mouse hover over the word if you don't see the blue line. You can place the mouse over the line to change it to a menu you can use to undo the change or set AutoCorrect options for the change.

**FIGURE 13.3**

You can use the AutoCorrect Exceptions dialog box to prevent certain AutoCorrect changes.

You can turn off automatic spell-checking if you prefer. You can also set other options to control other spelling options. In this case, choose Tools, Options to open the Options dialog box and then click the Spelling & Grammar tab, shown in Figure 13.4.

You can clear the Check Spelling as You Type check box if you don't want Word to check for spelling errors as you type. You can still press F7 at any time to check the spelling of a word or the entire document. Select the Hide Spelling Errors in This Document check box if you don't want Word to check spelling in this document. This setting is saved with the document, so if you select this option, the next time you open the document, automatic spell-checking will be turned off.

**FIGURE 13.4**

You can control spelling options with the Spelling & Grammar tab.

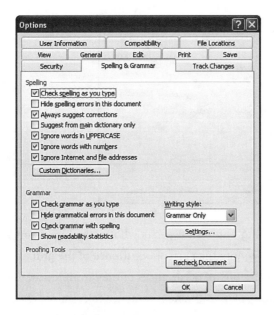

## USING AUTOCORRECT TO SAVE TIME

I write about many of the same topics frequently, and therefore I use certain words or phrases a lot. For example, I get tired of typing `Windows Server 2003`. Fortunately, I can use Word's AutoCorrect feature to quickly replace my own brand of shorthand with the correct words.

For example, I added an AutoCorrect entry that replaces w23 with Windows Server 2003. I just type w23 whenever I really want Windows Server 2003, and Word replaces it for me, saving me a lot of typing. I use a lot of other AutoCorrect entries for other common phrases, such as Control Panel, Network Neighborhood, and so on.

As you gain more experience with Word, think about the words you use often and create AutoCorrect shortcuts for them. Define enough shortcuts, and soon you'll be typing 300 words per minute!

# Checking That Grammar!

Word doesn't stop at checking your spelling; it also checks your grammar. When it finds a word or phrase it thinks is grammatically incorrect, Word underlines the word or phrase with a green squiggly line. As explained in the previous section, Word also checks grammar when it checks spelling. However, you might want to check grammar in an identified phrase immediately. If that case, you just click anywhere in the phrase and press F7 to open the Spelling and Grammar dialog box, shown in Figure 13.5.

**FIGURE 13.5**

You can use the Spelling and Grammar dialog box to check for grammatical errors.

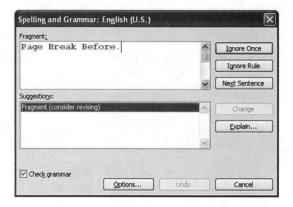

You can use the following buttons to specify what action you want Word to take:

- **Ignore Once**—Ignore the current occurrence of the grammatical error.
- **Ignore Rule**—Ignore all occurrences of the grammatical error.
- **Next Sentence**—Skip to the next sentence to continue checking.
- **Change**—Apply the change you have specified in the Fragment text box.
- **Explain**—Display a description of the problem and some suggested corrections.

You can set a handful of options that control Word's grammar-checking feature. Choose Tools, Options to open the Options dialog box and then click the Spelling & Grammar tab (refer to Figure 13.4). Then clear the Check Grammar as You Type option to prevent Word from checking grammar or underlining in green those words or phrases it considers grammatical errors. Use the Writing Style drop-down list box to choose between checking grammar only or checking grammar and style. See Word's Help documentation for more information on style and grammar checking.

# Can You Say "Thesaurus"?

Most days I can't say *thesaurus* without holding my mouth just right, but at least I know what it is. Fortunately, I can just press a couple keys in Word to bring up the thesaurus when I need to find a *synonym*—a different word with the same meaning. I don't often use Word's thesaurus when writing technical books, but it's great for finding just the right word for a bit of fiction. I'm sure you'll have other uses for it, as well.

To look up synonyms, first double-click the word you want to replace to highlight the word. Then press Shift+F7. Word opens a Research pane (shown in Figure 13.6) that offers suggested synonyms.

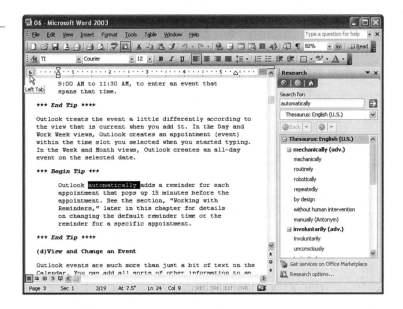

If you see the word you want to use, click the small arrow beside the word and
choose Insert to insert it in the document, replacing the selected word. Or you can
choose Copy to copy it to the Clipboard.

You can also look up a synonym to see synonyms for that word. Just click the word
to view its synonyms in the Research pane.

As you click through words, you'll realize two
things: You're hopelessly lost and want to get
back where you started, and the thesaurus also
offers *antonyms*—words that mean the opposite
of your selected word. To move back and forth
through the pages, you click the Previous Search
(Back) and Next Search buttons in the Research
pane. You can click an antonym to view its
synonyms.

**tip**

Word can translate words
and phrases between lan-
guages. To try this, select a
word or phrase and choose
Tools, Language, Translate to
open the Research pane
and view a translation. You
can choose the source and target
languages in the Research pane
and also view the translation
there.

# Using Other Languages and Custom Dictionaries

There are bound to be words that Word doesn't
recognize, even though they are correct. Names
and uncommonly used words are good examples.

The following sections explain how to customize the dictionary to add entries and also set the language that Word uses to check selected text.

## Customizing the Dictionary

Adding a word to the custom dictionary is easy:

1. Choose Tools, Options to open the Options dialog box and then click Custom Dictionaries on the Spelling & Grammar tab. The Custom Dictionaries dialog box (shown in Figure 13.7) appears.

2. Select the Custom.dic file and click Modify.

**FIGURE 13.7**

You can choose a custom dictionary from the Custom Dictionaries dialog box.

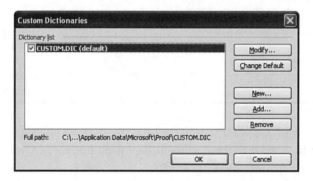

3. In the Word field, type the word you want to add to the dictionary and then click Add.

4. Add other words as needed and then click OK.

## Adding a New Custom Dictionary

A Word dictionary is a text file that has a .dic extension. You can create your own dictionary just by creating a text file with one word per line. Several companies offer custom dictionaries targeted to specific purposes, such as medical, legal, and technical fields. For example, you'll find one of the most popular medical dictionaries at www.stedmans.com. A search on Google or another search site for the keywords "Microsoft Word dictionary" should turn up lots of sites.

**tip**

You can select a dictionary and click Remove to remove it. Clear the check box beside a dictionary to leave it installed but not use it.

Follow these steps to add a dictionary to Word:

1. Choose Tools, Options to open the Options dialog box. Select the Spelling & Grammar tab and click Custom Dictionaries.

2. Click Add to open the Add Custom Dictionary dialog box.

3. Browse to the dictionary's `.dic` file and click OK.

## Setting Language for Selected Text

Word uses a particular language for proofing tools, which affects spelling and grammar rules. You can easily choose a different dictionary if you installed one version of Word but primarily write in a different language. To change language, choose Tools, Language, Set Language to open the Language dialog box, shown in Figure 13.8.

**FIGURE 13.8**

You can choose the desired proofing language in the Language dialog box.

The selection you make in the Language dialog box affects the selected text, marking that text as being the specified language. This means that Word will use that particular language when checking that selection of text. So you could mark a paragraph of French, for example, so that Word would check its spelling in French rather than in English.

To restore the text to its default language, click Default.

# THE ABSOLUTE MINIMUM

When you're ready to publish or print a document, it's likely that you will want to check the spelling—and perhaps grammar—in the document first. In this chapter you learned how to check spelling and grammar as you write a document, as well as how to check it at any other time.

In this chapter you also explored Word's thesaurus, which you can use to look up synonyms and antonyms. You also learned that you can use dictionaries in other languages to check spelling and grammar for documents written in those languages.

The next chapter takes you through the next logical step: saving, printing, faxing, and emailing documents.

# 14

# SAVING, PRINTING, EMAILING, AND FAXING DOCUMENTS

The past several chapters cover basic tasks in Word but not how to save Word documents. You probably already understand the concept of documents as files and how to save them on disk. I touch a bit on that in this chapter, but this chapter mainly focuses on tasks specifically related to saving Word documents.

This chapter also covers other tasks you will certainly want to perform with documents in Word, including printing documents, sending documents via email, and faxing documents.

# Filenames, Locations, and Formats

Each file has a name, and most files have file extensions. The *file extension* is usually three characters, and it identifies the type of file. For example, Word documents use the file extension .DOC. Word templates have the .DOT file extension.

File extensions not only help you identify the type of file but also help Word identify its own documents. When you select File, Open, for example, Word displays all the files with the .DOC extension in the selected folder. (It actually shows more than just DOC files, but let's simplify the discussion a bit.)

In addition to making it easy to identify documents in Word's Open dialog box, .DOC extensions on files also make it easy to identify documents in Windows Explorer. Windows uses a Word icon to display each file that has a .DOC extension, which gives you a visual cue as to the file's type. So although you can save Word documents with other extensions, using the default .DOC extension helps you organize and recognize Word documents.

## Choosing Filenames and Locations

Word uses certain folders by default for documents and other files. For example, Word uses your My Documents folder as the default location for files. So when you select File, Open, Word opens My Documents. You can navigate to other folders as needed with the controls in the Open dialog box.

Maybe you want to use a different folder to store your documents, however. For example, perhaps most of the documents you create or edit reside on a network server. You can configure Word to use a different default document location. To do so, choose Tools, Options, File Locations.

➪    For more information on how to change the default document location, see "Changing Default File Locations" in Chapter 16, "Word Settings to Change."

When you save a file, you specify a filename, much the way you do in any other Windows application. You don't need to add the file extension because Word adds it for you based on the file type you select. The operating system supports long filenames, so you can use truly descriptive document names, such as End-of-year sales report for 2003. You should still keep the filenames relatively short, however, because the longest filename in a folder sets the width of the Name column in the Open dialog box and in Windows Explorer, and a very wide Name column can make browsing through a long list of documents difficult.

## Choosing a Format for Saving a File

Word supports many different file *formats*. These different formats enable Word to make its documents portable to other applications, and they let you use Word to read documents created with other programs. For example, you can save a Word document as a WordPerfect file to enable WordPerfect users to open it.

To choose a file format, first choose File, Save As to open the Save As dialog box (see Figure 14.1). From the Save As Type drop-down list box, choose the file format you want to use. Then enter a filename in the File Name field and click Save to save the file.

**FIGURE 14.1**

You can choose a file type in the Save As dialog box.

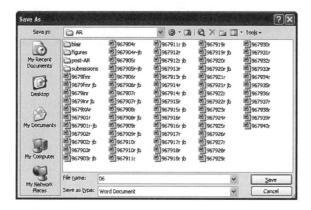

I don't cover each file type in detail here because you are likely to use the DOC format most often. Just keep in mind that if you need to make a file available to others who use Word version 2000 or earlier, you should save the file in the Word 97-2002 & 6.0/95 RTF format.

# Having Word Automatically Save Documents

Power goes out, computers crash, and, yes, people make mistakes. That's why Microsoft designed Word to automatically save a backup copy of documents as you work on them.

By default, Word saves an AutoRecover backup copy of a document every 10 minutes. If your system crashes for some reason, the most you lose is 10 minutes of work.

**note**

When you use Save As, Word saves the document to a different file. So if you open an existing document and then use Save As to save to a different file, you end up with two copies of the document.

➪ In some cases, 10 minutes can seem like hours, so you might want to have Word save the document more frequently. See Chapter 16 to learn how to do that.

When Word comes back up after a crash, it looks for the AutoRecover information. If it determines that previously opened documents were not saved, it shows a Document Recovery pane (see Figure 14.2) that lists the files that were open when Word crashed or shut down unexpectedly. You can click a document in this pane to open it. You can then save the file. You can repeat the process, clicking documents in the Document Recovery pane to open documents for recovery.

**FIGURE 14.2**

You can recover documents by using the Document Recovery pane.

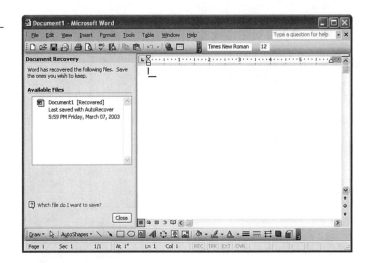

## Making Backup Copies

In addition to saving AutoRecover information, Word can also make a backup of a document for you. When you turn on this feature, Word actually saves two copies of the document: one as it was when you opened it before editing, and the other as it is after you make changes to it. Word saves the backup copy in the same folder as the current document, but it gives the file a .WBK file extension.

Why use backup copies? Let's say you open a document and make lots of changes to it. Several hours and several saves later, you realize you want to restore the document to its original state. You could repeatedly press Ctrl+Z to undo your changes, but that's a poor method at best. Instead, you can open the backup file Word created the first time you saved the document in the current editing session because that file represents the document's state before you made any changes.

Word does not enable automatic backups by default, so you need to turn on this feature if it appeals to you:

1. Choose Tools, Options. The Options dialog box appears. Select the Save tab (see Figure 14.3).

**FIGURE 14.3**

You can configure automatic backups on the Save tab.

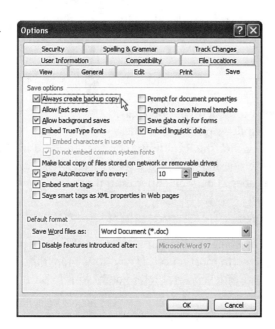

2. Select the option Always Create Backup Copy and click OK.

3. Save the document at least twice to trigger Word to save a backup copy.

When you need to open a backup file, follow these steps:

1. Open Word and choose File, Open.

2. In the Open dialog box, type *.WBK in the File Name field.

3. Select the folder where the backup file is located (the same folder as the primary document).

4. Click the small arrow beside the Views button in the toolbar and choose Details to display file details.

5. Click the Date Modified column to sort by date and time.

6. Locate the backup file based on the filename (which is the same as the primary document) and the date.

7. Select the file and click Open.

# Printing Documents

If you've used other Windows applications, you are probably familiar with printing. The following sections provide some tips for printing documents in Word, using a specific printer, printing only parts of a document, and changing some common print settings.

## Quick Printing

If you want to print one copy of an entire document to your default Windows printer, the quickest way to print is simply click the Print button on the Standard toolbar. Word starts printing immediately—it doesn't prompt you for any options at all. The printer just starts spitting paper! It doesn't get any easier than that.

## Using a Different Printer

Even if you're working at home, you might have more than one printer. Multiple printers are almost a given in most offices. If you have more than one printer available to you, it's a sure bet that sooner or later you'll want to print to a printer other than your default printer.

Follow these steps to print to a particular printer:

1. Open the document and choose File, Print to open the Print dialog box (see Figure 14.4).

**FIGURE 14.4**

You can choose a printer in the Print dialog box.

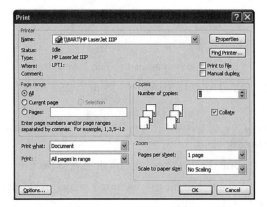

2. From the Name drop-down list box in the Printer group, select the printer you want to use.

3. Set other options, as needed, such as the number of copies to print.

4. Click the Properties button to open the properties for the printer.

5. Set options for the printer, such as paper source, color or black and white, and so on, and then click OK.

6. Back in the Print dialog box, click OK to start printing.

> **tip**
>
> Here's an easy way to add a network printer: Open My Network Places and browse to the computer to which the printer is attached (or to the printer itself, if it is connected directly to the network). When you find the printer, drag it to your desktop. Windows sets up your system to print to the printer.

## Printing Pages or a Selection of Text

Often, particularly with long documents, you need to print only a single page, a range of pages, or even just a paragraph or two. Word makes it easy to print just part of a document. Here's what you do:

1. Open the document.

2. If you want to print only a selection of text, select that text (click and drag over it) with the mouse.

3. Choose File, Print. The Print dialog box appears.

4. In the Print dialog box, find the Page Range group of controls and choose one of the following:

   - **All**—Print the entire document.

   - **Current Page**—Print only the page where the cursor is located.

   - **Selection**—Print the current selection of text.

   - **Pages**—Enter page numbers, separated by commas, to specify individual pages, or enter a page range to specify the lower and upper pages in the range, separated by a dash. For example, you'd enter 7-14 to print pages 7 through 14. You can also use a combination of methods, such as 2,4,6-9,12-15,20.

5. Set other print options and click OK to start printing.

## Changing Other Common Print Settings

There are a handful of options in the Print dialog box that you'll find useful in certain situations. To explore them, you can choose File, Print to open the Print dialog box. The following are some of the options you might find useful in this dialog box:

- **Number of Copies**—You can select the number of copies of the document to print.

- **Collate**—You can enable this option to have Word print one copy of the document before printing the next copy. Turn off this option to have Word print all copies of page 1, then all copies of page 2, and so on.

- **Print What**—Usually you want to print the document. However, you can print other items, such as a list of markups, document properties, styles, and so on. You can experiment with these to see what they do.

- **Print**—You can choose between printing both odd and even pages, printing only odd pages, or printing only even pages.

- **Zoom**—This option is handy for printing quick proofs. You can fit more than one page on a printed sheet and scale the print size up or down.

These aren't the only options you can set. In the Print dialog box, click the Options button to open the Print dialog box shown in Figure 14.5.

**FIGURE 14.5**

You can set a number of options for printing.

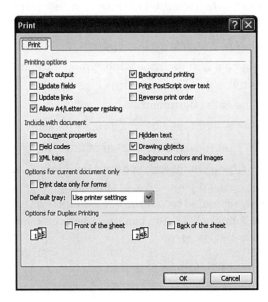

The following are the options in this dialog box that you will most likely want to change at some point:

- **Draft Output**—You can print the document by using the printer's draft mode, if it offers one. Draft mode prints faster but at a lower-quality output than standard mode, and it is handy for checking a document before you print the final copy.

- **Update Fields**—You can enable this option to have Word update fields in a document before it prints the document. For example, you can enable this option to update an index, a table of contents, or other elements that use field codes.

- **Reverse Print Order**—You can print the document from the last page to the first rather than first to last.

- **Background Colors and Images**—You can use this option with documents that have background elements in order to print those elements. If this option it turned off, Word does not print the background elements.

- **Print Data Only for Forms**—You can use this option with online forms to print only the data, not the form fields. You would typically use this option to print on a preprinted form.

- **Front of the Sheet**—You can set the print order (first-to-last or last-to-first) for odd pages in two-sided printing.

- **Back of the Sheet**—You can set the print order (first-to-last or last-to-first) for even pages in two-sided printing.

The remaining options on this Print dialog box are generally not very commonly used. You can click the question mark button and then click an option to learn more about it.

# Easy Ways to Email a Document

Sooner or later, you will need to send a Word document by email. It might be a simple recipe or an important report. Whatever the document, you have a couple ways to easily send the document.

➪  This chapter explains ways to email Word documents right from Word. The section "Working with Attachments" in Chapter 5, "All Your Email in One Handy Spot," explains how to attach files to an email message in Outlook.

## Just Email It!

If you want to include a document in the body of an email message, you choose File, Send To, Mail Recipient. Word's menu bar changes to include mail commands and the message fields (To, Cc, and so on), as shown in Figure 14.6.

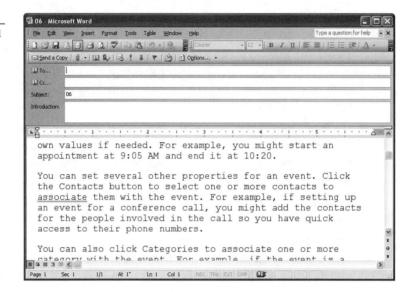

The Introduction field is the place where you type some notes about the document. The introduction appears in the message above the Word document, separated from it by a horizontal line.

You need to specify the address, subject, and other items and then click Send a Copy. If you change your mind and decide not to send the message, just choose File, Send To, Mail Recipient to turn off the message fields.

## Sending a Document as an Attachment

If you want the recipient of your message to be able to open the document for editing or view it in Word instead of Outlook, you need to send the document as an attachment. To do this, choose File, Send To, Mail Recipient (As Attachment). Word opens a new message form and attaches the document to it. Fill in the address and other required information and then click Send to send the message.

## Routing a Document with a Routing Slip

Word lets you send a document to a *routing list*, or a group of recipients who need to receive the document in turn. For example, let's say you have an approval process for documents in which three other people need to review and approve the document. You specify the list of people and their order in the list, and Outlook takes care of routing the message.

Follow these steps to send a document through a routing list:

1. Open the document and choose File, Send To, Routing Recipient.

2. If you receive a dialog box warning you that a program is trying to access email addresses in Outlook, click Yes.

3. In the Routing Slip dialog box (see Figure 14.7), Click Address and select the recipients, click To, and then click OK.

**FIGURE 14.7**

Use a Routing Slip to send the document to a series of recipients.

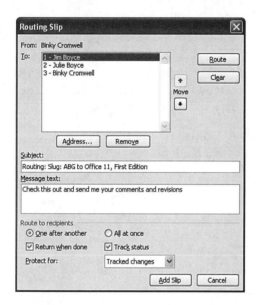

4. Use the Up and Down arrow buttons to rearrange the recipient order, if needed.

5. Change the Subject field, if needed, and add some descriptive text (if needed) in the Message Text field to explain why the document is being routed and what the recipients should do with it.

6. Choose from the following options:

   ■ **One After Another**—You can select this option if you want to send the document to the first person in the list, have that person send it to the second, the second send it to the third, and so on.

   ■ **All At Once**—You can select this option to send a copy of the document to each person on the list.

   ■ **Return When Done**—You can select this option to receive a copy back from the last recipient if One After Another is selected or receive a copy back from all recipients if All At Once is selected.

- **Track Status**—You can choose to receive an email notice when each recipient forwards the message to the next person in the routing list.

- **Protect For**—You can select an option from the Protect For drop-down list to specify how (if at all) the recipients can mark up the document.

- **Add Slip**—You can click this button to add the routing slip to the document when you're satisfied with the options and recipient list.

7. When you're ready to route the document, choose File, Send to, Next Routing Recipient.

When you receive a document from someone else for review, you open the attachment, perform your review, and choose File, Send To, Next Routing Recipient.

# Faxing a Document

Both Window 2000 and Windows XP include a Fax service that lets you send faxes by using a fax modem. You can also install third-party programs that do the same thing, and they generally offer features that are not offered by the Windows Fax service.

You can fax a document from Word by using one of two methods: You can send it from the File menu or print it to the Fax printer.

## Faxing from the File Menu

Follow these steps to send a fax by using the File menu:

**tip**

If you change your mind and want to remove the routing slip, you can choose Tools, Options to open the Options dialog box. Then you click the Security tab, select Remove Personal Information from This File on Save, and click OK. Then you can save the document. You can turn this option off again if you want personal information, including a routing slip, to be saved with the document.

**note**

This section on routing slips is included because routings slips can be very useful. However, in order to use it, you need to have a good understanding of the Track Changes feature in Word, which is not covered in this book. You should read through Word's Help documentation to learn more about Track Changes and how to use it, as well as how to merge changes between documents, before you go crazy routing documents around your office.

1. Open the document in Word and choose File, Send To, Recipient Using a Fax Modem. Word starts the Fax Wizard.

2. Follow the prompts in the wizard to enter the fax number and other information.

3. Click Finish when you're ready to send the fax.

## Printing to the Fax Printer

When you install the Windows Fax service or a third-party fax application, a Fax printer driver is added to your computer. You can send the fax simply by printing to the Fax printer. Here's how:

1. Open the document in Word and choose File, Print.

2. In the Print dialog box, choose Fax from the Name drop-down list box.

3. Click OK to start the Fax Wizard. Follow the prompts in the wizard to send the fax.

**note**

This chapter assumes that you have already installed a fax modem and that it is working. You should see the Windows Help documentation if you're not sure how to install or configure a fax modem. You can use the Add or Remove Programs applet in the Control Panel to add the Fax service to your computer if it is not already installed.

# THE ABSOLUTE MINIMUM

In this chapter you learned how easy it is to save and print documents in Word. Word supports several file types, and you can convert to a particular type simply by choosing that file type from the Save As dialog box. Word also offers lots of control over printing options to help you control the way a printed document will look.

This chapter explains how to send a document via email right from Word. You can send a document as an attachment or route a document by using a routing slip. Faxing a document is as easy as printing to the Fax printer.

In this and previous chapters you've learned how to apply most of the basic features in Word. In the following chapter you'll learn about some of the features in Word that make it easy to create and print special types of documents, including mailing lists, form letters, and envelopes.

**15**

# MAILING LISTS, FORM LETTERS, ENVELOPES, AND LABELS

Word is well suited to several tasks in an office setting besides just creating letters, reports, and other types of documents. For example, you might need to maintain a mailing list of clients, friends, family members, or members of an organization. You might also want to create form letters, envelopes, or labels. Word is a great tool for handling these tasks because it does most of the work itself!

This chapter explains how to set up mailing lists, create form letters, and print envelopes and labels.

# Mailing Lists: Using Outlook or Access Instead of Word

Before you start creating a form letter, you need a mailing list to store the addresses that will go on the form letter.

A *mailing list* is really just a collection of addresses. You could certainly use Word to keep a mailing list, entering addresses one page after another. The problem arises when you try to actually use those addresses. Although you can use a Word document as the address source for a mail merge (that is, a mass mail form letter), you can't do much else with the address list.

If you need to manage an address list, I recommend that you use either Outlook or Access to create and manage the list. The following section provides some tips for using Outlook to store mail merge contacts.

> **note**
>
> You can use either Outlook or Access as an address source for form letters and mail merge in Word. This chapter focuses on Outlook rather than Access.

## Using Outlook for a Mailing List

Outlook is a good choice for storing mail merge contacts if you also need to send email to the people on the list or if the list comprises mainly the people already in your Contacts folder.

You can use your main Contacts folder to hold mailing list addresses, as shown in Figure 15.1, or you can create a separate folder to hold a mailing list. You should use the former if most of the people in the list are also contacts you deal with frequently via email, phone, and so on. You should use a separate folder if you don't work with the people in the list very often.

For example, let's say you maintain your main business contacts and addresses for other people in your business in your Contacts folder. You want to maintain a list of your clients, but you want to keep them separate from your other contacts. In this case, you can create a separate folder to hold the client list and continue to use your main Contacts folder for your other contacts.

> **tip**
>
> To create a new contact folder in Outlook, first open the Contacts folder. Choose File, Folder, New Folder to open the Create New Folder dialog box. Then enter a name for the new folder (for example, Clients). Next, click the folder in which you want the new folder created (for example, click Contacts to create the Clients folder under the Contacts folder). Finally, make sure Contact Items is selected in the Folder Contains drop-down list and click OK.

**FIGURE 15.1**

You can use the Contacts folder to hold mailing list addresses, or create a separate contact folder.

After you decide what contact folder to use, you can start creating the contacts in the folder. You need to take care to enter the names with the last name in Last field, first name in the First field, and so on. Click Full Name in the contact form to open the Check Full Name dialog box to enter the name, as shown in Figure 15.2. Entering the name correctly will ensure that the names sort properly and work as they are supposed to in a mail merge.

**FIGURE 15.2**

You can use the Check Full Name dialog box to make sure you get the name fields in the right spots.

⇨ See Chapter 4, "Keeping Track of People and Places by Using Contacts," to learn more about managing contacts by using Outlook.

# Working with Form Letters

At this point, I'll assume that you have created a contact list either in Outlook or Access. Now you want to create a form letter and print customized copies by using your contact list. First, you need to set up the form letter.

## Setting Up a Form Letter

A form letter includes text that appears on every copy of the letter, with fields that are replaced by information when you print. For example, the name in the address and salutation might come from your contact list.

You can start the Mail Merge Wizard and then create the body of a form letter, but I prefer to create most of a form letter first and then insert the dynamic pieces, such as address block, salutation, and other items that will come from the contact list or database. To create a form letter in this way, start a new document and type the body of the letter. At this point, you don't need to worry about the address block, salutation, or other items that will change from one letter to the next. You should concentrate on creating the boilerplate text that will be the same on all copies of the letter. You should save the letter when you've finished the draft and leave the document open.

## Creating the Merged Document for an Outlook List

With the body of a form letter document ready to go, it's time to start building the dynamic parts of the letter. Follow these steps to create a form letter if you are using addresses from Outlook:

1. Open the letter in Word and choose Tools, Letters and Mailings, Mail Merge Wizard. The Mail Merge pane (see Figure 15.3) appears.

2. Make sure Letters is selected and click Next: Starting Document at the bottom of the Mail Marge pane.

3. Select Use Current Document and click Next: Select Recipients.

4. Click Select for Outlook Contacts and click Choose Contacts Folder.

5. Select the Outlook profile that contains the needed contacts folder and click OK.

6. Select the folder that contains the contacts (see Figure 15.4) and click OK.

**FIGURE 15.3**

The Mail Merge pane helps you set up a form letter.

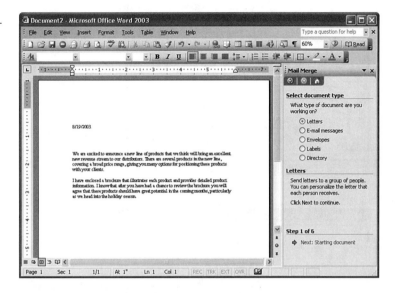

**FIGURE 15.4**

You can use the Select Contact List Folder dialog box to select the contacts folder that contains the mailing list.

7. In the Mail Merge Recipients dialog box (see Figure 15.5), click the arrow beside the Last column head and choose one of the following:

   ■ **All**—Use all entries, even if they are blank.

   ■ **Blanks**—Use only entries that have blank Last Name fields.

   ■ **Nonblanks**—Use only entries that have something in the Last Name field.

   ■ **Advanced**—Open the Filter and Sort dialog box, shown in Figure 15.6, to specify advanced filter options.

Let's stop the steps here for a bit. What you need to accomplish in the Mail Merge Recipients dialog box is define which recipients will be included. In most cases, you will want to be sure you select Nonblank for Last and First, which would filter the list to include only contacts that have something in the First Name and Last Name fields. You might not always have data in these fields, however.

**FIGURE 15.5**

You can set up which recipients to use in the Mail Merge Recipients dialog box.

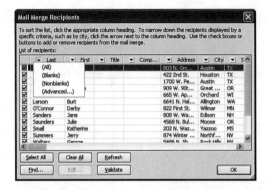

**FIGURE 15.6**

You can use the Filter and Sort dialog box to set conditions for contacts to be included or excluded.

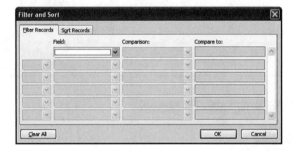

You can use the All, Blanks, and Nonblanks options for each column to whittle down the list to include the right contacts for the mail merge, or at least build a rough set.

Next, use the Advanced option to open the Filter and Sort dialog box (refer to Figure 15.6). This is where you can exercise much more control over who is included and who isn't.

For example, let's say you want to include only contacts with addresses in the states Texas and Minnesota. Here's how you'd filter the list to accomplish that:

1. In the Mail Merge Recipients dialog box, click the arrow beside the State column header and choose Advanced.

2. In the Filter and Sort dialog box, select State from the Field drop-down list in the third row (see Figure 15.7). In Figure 15.7, I've specified that the Last and First fields must not be blank.

3. Select Equal To from the Comparison drop-down list.

4. Click in the Compare To field and type **TX**.

5. In the fourth row, click Or instead of And from the first drop-down list.

**FIGURE 15.7**

These conditions would include only contacts in Texas with entries in the Last and First fields.

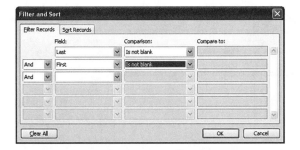

6. Choose State from the Field drop-down list, choose Equal To from the Comparison field, and type **MN** in the Compare To field.

7. Click OK. The Mail Merge Recipients list should now show only the contacts that meet your filter conditions—in this case, only contacts in Texas and Minnesota.

8. Remove the check mark beside any individual contacts you do not want included.

9. Click a column head to sort the list by that column. For example, click Last to sort by last name.

10. Click OK to close the dialog box.

Up to this point, you have created the body of the letter and specified which recipients will be included in the final merged letter. The next step is to add the dynamic elements, such as the address block, salutation, and other areas that will be filled in from the recipient list. Here's what you do now:

1. Click Next: Write Your Letter to show the options in Figure 15.8.

2. Click in the letter where you want the address block inserted and click Address Block to open the Insert Address Block dialog box, shown in Figure 15.9.

3. Select the name format and other options to control how the address block appears and then click OK.

4. Click in the letter where you want the salutation and click Greeting Line to open the Greeting Line dialog box.

5. Select the format for the name as you want it to appear on the salutation line and select the greeting for any contacts that don't have valid recipient names. Click OK.

6. Click Next: Preview Your Letters and click the forward and back buttons in the Mail Merge pane to preview the letter with actual contacts.

**FIGURE 15.8**

The Write Your
Letter portion of
the wizard helps
you insert
dynamic items
such as the
address block.

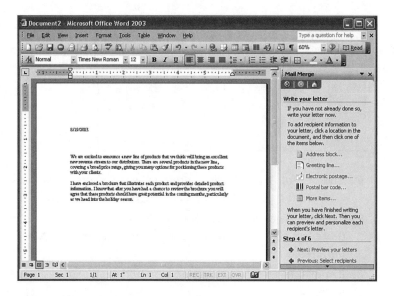

**FIGURE 15.9**

You can set
options for the
address block by
using the Insert
Address Block
dialog box.

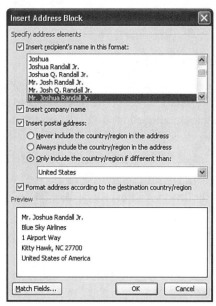

7. When you're satisfied with the results, click Next: Complete the Merge. In the
Mail Merge pane, click Print to print the letters or click Edit Individual Letters
to open the letters as documents for editing or saving.

# Printing Envelopes

Even if you never perform a mail merge, you are likely to print envelopes now and then. Printing envelopes is easy with Word. You can even add electronic postage if you have electronic postage software installed on your computer. You can also add a delivery point bar code and FIM-A courtesy reply mail bar code (the bar code just to the left of the stamp area).

⇨   You can find information about electronic postage software at the Microsoft Office Web site (www.microsoft.com/office).

You can simply print an envelope and not save it, or you can save an envelope as a part of a document, such as a letter. If you add an envelope to a document, Word adds the envelope as page 0 of the document.

## Printing a Single Envelope

Follow these steps to create, save, and print an envelope:

1. Open the letter or other document for which you need an envelope.

2. If you already have the recipient address in the letter, highlight the address.

3. Choose Tools, Letters and Mailings, Envelopes and Labels to open the Envelopes and Labels dialog box, shown in Figure 15.10.

**FIGURE 15.10**

You can set envelope options in the Envelopes and Labels dialog box.

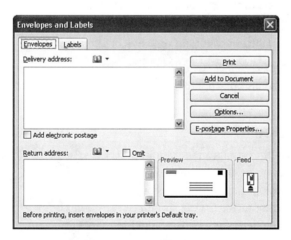

4. Edit the address in the Delivery Address field, if necessary.

5. Type the return address in the Return Address field.

6. Click Options to open the Envelope Options dialog box, shown in Figure 15.11.

**FIGURE 15.11**

You can set
options for the
envelope in the
Envelope Options
dialog box.

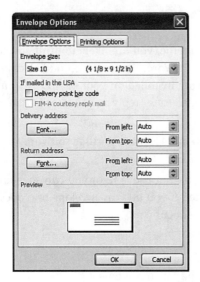

7. Use the options on the Envelope Options tab to add a bar code, if needed, and set the font for the address text. If you don't specify a font, Word uses the font that was active in the selected paragraph when you opened the Envelopes and Labels dialog box.

8. Use the options in the Printing Options dialog box to specify the way the envelope will enter the printer and then click OK.

9. Click Add to Document to add the envelope as page 0.

10. Click File, Print to open the Print dialog box.

11. Choose the Pages option, enter **0** in the Pages field, and click Print.

## Printing Many Envelopes

Word makes it easy to create a mass mailing through the Mail Merge Wizard. You can also easily print the envelopes for your letters by using the wizard. The process is very similar to creating a mail merge letter, which is covered in the section "Creating the Merged Document for an Outlook List," earlier in this chapter. Assuming that you've read that section, this section just covers the subtle differences to get you started.

**tip**

You can just click Print if you want to print an envelope without saving it with a document.

Follow these steps to start the process of creating mail-merge envelopes:

1. Open a new document to contain the envelopes.

2. Choose Tools, Letters and Mailings, Mail Merge to open the Mail Merge pane.

3. Select Envelopes in the Select Document Type area and click Next: Starting Document.

4. Click Envelope Options to open the Envelope Options dialog box (refer to Figure 15.11). Set printing and font options and then click OK.

5. Click Next: Select Recipients.

6. Click Select from Outlook Contacts, click Choose Contacts Folder, select the profile, and select the Contacts folder.

7. Use the same process to select recipients as you did for your letter (see the section "Working with Form Letters," earlier in this chapter) and then click OK.

8. Click Next: Arrange Your Envelope.

9. Add your return address to the envelope and then click where you want the recipient address to be added.

10. Click Address Block to insert the address block.

11. Click Next: Preview Your Envelopes, and if all looks good, click Next: Complete the Merge.

12. Click Print to print the envelopes or click Edit Individual Envelopes to save them to the document for fine-tuning or to save them to disk.

> **tip**
>
> If you need to change an envelope's properties or print another copy, you can click page 0 of the document and choose Tools, Letters and Mailings, Envelopes and Labels. Then you can make the changes and click Change Document to apply the changes or click Print to print the envelope.

# Creating and Printing Labels

In some cases you aren't able to print envelopes directly or you might simply prefer to use labels for a mass mailing. Or, perhaps you need to print some disk labels, shipping labels, or other labels. Printing labels is a snap with Word.

Just as with envelopes, you can save a sheet of labels or you can simply print them without saving them. You would save them in a document if you needed to reprint them later or needed to fine-tune them before printing.

Word includes definitions for many different labels from a range of label manufacturers. In most cases, you will be able to create your labels without actually specifying the label layout—you just select the brand and type of label, fill in the blanks, and save or print.

Follow these steps to create a set of labels using a standard label layout:

1. Open a new document and choose Tools, Letters and Mailings, Envelopes and Labels. The Envelopes and Labels dialog box appears (see Figure 15.12).

**FIGURE 15.12**

You can set up labels by using the Labels tab.

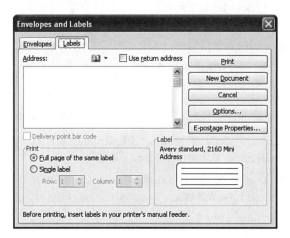

2. In the Labels tab, click Options to open the Label Options dialog box, shown in Figure 15.13.

**FIGURE 15.13**

You can choose the label type from the Label Options dialog box.

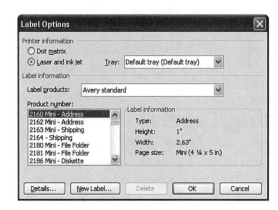

3. Choose the manufacturer from the Label Products drop-down list box.

4. Choose the label type from the Product Number list box. You should find this number on the label packaging.

5. Click OK.

6. Click in the Address field and type the text for the label.

7. Click New Document to create a page of labels.

8. Change the labels as needed and then print the document to print the labels.

You can also perform a mail merge to labels, if needed. You follow the steps in the section "Working with Form Letters," earlier in this chapter, to print a mail merge envelope, but select Labels from the Select Document Type area of the Mail Merge pane. The rest of the process is almost identical to creating mail-merged envelopes.

# THE ABSOLUTE MINIMUM

If you ever need to create a form letter or similar type of document for which you need to customize and print multiple copies, you'll really appreciate Word's mail-merge capabilities. This chapter explains how to create a mail-merge letter, use contacts from Outlook as your mailing list, and print the document. You also learned how to add envelopes to letters and create and print labels.

The next chapter rounds out the Word part of the book, with a look at the most common settings you will likely want to change for Word, where to find them, and suggestions for changing them.

- Adding more recently used files to the File menu

- Editing text by using the mouse

- Controlling how Word selects text

- Setting backup and recovery options

- Changing the default location for templates and other files

- Changing your personal information

- Setting spelling options

- Controlling macro security

16

# WORD SETTINGS TO CHANGE

Like the other Microsoft Office applications, Word gives you a wealth of settings to change that control the way the program looks and functions. For example, you might want to use a program such as Adobe Photoshop to edit pictures, add more recently used documents to the File menu, or change the personal information stored with your documents.

This chapter covers the most common settings you will likely need or want to change as you start working with Word.

# Adding More Recently Used Files

By default, Word's File menu shows the four documents on which you have most recently worked. This recently used document list makes it easy to open a document—you just click it in the File menu rather than hunt through your folders for it. Figure 16.1 shows the recently used file list.

**FIGURE 16.1**

The File menu provides quick access to recently used documents.

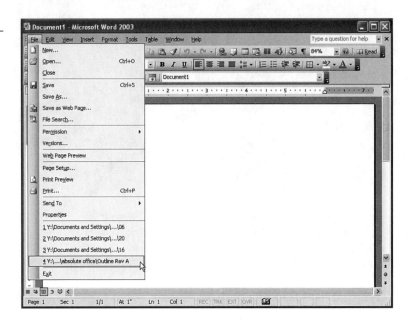

By following these steps, you can configure Word to show up to nine recently used documents in the File menu:

1. Choose File, Options to open the Options dialog box, shown in Figure 16.2.

2. Click the General tab.

3. Be sure the Recently Used File List option is selected and then set the desired value by clicking the numeric spin control. When you're done, click OK.

**FIGURE 16.2**

You can use the
Options dialog
box to add
recently used
files to the File
menu.

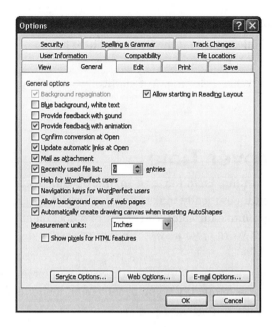

# Editing Text by Using Drag-and-Drop

You might not realize it, but you can use the mouse to move and copy text in Word.
To move some text, you just highlight the text and drag it into its new location by
using the mouse. To copy the text rather than move it, you hold down the Ctrl key
while you drag the text.

Word enables drag-and-drop text editing by default. If you don't use this feature,
you might want to turn it off to prevent unwanted text moves when you are high-
lighting text. Here's how you turn it off:

1. Choose Tools, Options to open the Options dialog box and then click the
   Edit tab.

2. Clear the Drag-and-Drop Text Editing option and click OK.

# Controlling Text Selection

When you select text in Word, the program automatically selects an entire word
even though you might have dragged over only part of a word. Word also selects the
space following the word, if there is one. This behavior can save time and make it
easier to select text, but it can also drive you nuts if you prefer to select the text
yourself.

Here's how you turn off this behavior:

1. Choose Tools, Options to open the Options dialog box and then click the Edit tab.

2. Clear the option When Selecting, Automatically Select Entire Word.

3. Click OK.

# Changing AutoRecover Time

Chapter 14, "Saving, Printing, Emailing, and Faxing Documents," explains how you can configure Word to automatically make backup copies of documents as you work on them. Word will also make an *AutoRecover* copy of a document that enables Word to recover a document if Word or your system hangs while you are working on the document.

The default AutoRecover period is 10 minutes. However, you might want Word to save your documents more frequently if you usually get a lot done in 10 minutes.

Here's how you change the AutoRecover period:

1. Choose Tools, Options to open the Options dialog box and then click the Save tab (see Figure 16.3).

**FIGURE 16.3**

You can use the Save tab to configure AutoRecover options.

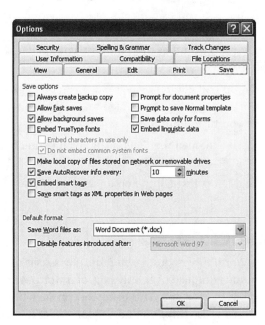

2. Make sure the option Save AutoRecover Info Every is checked and then change the time by using the numeric spin control.

3. Click OK.

# Changing Default File Locations

Word uses your My Documents folder as the default location for documents. So when you click File, Open, the Open dialog box shows the contents of My Documents. Word also sets other default file locations, such as the locations of templates, clip art, and AutoRecover files.

You can change these default locations to help better organize your documents and other files or to adjust Word to the way you store your documents. For example, maybe you use a particular folder in My Documents for all your Word documents. Why not open that folder by default instead of opening My Documents? Or you might have a collection of templates on a server that you want Word to use. You can point Word to the server for those templates.

Follow these steps to change file locations:

1. Choose Tools, Options to open the Options dialog box and then click the File Locations tab (see Figure 16.4).

**FIGURE 16.4**

You can change the places that Word looks for files on the File Locations tab.

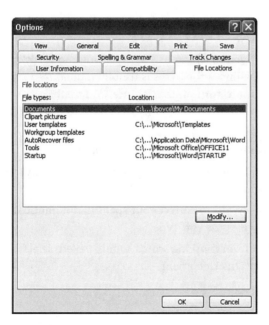

2. Click a file type and then click Modify to open the Modify Location dialog box, which is a lot like the common Open dialog box.

3. Select the folder you want to use and click OK.

4. Click OK to close the Options dialog box.

# Changing Your User Information

Word stores some information about you and uses that information when you make changes to a document, create letters, address envelopes, and do a few other tasks. For example, if you turn on the Track Changes feature and add some comments or otherwise edit a document, Word marks those edits with your name so other people can see who made the edits.

Word stores your name, initials, and mailing address. Follow these steps to change this information:

1. Choose Tools, Options to open the Options dialog box and then click the User Information tab.

2. Change your name, initials, or address and then click OK.

3. Click OK to close the Options dialog box.

# Checking Spelling as You Type

By default, Word checks your spelling as you type, automatically making corrections to typographical and spelling errors. This is usually a good thing, but there might be situations when you want to turn off this feature. You might also want Word to ignore spelling in a document that contains lots of words that Word doesn't have in its dictionary.

Follow these steps to configure these two spelling options:

1. Choose Tools, Options to open the Options dialog box and then click the Spelling & Grammar tab (see Figure 16.5).

2. If you don't want Word to correct your spelling automatically, clear the option Check Spelling as You Type.

3. To prevent Word from marking words as misspelled, select the option Hide Spelling Errors in This Document.

4. Click OK.

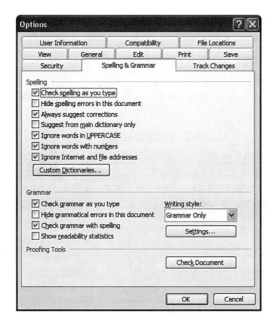

# Understanding Macro Security

This last change in this chapter is certainly not the least important, so pay attention!

Word documents can contain macros that automate many different tasks. These macros are stored with the document. Depending on how Word is configured, macros can execute automatically when you open a document. This can be a good thing, but it can also be a really bad thing if the macro is a malicious one that, say, deletes a bunch of files from your hard disk. You might open an innocent-seeming document that someone has sent you as an email attachment, only to have it really cripple your computer.

If you don't have a virus scanner that can scan documents for macro viruses, put this book down and go buy one. Go ahead, I'll wait....

Ah, you're back! Well, even if you do install a virus scanner that identifies macro viruses, you should also configure macro security to prevent macros from running unless you let them. Here's how:

1. Choose Tools, Options to open the Options dialog box and then click the Security tab.

2. Click Macro Security to open the Security dialog box, shown in Figure 16.6.

3. Select the High option if it is not already selected.

4. Click OK to close the Macro Security dialog box and then click OK to close the Options dialog box.

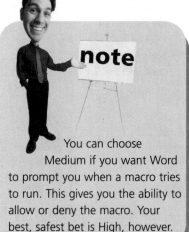

You can choose Medium if you want Word to prompt you when a macro tries to run. This gives you the ability to allow or deny the macro. Your best, safest bet is High, however.

**FIGURE 16.6**

You can configure the security level for macros by using the Security dialog box.

# THE ABSOLUTE MINIMUM

Like all the other Microsoft Office applications, Word provides numerous settings and options that you can change to control the way Word looks and functions. This chapter explains the most common changes that you're likely to want to make as you begin to become more comfortable using Word. Spend some time exploring the other options in the Options dialog box and scanning the Help and Support information to learn more.

This chapter completes the Word portion of this book. In the next chapter you'll begin your exploration of Microsoft Excel, the spreadsheet program included with Microsoft Office 2003.

# PART IV

# NUMBER-CRUNCHING WITH EXCEL

**17**

# ONCE AROUND THE WORKSHEET

In the good old days of bookkeeping and accounting, Bob Cratchet entered numbers by hand in a big ledger book and totaled them by the light of a flickering candle.

Fortunately, those days are gone, and we have much better ways to keep track of numbers, charts, formulas, and all sorts of other information. Microsoft's answer is Excel, one of the applications included in the Office suite. This chapter takes you on a tour of spreadsheets in general and Excel in particular to help you learn what this handy application is all about.

# Spreadsheets 101

In a nutshell, Microsoft Excel (see Figure 17.1) is a *spreadsheet* application. You can use Excel to enter, manipulate, summarize, and analyze numbers for all sorts of situations. For example, you might use a spreadsheet to keep track of sales figures for different products in different sales regions. You might go a bit further and keep track of sales for individual salespeople, calculate their commissions, and generate weekly or monthly sales reports based on that information.

**FIGURE 17.1**

You can use Excel to manipulate and analyze numbers.

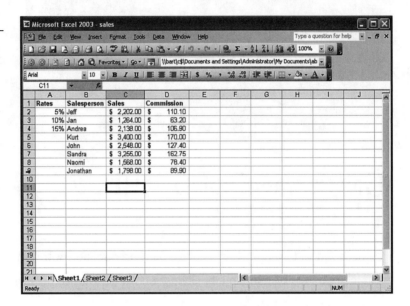

Excel lends itself to lots of other uses, too. Although I use Microsoft Money to manage my bank accounts, business receivables, and household bills, I use Excel to keep track of my monthly bills and credit cards. Excel helps me organize the bills and keep track of balances, amounts paid each month, and so on. I could do some of this in Money, but like having the information in Excel, where I can play what-if scenarios.

A spreadsheet doesn't hold only numbers, and certainly not just static numbers. You can enter formulas—from simple to complex—to manipulate those numbers. For example, you could use a formula to total daily sales figures for the month and then use another formula to multiply that total by a certain percentage to determine commission.

Spreadsheets can do a lot more than just manipulate numbers and show the results. You can use them to easily create complex, professional-looking charts and graphs, add and format text, and add lines, pictures, and other graphical elements, all to spruce up a spreadsheet's appearance and make it more useful and convey more information.

The best way to learn about a topic is to dig in and experience it. The following section takes you on a hands-on tour of some of the elements you'll see in Excel.

# Using Cells and Other Interesting Things

A spreadsheet is made up of rows and columns of cells. Each cell can contain a unique item of information, such as a number, formula, or text string. By default, the rows in an Excel spreadsheet are numbered top-to-bottom, starting at 1. Columns are labeled with letters, left-to-right, starting with the letter A. Figure 17.2 shows an example of rows and columns.

**note**

You can even use a spreadsheet as a simple, flat database, and you can then search and sort information in the spreadsheet. Access does a much better job of managing data, however, so this book doesn't talk about using Excel as a database application.

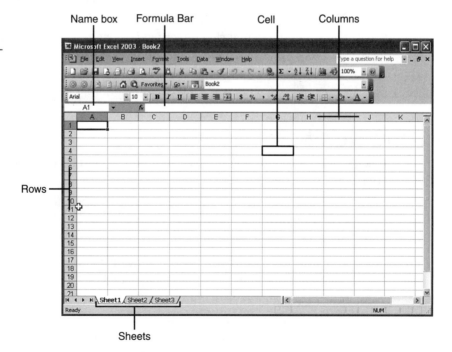

**FIGURE 17.2**

Excel uses rows and columns to organize information.

The intersection of a row and column is called a *cell*. For example, Cell B8 references Column B, Row 8. You'll see that cell references are important in Chapter 18, "From

Simple Addition to What-ifs: Formulas," where you'll learn how to create formulas to manipulate data. The cell reference is like the address of the data in the cell and the means by which you work with that data.

A single spreadsheet can contain more than one sheet. By default, Excel creates three sheets in a new spreadsheet, as Figure 17.2 shows. The sheets don't need to be related to one another, but generally they are. For example, let's say you need to analyze sales figures for your East, West, North, and South divisions. Each division could have its own sheet, with a fifth sheet to summarize all the information.

The mouse pointer changes in different areas of Excel. For example, it appears as a large addition sign when it's over a cell. The pointer changes to a right arrow when it hovers over a row heading and to a down arrow when it hovers over a column heading. If you place the pointer between two column headings, the pointer changes to a left-right arrow for dragging the column's edge to make it wider or narrower.

You can enter information, including formulas, right in a cell. The Formula Bar is the place to go when you need to edit some information or a formula without retyping it.

Finally, like other Office and Windows applications, Excel includes a menu bar and toolbars that give you quick access to its commands and features.

> **tip**
>
> You can easily use information and results from one sheet on another so that when one sheet changes, the contents of another change automatically. You can enter new sales figures for the West division, for example, and have the totals automatically change on the Sales Summary sheet.

# Entering Numbers

It doesn't take much to enter numbers in a cell. You just click in the cell and type! Try it out:

1. Open Excel by selecting Start, All Programs, Microsoft Office, Microsoft Office Excel 2003.

2. When Excel opens, click in Cell B3.

3. Type **7862** and press Enter. Notice that the text jumps to the right edge of the cell (that is, the number is right-aligned) and Cell B4 is automatically selected.

4. Type **2364** and press Enter. This places the number in Cell B4.

5. Type **8734** in Cell B5 and press Enter.

That's too easy! Here's what you do to change some of these numbers:

1. Click in Cell B3, type **4567**, and press Enter.

2. Click in cell B5, click in the Formula Bar, press Backspace, and change the 4 to 2.

3. Press Enter. Cell B5 should now read 8732 (see Figure 17.3).

**FIGURE 17.3**

Excel makes it
easy to change
the contents of a
cell.

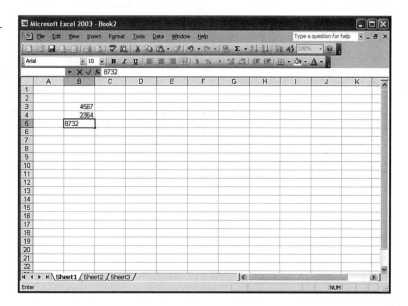

As shown in the second set of steps, you can use two different methods to change a value in a cell. You can simply click a cell and type a new value, or you can use the Formula Bar to edit the values in a cell without completely replacing them.

We'll save formulas for Chapter 18. For now, let's add some text to the spreadsheet.

# Entering Text in Cells

As mentioned earlier in this chapter, you can add text to a spreadsheet just as easily as you can add numbers. For example, let's say you're building a spreadsheet to keep track of sales figures for each division. Here's how you add a title to the spread-sheet:

1. Continue with the spreadsheet from the previous section and click in Cell A1.

2. Type the text **Sales Totals** and press Enter.

3. Click in Cell A3 and type **North**. Then press Enter.

4. Type **South** and press Enter to add text to Cell A4.

5. Type **West** and press Enter to add text to Cell A5.

**tip**

When you press Enter, Excel moves to the next cell. If you want to start a new line in a cell, you press Alt+Enter.

At this point you could add some formatting to the text; for example, you could make the title bold or left-justify the region names so they move to the left sides of their cells. However, let's leave those tasks for Chapter 18 and take a look at how you can work with cells.

# Selecting Cells

If you have followed along with this chapter so far, you already have some experience in selecting cells. To enter a value, formula, or text in a cell, you must first select the cell. Just click in a cell to select that cell.

In many situations, you need to select more than one cell. For example, perhaps you want to select a range of numbers to add. Or perhaps you need to format the text in several cells as bold.

Selecting multiple cells is really no different from selecting multiple paragraphs in a Word document. Just click one cell, hold down the mouse button, and drag the pointer to select other cells. You can select cells in a rectangular area by using this method, whether in a single column, single row, or more than one row or column. Figure 17.4 shows a range of cells selected in a spreadsheet.

**FIGURE 17.4**

You can click and drag to select cells in a rectangular range.

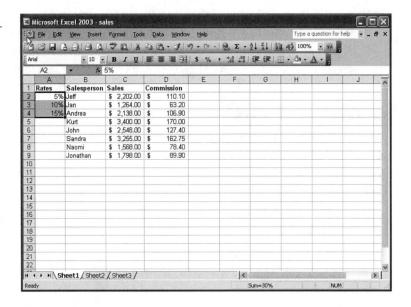

Sometimes it is necessary to select multiple cells that are not in a rectangular range. For example, you might want to format several cells that contain text with a particular font, font color, or background color, but those cells are not side by side. To select multiple cells in this type of situation, click the first cell, hold down the Ctrl key, and click another cell. Continue to hold down Ctrl while you select all the needed cells.

# Changing Row and Column Properties

Excel starts with a default row and column size, but you are certainly not locked in to using those properties. For example, you might need to make a column wider to show the numbers it contains or make a row taller to fit multiple lines of text.

**tip**

When you click and drag to select cells, the Name box just to the left of the Formula Bar shows the width and height of your cell selection. For example, 6R×3C indicates a cell area of six rows by three columns.

Resizing a column or row is easy: Just click on the edge of the column or row header and drag with the mouse to change the width or height, respectively. When the pointer is over the column or row edge, the pointer changes to an up/down or left/right resize arrow, as shown in Figure 17.5.

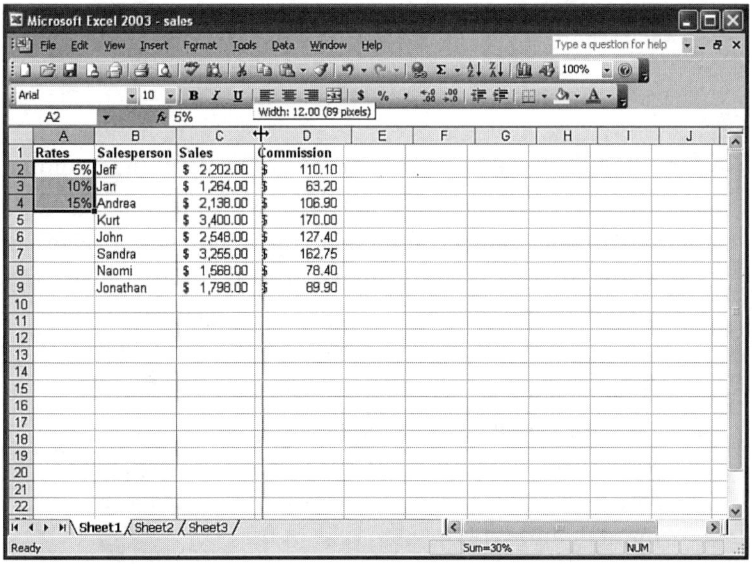

**FIGURE 17.5**

You can easily resize rows or columns by using the mouse.

Resizing rows and columns in this way isn't very precise. Sometimes you might want an exact size or you might want to reset a row or column size back to the default setting. Excel provides a handful of commands to accomplish these tasks.

First, let's look at rows. You can click in a row and choose Format, Row, followed by one of these commands:

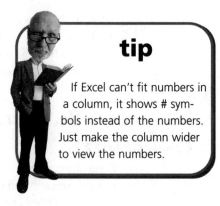

**tip**

If Excel can't fit numbers in a column, it shows # symbols instead of the numbers. Just make the column wider to view the numbers.

- **Height**—Select this command to open the Row Height dialog box (shown in Figure 17.6) and enter a value, in points, between 0 and 409.

- **AutoFit**—Select this command to automatically resize the row to accommodate the tallest data in the row. For example, if one cell contains three lines of text and all others contain one or two rows, Excel resizes the cell to the minimum needed to contain the three lines.

**FIGURE 17.6**

You can change the height of a row by using the Row Height dialog box.

You can change the width of a column by clicking in the column and choosing Format, Column, followed by one of these commands:

- **Width**—Select this command to open the Column Width dialog box, with which you specify the column width, in points, from 0 to 255.

- **AutoFit Selection**—Select this command to automatically resize the column to accommodate the text or numbers in the currently selected cell or range of cells.

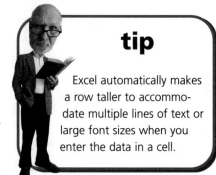

**tip**

Excel automatically makes a row taller to accommodate multiple lines of text or large font sizes when you enter the data in a cell.

- **Standard Width**—You can choose the Standard Width command to open the Standard Width dialog box. In this dialog box, you specify a width, in points. When you click OK, Excel resizes all columns that do not already have the width explicitly set.

# Using Ranges and Names

A *range* of cells is not, as you might think, a rectangular selection of cells. Although a range can certainly specify a rectangular selection of cells, a range need not necessarily be a *single* rectangular group of cells. Figure 17.7 illustrates this idea by showing a range that comprises five different groups of cells.

**FIGURE 17.7**

This single range comprises five groups of cells.

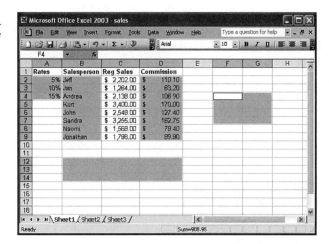

Why define and use ranges? A range can be useful in enabling you to reference data from one sheet in another or within the same sheet. Ranges are also helpful in navigating complex sheets. Rather than hunt through page after page of data to find a single value, for example, you can name a cell or a range around it. When you need to view that information, you just direct Excel to go to that named range or cell.

At the left of the Formula Bar is the Name box (refer to Figure 17.2). Naming a cell or range of cells is easy: You just click the cell or click and drag to select a range of cells. Then you click in the Name box and type a name for the range.

If you need to assign multiple names, you can assign them in the Define Name dialog box rather than use the Name box. Here's how you do it:

1. Choose Insert, Name, Define to open the Define Name dialog box (shown in Figure 17.8).

2. Click in the Names in Workbook field and type a new name.

3. Highlight the existing range in the Refers To field and click or drag to select the range. You can also type the cell or range reference.

4. Click Add.

5. Repeat the process for other names and click Close.

**FIGURE 17.8**

You can define
multiple names
by using the
Define Name
dialog box.

## Jumping to a Named Cell or Range

After you name a cell or range, you can quickly jump to that place in the spread-
sheet, whether it is on the current sheet or a different sheet. To do so, you choose
Edit, Go To or press Ctrl+G to open the Go To dialog box (shown in Figure 17.9).
Then you click the name and click OK.

**FIGURE 17.9**

You can use the
Go To dialog
box to jump to
a named range.

## Identifying a Named Cell or Range

As you work with named cells and ranges, you will probably need Excel to refresh
your memory about which names refer to which cells or ranges. This is particularly
true if you have lots of names defined.

Use these steps to identify a cell or range:

1. Choose Insert, Name, Define to open the Define Name dialog box.

2. Click a name and view the cell reference in the Refers To field.

3. Click Close.

## Referencing a Named Cell in a Formula

In addition to using ranges as a means of moving around a spreadsheet, you can also use names in formulas. For example, assume that you are setting up a spreadsheet to calculate commissions for your sales staff. You have three different commission levels, which depend on the tenure of the salesperson. You can enter the commission rates in three different cells and reference those cells when you need to calculate a commission, but maybe you find it easier to use a name.

This section uses formulas to a limited extent to illustrate some of this chapter's concepts. Formulas are covered in detail in Chapter 18.

For example, assume that you've entered the commission rates in Cells B3, B4, and B5 and that these represent low, medium, and high commission rates, respectively. Why not name the cells CLow, CMed, and CHigh and use those names in your formulas? That way, you don't need to remember the cell locations as you work in the sheet.

Follow these steps to set up the sheet in this example:

1. Click in Cell B3, click the Name box, and type **CLow**.
2. Click in Cell B4, click the Name box, and type **CMed**.
3. Click in Cell B5, click the Name box, and type **CHigh**.
4. Enter the numbers **.05**, **.10**, and **.15** in Cells B3, B4, and B5, respectively.
5. Click in Cell D3 and type **=C3*CLow**.
6. Click in Cell D4 and type **=C4*CMed**.
7. Click in Cell D5 and type **=C5*CHigh**.
8. Enter values of your choosing in Cells C3, C4, and C5.

In this example, Excel multiplies the values you enter in Cells C3, C4, and C5 by the values in the cells referenced by the names CLow, CMed, and CHigh.

## Using Row and Column Labels

You can label rows and columns in Excel. Figure 17.10 shows an example in which two columns are labeled Sales and Commissions.

Let's assume that you're not sure at this point how many salespeople you will enter in the spreadsheet. So you want to use the label Commissions in a formula to add up the values in the Commissions column.

**FIGURE 17.10**

You can label rows and columns in a spreadsheet.

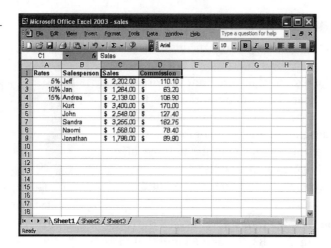

First, you need to configure Excel to accept labels in formulas:

1. In Excel, choose Tools, Options to open the Options dialog box and then click the Calculation tab, as shown in Figure 17.11.

**FIGURE 17.11**

You can enable labels in formulas on the Calculation tab.

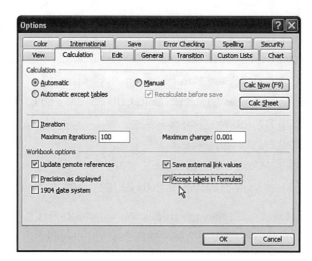

2. Select the option Accept Labels in Formulas and click OK.

Now, you can define and use the label in a formula:

1. Click in Cell D1 and type **Commissions**.

2. Click the column header for Column D (that is, click on the D above Commissions).

3. Choose Insert, Name, Create to open the Create Names dialog box, shown in Figure 17.12.

**FIGURE 17.12**

You can create a
name by using
the Create
Names dialog
box.

4. Choose Top Row and click OK.

5. Click in Cell F5 and type `=sum(commissions)`.
   Then press Enter. Note that Excel highlights
   the column when you finish typing the label
   name.

6. Enter values in Column D and notice that
   Excel sums the values in Cell F5.

The option you select in
the Create Names dialog
box identifies the location in your
selection where the label is
located. In this case, the label
`Commissions` is located in the top
row of the selection, so you select
the Top Row option.

After you read Chapter 18 and learn about formulas in more detail, you should take some time to
experiment with naming rows and columns and using those columns in formulas.
Labels can be very useful for helping you keep track of information in complex
spreadsheets.

## Defining Constants

Depending on the types of information with which you work in Excel, you might
need to define some constants. For example, if you needed to calculate sales tax on
sales, the tax rate would be a constant. You could use
the constant in formulas where you needed to calculate the tax.

In this example, assume that the constant will be
named TAX and be set to 6%:

1. Choose Insert, Name, Define to open the
   Define Name dialog box.

2. In the Names in Workbook field, type **TAX**.

3. Click in the Refers To field, remove any
   existing text, and type `=.06`.

4. Click Add and then click Close.

5. Click in the cell where you want to use the
   constant and type a formula that includes

Names in formulas are
not case sensitive, so Excel
would treat `commissions` and
`Commissions` as the same label.

the constant. For example, assume that you have defined a column label as `Sales` that totals the `Sales` column. To calculate the sales tax on that total, use the formula `=sum(Sales)*TAX`.

# THE ABSOLUTE MINIMUM

This chapter introduces you to Excel, the spreadsheet program in Office 2003 that you can use to analyze numbers and perform similar tasks. This chapter explores the very basics of using Excel, including common terms, how to enter values in cells, and how to work with ranges.

In the next chapter you'll begin to really unleash the power of Excel by adding formulas to worksheets.

## IN THIS CHAPTER

- Using basic math functions in Excel
- Reusing formulas in a spreadsheet
- Using values or results from other sheets or files
- Playing what-if to analyze figures

18

# FROM SIMPLE ADDITION TO WHAT-IFS: FORMULAS

A spreadsheet would be mostly useless if all you could do with it was enter numbers and text in cells. The main purpose of a spreadsheet is to analyze information, and without formulas, most analysis would be impossible.

This chapter describes basic math functions and how to use them in Excel, as well as how to create formulas to manipulate and analyze the information in a spreadsheet.

# Understanding Cell References and Operators

Before you can start building formulas, you need to understand two key topics: cell references and operators.

## Understanding Cell References

In Chapter 17, "Once Around the Worksheet," you learned a little about cell references. A *cell reference* is simply a reference to a cell. For example, Cell B5 refers to Column B, Row 5 in a spreadsheet. Likewise, Cell D8 means Column D, Row 8.

You can combine cell references to create range references. A range reference includes two or more cell references and one or more *reference operators*. You'll learn more about reference operators in the following section. For now, you should understand that the most common reference operator is the colon (:), which specifies the range of cells between two bracketing cells. For example, the reference B3:B7 refers to the range of cells B3, B4, B5, B6, and B7.

References can be either absolute or relative. An *absolute reference* specifies the exact address of a cell. An absolute cell reference takes the following form:

> $c$r

In this case, *c* represents the column and *r* represents the row. For example, the cell reference $B$6 identifies Column B, Row 6.

A *relative reference* specifies the address of a cell based on the relative position of the cell that contains the formula and the referenced cell. A relative reference takes the following form:

> *cr*

Again, *c* represents the column and *r* represents the row. Using the previous example, a relative reference would be B6 rather than the absolute $B$6.

So, what's the difference? None really, until you try to move the formula or insert rows or columns. If you specify an absolute reference, the formula will continue to use the value of the explicit cell. If you move or copy the formula and it contains relative references, the cell to which the formula refers will change.

Take the sheet in Figure 18.1 as an example. The formula =A2*C2 in Cell D2 multiplies A2 by C2 to derive a commission.

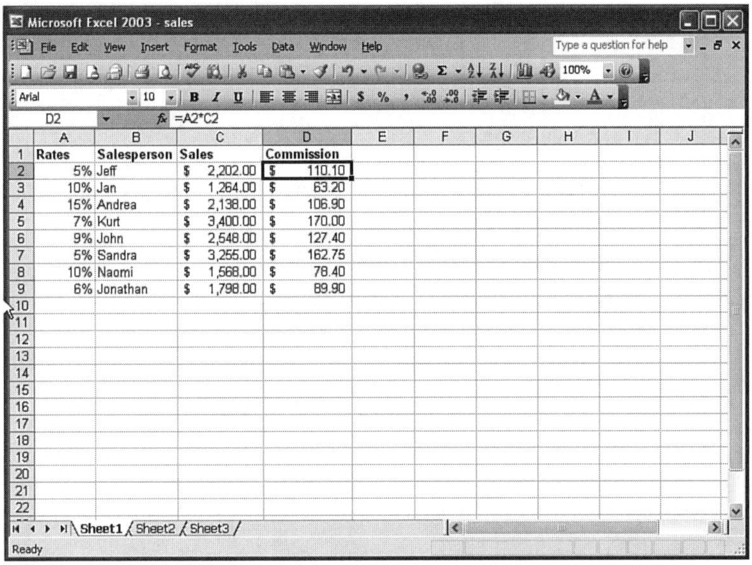

**FIGURE 18.1**

This formula includes a relative reference.

If you copy the formula down into the following four cells, these are the resulting formulas:

=A3*C3

=A4*C4

=A5*C5

=A6*C6

Excel copies the formulas relative to the positions of the cells in the relative reference. In this case, that is the result you want because each person's commission is based on his or her sales multiplied by his or her commission rate.

But let's say that everyone has the same commission rate. Figure 18.2 shows the spreadsheet for this case. In this example, the commission rate is stored in A2. The formula in D2 is an absolute reference to Cell A2 and a relative reference to Cell C2. When you copy the formula to fill the other cells, the relative reference changes, but the absolute reference remains, giving you the following formulas in the other four cells:

=$A$2*C3

=$A$2*C4

=$A$2*C5

=$A$2*C6

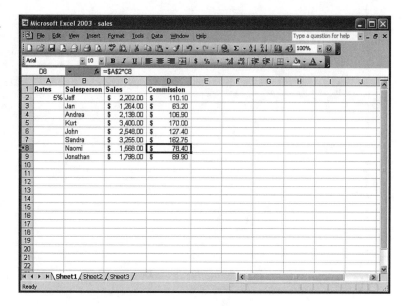

Finally, you can combine relative and absolute references. The reference $A2 absolutely references Column A but relatively references Row 2. If you used $A2 in the formula rather than $A$2 and then copied the formula, these would be the resulting formulas:

=$A3*C3

=$A4*C4

=$A5*C5

=$A6*C6

Each subsequent formula increases the row by one, but Column A remains in each formula.

Whether you use absolute or relative references depends entirely on what you need to accomplish with your formulas. You might need to change references from relative to absolute, or vice versa, before copying or moving formulas.

## Understanding Operators

If you have never worked with a spreadsheet program before or done any programming, you might not be familiar with math operators and

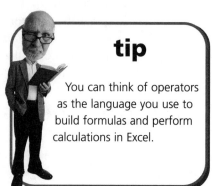

**tip**

You can think of operators as the language you use to build formulas and perform calculations in Excel.

how you use them. Excel actually supports four types of operators—arithmetic operators, comparison operators, text operators, and reference operators—which are explained in the following sections.

### Arithmetic Operators

Excel supports several *arithmetic operators* that enable you to perform math operations on values. For example, you could use math operators to add sales figures, calculate sales tax and commissions, average grades, and so on. Table 18.1 lists the arithmetic operators, their functions, and an example of each operator.

**Table 18.1**   Arithmetic Operators

| Operator | Purpose | Example |
|---|---|---|
| + | Addition | B2+C4 |
| - | Subtraction | C3-431 |
| * | Multiplication | A2*B6 |
| / | Division | C5/3 |
| % | Percent | A4*15% |
| ^ | Exponentiation | 3^3 |

As you examine the examples in Table 18.1, you will find cell references. For example, the + operator example adds the contents of cell B2 and C4. The - operator example subtracts 431 from the value in cell C3.

⇨   For more information on formulas, see the section "Creating Simple Formulas," later in this chapter.

### Comparison Operators

*Comparison operators* are used to compare two values and return either TRUE or FALSE. For example, you might want a spreadsheet to indicate, in a summary area, whether the sum of a long column of numbers is greater than a certain amount or less than the value in another cell.

Table 18.2 explains the comparison operators you can use in Excel.

**Table 18.2**   Comparison Operators

| Operator | Purpose | Example |
|---|---|---|
| = | Equal to | B3=C3 |
| > | Greater than | B5>10 |
| < | Less than | C4<100 |

**Table 18.2**  (continued)

| Operator | Purpose | Example |
|----------|---------|---------|
| >= | Greater than or equal to | B4>=100 |
| <= | Less than or equal to | R3<=75 |
| <> | Not equal to | B3<>C5 |

### Text Operators

There is only one *text operator* in Excel: the ampersand (&). The ampersand concatenates text strings into a single string. For example, the formula ="hob"&"nob" would result in the cell displaying *hobnob*. You should use this operator any time you need to merge two text strings.

### Reference Operators

*Reference operators* combine cells or ranges of cells. For example, assume that you want to add up Cells D3 through D19. You don't have to use =SUM(D3+D4+D5+D6...) and include all cells in the range. Instead, you can specify the first and last cells, separated by a colon, such as =SUM(D3:D19). Table 18.3 describes the reference operators.

**Table 18.3**  Reference Operators

| Operator | Purpose | Example |
|----------|---------|---------|
| : | Range operator, specifies a range between two cells | B4:B18 |
| , | Union operator, combines multiple references into one reference | SUM(C4:C6,D6:D8) |
| (space) | Intersection operator, produces one reference to cells common to two ranges | (C3:E8 A4:D5) |

Let's briefly look at a few examples to help you better understand reference operators. I've already given some examples that use the range operator.

The union operator combines multiple references into one reference. For example, assume that you want to sum the contents of B3:B9 and E7:E12. You could create a formula that looks like this:

(SUM(B3:B9)+SUM(E7:E12))

You can simplify that formula by using a union operator:

SUM(B3:B9,E7:E12)

The result is that Excel sums the range B3:B9, sums the range E7:E12, and adds the ranges together for a total sum.

The intersection operator produces a single reference that includes the common elements of other ranges. I'll illustrate this one with a figure to help you understand it. Figure 18.3 shows two ranges, B3:E9 and D6:G12. The shaded intersection of these two is D6:E9.

**FIGURE 18.3**

The shaded cells are the intersection of the two boxed ranges.

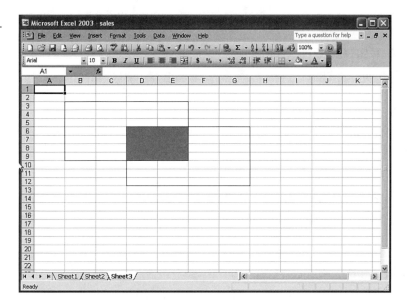

# Creating Simple Formulas

Now that you have some background in cell references and operators, you're ready to start creating formulas.

## Simple Formulas

You can use the math operators explained earlier to create simple formulas. For example, assume that you want to add Cells B2 and B3. Here's a simple formula to do that:

    =B2+B3

Notice the = sign at the beginning of the formula. It indicates to Excel that this is a formula and not next. If you omit the = sign, Excel treats the formula as simple text and does not perform any calculation.

You can use other operators, as well, and you can nest operations. The following example adds Cells B2 and B3, multiplies the result by 4, and then divides by the value in Cell D5:

=((B2+B3)*4)/D5

You don't have to do anything special to make Excel calculate a formula; you just click in the cell where you want the value to appear and type the formula. When you press Enter, Excel performs the calculation and displays the results in the cell.

## Understanding Functions

If you had to rely solely on math operators to create complex formulas, you'd have an extremely difficult time doing anything other than basic math operations. That's where Excel's *functions* come into play.

I've already used one function a few times in this chapter and in Chapter 17: the SUM function. The following formula adds the contents of Cells C5 through C9:

=SUM(C5:C9)

There are lots of functions available in Excel, so I won't cover them all in this chapter. Instead, I'll explain how to use them and where to find a listing and explanation of the functions.

## Where Are Those Functions?

You could rummage through the Excel Help documentation to find a list of functions, but here's a more direct method: Click in any cell and press Shift+F3 or choose Insert, Function to open the Insert Function dialog box (see Figure 18.4).

**FIGURE 18.4**

You can use the Insert Function dialog box to insert functions.

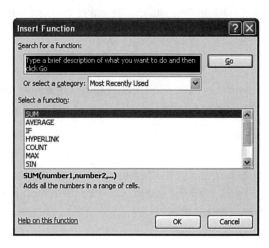

Excel offers several categories of functions. You can choose a category from the Or Select a Category drop-down list box in the Insert Function dialog box, and Excel displays the associated functions. After you select a function and click OK, Excel prompts you for function arguments (see Figure 18.5).

**FIGURE 18.5**

You can specify the arguments for a function by using the Function Arguments dialog box.

| Function Arguments | ✕ |
| --- | --- |

IF

Logical_test [                    ] = logical
Value_if_true [                    ] = any
Value_if_false [                    ] = any

=

Checks whether a condition is met, and returns one value if TRUE, and another value if FALSE.

**Logical_test** is any value or expression that can be evaluated to TRUE or FALSE.

Formula result =

Help on this function               [ OK ]   [ Cancel ]

What argument(s) you provide depends on the function. Some functions require a cell or range reference, some require numbers, and so on.

You can also simply type a formula and include whatever functions are necessary. Before you can use a function, however, you need to know the structure for the function and what arguments it requires. Perhaps the easiest way to learn the right structure is to simply insert a function by using the Insert Function dialog box.

## Combining References and Functions

Now, let's put it all together. In many cases you will use references along with functions to create a formula. You can specify values for the arguments for a function, or you can specify a cell or range reference. This example calculates the sine of the value in cell A5 and divides it by the sum of C3:C6:

=SIN(A5)/SUM(C3:C6)

If you enter an invalid formula, Excel displays an error message, such as #DIV/0!, which in this example indicates a division-by-zero error. If you simply get lots of # signs, you need to widen the column; the likely problem is that the results will not fit within the column as it is currently sized.

# tip

You can enter function names in lowercase. Excel automatically converts them to uppercase.

# Copying Formulas Between Cells

Many times you will want to use the same formula in more than one place in a spreadsheet. In the sales commission example from earlier in this chapter, for instance, it would save time to be able to create one formula and then copy it to calculate the commissions for other salespeople.

Copying a formula is simply a matter of selecting the cell containing the formula, copying it to the Clipboard, selecting a destination cell or range, and copying from the Clipboard.

Before you copy a formula, however, you should consider whether it uses absolute or relative references. Remember that absolute references in the formula will continue to reference the same absolute cell, row, or column after the formula is copied to other locations. Relative references will adapt within the copied formulas to reference other cells, rows, or columns.

Follow these steps to copy a formula:

1. Click in the cell where the formula is located.
2. Press Ctrl+C or choose Edit, Copy.
3. Click in the cell where you want the formula copied or select a range of cells in which to copy the formula.
4. Press Ctrl+V or choose Edit, Copy to paste the formula.

# Pulling Numbers from Other Worksheets

Excel enables you to work with values all over a worksheet. For example, you might pull values from several cells and add them together in a formula.

A single spreadsheet file can comprise multiple sheets, and this collection of worksheets is called a *workbook*. You are not limited to using values from a single worksheet. Instead, you can easily reference cells or ranges from one worksheet to another in a workbook.

# Naming and Referencing Other Worksheets

Assume that you need to manage commissions for several salespeople in four different divisions. You set up a worksheet for each division, and then you add a fifth worksheet to serve as a Summary sheet. The Summary sheet needs to pull values from each of the division sheets to total the sales, commissions, and so on.

One of the easiest ways to reference cells on other sheets is to simply click them. Follow these steps to create a formula using cells on different worksheets:

1. On Sheet1, enter the value **2** in Cell A12.
2. Click the Sheet2 tab, click in Cell B1, and type = to start a formula.
3. Click the Sheet1 tab and click Cell A12.
4. Type * and click the Sheet2 tab.
5. Click Cell A1 and press Enter. You have created a formula that multiplies the value in Cell A12 on Sheet1 by the value in Cell A1 on Sheet2. At the moment, Cell B2 shows a value of 0 because A1 is empty.
6. Click in Cell A1 on Sheet2 and enter the value **4**. Cell B1 now shows the value 8.

You don't have to click cells on other sheets to reference them in a formula. Instead, you can just include a sheet reference along with the cell reference. You simply specify the sheet name followed by an exclamation point to reference a different sheet. For example, the following references Cell B12 on Sheet3:

Sheet3!B12

By default, Excel names worksheets Sheet1, Sheet2, Sheet3, and so on. However, you don't have to live with the default sheet names in a spreadsheet. In this chapter's commission example, the sheets need to be named North, South, East, West, and Summary. To rename a sheet, right-click the sheet's tab and choose Rename, and then type the new name for the sheet. When you specify a reference to the sheet, you just use its name. The following example adds values in cells from four different sheets:

=North!B12+South!B6+West!C19+East!D7

What if you rename a sheet? That's not a problem. Excel automatically renames the sheet in any references where it is used. You don't need to worry about breaking your formulas when you rename a sheet.

## Copying and Linking Between Worksheets

You can copy values from one worksheet to another. To do so, you just click a cell in one sheet, copy the cell to the Clipboard, select a cell on another worksheet, and paste the value.

When you copy values like this, the data is duplicated from one sheet to the other. Changing the value on the source sheet does not affect the value on the destination sheet.

When you need values to change across sheets when a change is made to one cell, you should *link* the value rather than copy it. Here's how you do that:

1. Click the cell or range you want to copy.

2. Choose Edit, Copy to copy the cell or range to the Clipboard.

3. Select the cell or range on the destination sheet.

4. Choose Edit, Paste Special to open the Paste Special dialog box (see Figure 18.6).

**FIGURE 18.6**

You can use the Paste Special dialog box to link data between sheets.

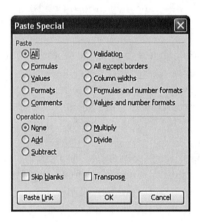

5. You don't need to choose any options in the dialog box—just click Paste Link to create a link.

## Referencing Other Workbooks

Up to this point I've explained how to reference cells on other worksheets within the current workbook. In some situations you might find it useful to reference cells and their values in other workbooks. Using this chapter's commission example, assume that division managers each create and manage their own sales workbooks and send them to you, the corporate sales manager, on a monthly basis. You need to bring all that information together into a summary workbook.

Use these steps to reference another workbook:

1. Open the source and destination workbooks and save the destination workbook before proceeding.

2. Switch to the source workbook and select the cell or cells you want to copy or link.

3. Switch to the destination workbook and select the destination cell or cells for the incoming data.

4. To copy the information, press Enter or choose Edit, Paste. Choose Edit, Paste Special, and click Paste Link if you want to link the information instead of copy it. Remember that linking the information allows it to be updated in the destination workbook if the values change in the source workbooks.

You can also create a reference yourself, such as when you need to build a formula that references another workbook. The source workbook need not be open to reference its contents. Just specify the workbook name in brackets, the worksheet name, and the reference. The following example references Cell A12 of Sheet1 in the workbook North.xls:

'[North.xls]Sheet1'!A12

You can simplify the task of creating a reference by using sheet names and creating names within the workbook. For example, assume that each of the four division workbooks from the commission example contains a named reference TotalSales on a sheet named Sales that sums all sales for the division. You want to add those values from each workbook. You could use the following formula to do so:

='[North.xls]Sales'!TotalSales+

[South.xls]Sales'!TotalSales+

[East.xls]Sales'!TotalSales+

[West.xls]Sales'!TotalSales

In this example, changes to the values in the division workbooks are automatically reflected in the Summary workbook. Your ability to reference cells in other worksheets and other workbooks is extremely powerful.

Excel asks if you want to update links when you open a workbook that contains links. If the workbook is already open, you choose Edit, Links to open the Edit Links dialog box (see Figure 18.7).

**tip**

Excel adds the path to the workbook for you if it finds the file. Excel displays an error message if it cannot locate the workbook. You can specify the path yourself, including specifying a uniform naming convention (UNC) path that specifies a location on a network server.

**FIGURE 18.7**

You can use the
Edit Links dia-
log box to
update or
change links.

You can click the source and click Update Values to update the linked values in the
current workbook from the linked workbook(s).

# Playing What-if

One of the great things about Excel is the ability it gives you to play what-if. What if
sales increased by 5% over last quarter? What if the load increased on this span by
2,000 pounds? What if output dropped by 10%?

Analyzing data in this way is not difficult at all. Just open the workbook and change
values, and then view the results within the workbook as Excel recalculates the
worksheets. You don't even have to save the
changes; just close the workbook and click No
when Excel asks if you want to save the changes.

In some cases you want to reach a certain value
in a cell but don't want to go through the trial-
and-error of fiddling with values to achieve the
result. In the commission example, assume that
you want to pay a bonus to all salespeople that
won't exceed a total of $10,000. You want to
base the commission on a percentage of total
sales. In this case, you want to adjust the bonus
rate until the total bonus value reaches $10,000.

You can use the Goal Seek feature to find this type
of answer. You click in the cell in which you want
to reach your goal (in this case, the total bonus)
and choose Tools, Goal Seek to open the Goal
Seek dialog box (see Figure 18.8).

**tip**

You can open a workbook
in read-only mode, which
prevents you from saving
changes. This is a good
approach to take to ensure
that you don't accidentally
change a workbook. To
open a workbook in read-only
mode, in the Open dialog box,
click the down arrow beside the
Open button and choose Open
Read-Only.

**FIGURE 18.8**

You can use the Goal Seek dialog box to find a specific solution.

In the To Value field, enter the value to be reached, which in this case is **10000**. Then click in the By Changing Cell field and type the cell reference of the value to be adjusted to reach the goal. Or you can click in the cell to select it. Then click OK to start the goal seek. Excel adjusts the specified value until it reaches the specified value in the goal cell.

There are other tools you can use in Excel to play what-if. In particular, scenarios and PivotTables are extremely useful tools for analyzing information and evaluating what will happen in various situations. As you gain more experience with Excel, you should check out these two features in the Help documentation to learn more about them.

# THE ABSOLUTE MINIMUM

Formulas enable Excel to perform calculations, from simple to complex, on values in a worksheet. In this chapter you learned how to create basic math functions and reuse formulas in a worksheet. You also learned how to use values and results from one worksheet on another, as well as perform what-if analysis on data by using the Goal Seek feature.

After you become comfortable working with text, values, and formulas in Excel, you will probably want to start adding formatting, lines, and other elements to worksheets to give them more visual appeal and make them more useful. The next chapter explains how to accomplish these tasks.

## IN THIS CHAPTER

- Adding pizzazz by formatting numbers and text
- Adding lines, borders, and shading
- Formatting cells
- Splitting, merging, hiding, and unhiding cells
- Using automatic formatting
- Adding comments and other items
- Filling a series of cells

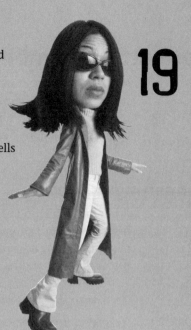

# JAZZING UP WORKSHEETS IN EXCEL

You could certainly create a spreadsheet without adding any text, special formatting, graphics, or other elements. Adding these types of elements, however, not only makes a spreadsheet look more professional but can also make it more useful and easier to read. Formatting column headings or key values in a worksheet as bold, for example, makes those headings and values easier to spot.

This chapter describes several steps you can take to format numbers and text in a worksheet, add borders and shading, and improve a worksheet's appearance in other ways. This chapter also explores a few methods for modifying cells and quickly filling a range of cells with a series of values.

# Formatting Numbers and Text

Excel makes it easy to apply formatting to data in a worksheet. For example, you can format cells so they display as currency, such as with a $ sign. You can format numbers to display with a certain number of decimal places. You can apply different fonts and other font characteristics to text. Many other formatting choices are available, as well. The following sections examine some of the most common ones.

## Formatting Numbers

The main reason to format numbers in a worksheet is to control the way the numbers appear. For example, you might want some numbers to appear as currency and others to appear as percentages. Figure 19.1 includes cells formatted to display numbers using both of these formats.

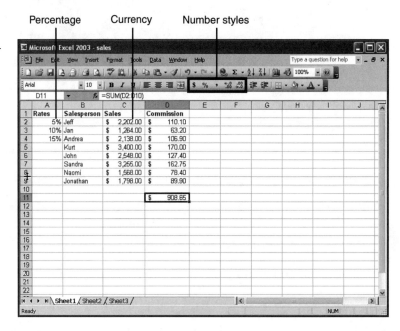

**FIGURE 19.1**

A worksheet can include cells formatted for currency and percentage.

It's relatively easy to format cells for a certain number format, and you can apply the formatting whether a cell is empty or contains a value or formula.

Excel's Formatting toolbar includes five number styles that you can apply quickly. You just select a cell or range of cells and click a style on the toolbar. These are the five number style buttons:

■ **Currency Style**—You can select this button to add a currency symbol, use commas as separators, and include two decimal points.

■ **Percent Style**—You can select this button to display the value as a percentage. If you enter **.05**, for example, Excel displays 5%.

■ **Comma Style**—You can select this button to use commas for separators and include two decimal places but exclude a currency sign.

■ **Increase Decimal**—You can select this button to add one decimal place.

■ **Decrease Decimal**—You can select this button to remove one decimal place.

You can follow these steps if you need a style not represented by the five number style buttons:

1. Click the cell or select the range of cells and choose Format, Cells to open the Format Cells dialog box (see Figure 19.2).

**FIGURE 19.2**

You can use the Format Cells dialog box to format numbers and other cell properties.

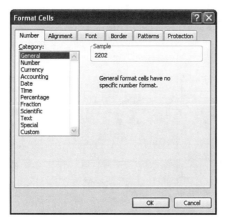

2. Select the Number tab.

3. Select an option from the Category list and then specify other options on the Number tab, which vary depending on which category is selected.

4. Click OK to apply the formatting.

As Figure 19.2 illustrates, you have several categories from which to choose. As mentioned in step 3, each category offers its own options. Figure 19.3, for example, shows the options that are available for the Currency category. As the figure illustrates, you can choose the currency symbol, number of decimal places, and how negative numbers should appear.

**FIGURE 19.3**

**FIGURE 19.3**

You can choose a currency symbol and other options for currency values.

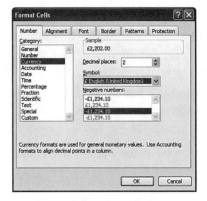

## Formatting Text

As you might expect, you have several options for formatting text in an Excel worksheet. The options you can set include font, font style, size, and color. To format text, you select a cell or range and choose Format, Cells to open the Format Cells dialog box. Then you should select the Font tab (see Figure 19.4).

**FIGURE 19.4**

You can use the Font tab to format text.

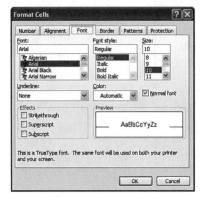

The options on the Font tab are generally self-explanatory. One option bears mention, however: You can select the Normal Font option to change the font back to its default settings, such as Arial, Regular, 10 point.

## Setting Alignment

Whether a cell contains text, numbers, or a formula that creates a text or numeric value, you

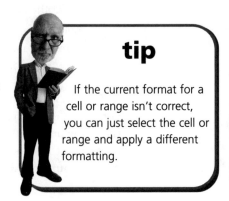

**tip**

If the current format for a cell or range isn't correct, you can just select the cell or range and apply a different formatting.

can control the cell's alignment. The *alignment* determines where in the cell the value appears.

By default, Excel left-aligns text, right-aligns numbers, and centers errors. For vertical alignment, Excel aligns the data at the bottom of the cell.

To set alignment, select a cell or range and choose Format, Cells. When the Format Cells dialog box appears, you select the Alignment tab, as shown in Figure 19.5.

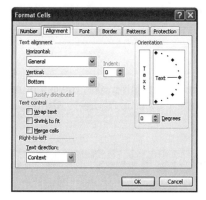

You use the Horizontal and Vertical drop-down list boxes to set the horizontal and vertical alignment, respectively. The options are mostly self-explanatory.

The Alignment tab includes some other options, as well:

■ **Wrap Text**—You can select this option to wrap the text to multiple lines if the column isn't wide enough to accommodate the text on one line. Enabling this option prevents the text from covering other cells or being hidden by the cell edge.

■ **Shrink to Fit**—You can select this option to shrink the width of the characters to fit the data in the cell. The character width adjusts as you adjust the column width

■ **Merge Cells**—You can combine two or more selected cells into a single cell. The upper-left cell in the range becomes the cell reference.

■ **Text Direction**—You can use this drop-down list box to control text direction.

■ **Degrees and Orientation**—You can use these controls to change the orientation angle of the data shown in the cell.

Why would you want to change alignment? Some situations are probably obvious to you. For example, you might want to move multiline text to the top of a cell and left-align the text. Or you might want to center column labels. Whatever the case, you just select the desired alignment and other properties from the Alignment tab. You can press Ctrl+Z or choose Edit, Undo if you don't like the results and then try again. Use Ctrl+Y to redo the last undo (that is, bring back whatever was changed).

# Using Borders, Boxes, Shading, and Other Jazz

One way to improve a worksheet's look is to add lines, boxes, color, shading, and other characteristics to cells. For example, instead of just using bold on an important sum, you can put a big red box around it.

## Using Borders

Adding a border around a cell or group of cells makes the cell or cells stand out or become separate from other cells. For example, Figure 19.6 shows a range of cells surrounded by a thick box.

**FIGURE 19.6**

A range of cells can have a thick border.

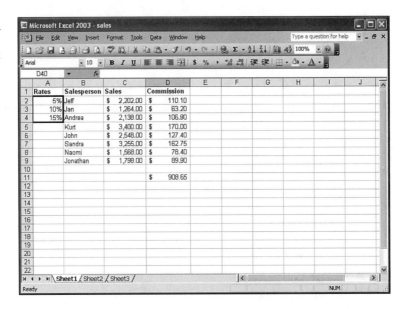

You don't have to put border lines all the way around cells. Instead, you can add border lines only to specific edges. For example, Figure 19.7 shows cells that have a thick border line on the bottom edge but not the other edges.

To add border lines to a cell or range of cells, you follow these steps:

1. Select the cell or range.

2. Choose Format, Cells to open the Format Cells dialog box. Select the Border tab (see Figure 19.8).

**FIGURE 19.7**

A range of cells can have only a bottom border line.

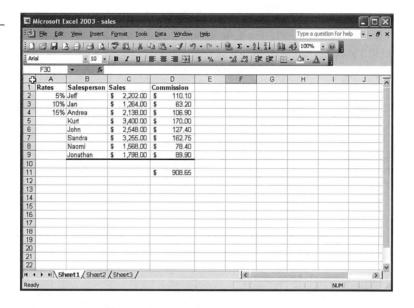

**FIGURE 19.8**

You can use the Border tab to add border lines to cells.

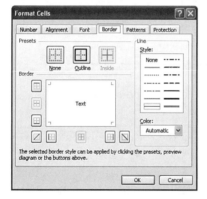

3. Click a line style from the Line group and then choose a color from the Automatic drop-down list box.

4. Click one of the three buttons for the preset modes in the Presets group or click one of the buttons in the Border group.

5. Click OK to apply the border.

## Applying Shading and Patterns

You can add color or patterns to the background of a cell in addition to or instead of a border. For

**tip**

Is Excel not giving you the line type you want, even though you have clicked it? If this is the case, make sure you click the line type first and then click the border style. Excel ignores the line style selection unless you also click a border style.

example, maybe you want an important sales total to appear as white text on a blue background to make it stand out. Or maybe you want to highlight a range of cells by giving them a yellow background. Figure 19.9 shows a worksheet with a range of cells highlighted with a pattern.

**FIGURE 19.9**

A worksheet can include cells that have background patterns.

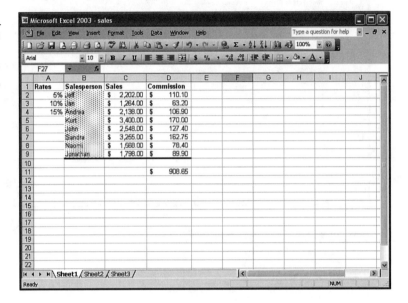

Follow these steps to add color or a colored pattern to cells:

1. Select the cell or range.

2. Choose Format, Cells to open the Format Cells dialog box. Select the Patterns tab (see Figure 19.10).

**FIGURE 19.10**

You can use the Patterns tab to apply color or a pattern to cells.

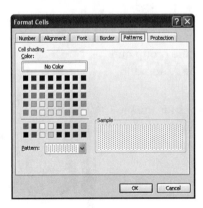

3. To apply a color, click a color in the Color selector.

4. Click the Pattern drop-down list box to show the pattern list shown in Figure 19.11.

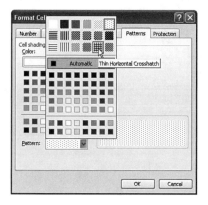

5. Click OK to apply the color and/or pattern to the selected cell(s).

# Other Ways to Work with Cells

The previous sections explain how to format cells to control the way the data in those cells appears. There are some other ways to work with cells, however, and the following sections discuss the most interesting of them.

## Merging and Splitting Cells

Sometimes you want to merge cells into one big cell. For example, to make multiline text fit in a single cell, you need to resize the cell. This resizing affects the cells on either side of the resized cell. So rather than make the cells on either side too big, you can just merge some cells together to suit the text. Figure 19.12 shows some cells that have been merged.

You merge cells by following these steps:

1. Select the cells you want to merge.

2. Choose Format, Cells to open the Format Cells dialog box. Select the Alignment tab.

3. Select Merge Cells and click OK.

**tip**

You can apply a color and a pattern, a pattern with no color (Automatic color), or a colored pattern. To apply a colored pattern, you click the Pattern drop-down list box, choose a color from the pop-up list, and then click the Pattern drop-down list box again and choose the pattern.

**FIGURE 19.12**

A worksheet can
include cells
that have been
merged.

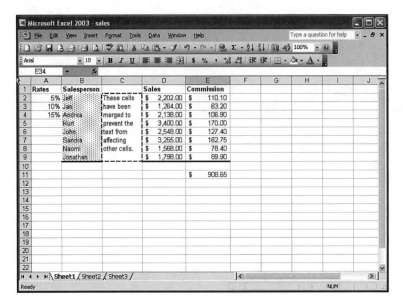

When you merge a range of cells, the cell takes on a single cell reference—the cell reference of the upper-left cell in the range. For example, if you merge cells B4 through E6, the cell reference for the resulting cell is B4.

If you later decide you want to split the merged cell back into individual cells, you just reverse the process: Click the cell and choose Format, Cells to open the Format Cells dialog box, and then you select the Alignment tab, clear the Merge Cells option, and click OK.

## Locking and Hiding Cells, Rows, and Columns

As a worksheet becomes increasingly complex, the information it contains becomes more difficult to follow. You can simplify a complex worksheet by hiding rows or columns. The hidden cells essentially collapse behind the other cells. Figure 19.13 shows a worksheet in which some cells are hidden.

You can hide rows and columns in a worksheet, and you can hide multiple sets of rows and columns, as needed. Follow these steps to hide rows or columns:

1. Click and drag the column headers or row headers to select the columns or rows you want to hide.

2. Choose Format, Column, Hide to hide columns or choose Format, Row, Hide to hide rows.

**FIGURE 19.13**

You can hide cells to simplify a worksheet.

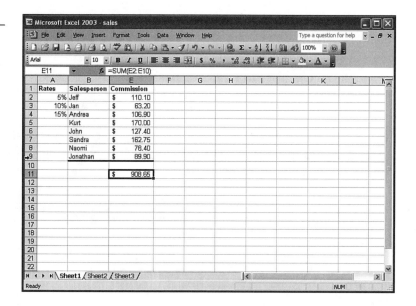

You can reference cells in hidden rows or columns, but you can't work with them directly by selecting them because they are hidden. Sooner or later you might need to unhide some hidden cells, and here's how you do it:

1. Click and drag to select the rows or columns on either side of the hidden ones.

2. Choose Format, Column, Unhide to unhide hidden columns or choose Format, Row, Unhide to unhide hidden rows.

How can you locate the hidden columns or rows? It's easy! The column letters and row numbers are sequential. Just look for nonsequential headers.

## Quickly Filling Cells with a Series

Many worksheets contain serial data of one type or another. This serial data might be days of the week, months of the year, sequential numbers, or other data. You don't need to enter this information yourself; instead, you can take advantage of your computer's ability to perform repetitive tasks.

The serial data need only fit a pattern. For example, if you enter 1, 2, 3, Excel extends the pattern with 4, 5, 6, and so on. Excel also looks for more complex patterns. If you enter Jan, April, July, October, Excel repeats that pattern by continuing with each fourth month.

Follow these steps to fill cells with a pattern of data:

1. Enter enough in sequential cells to define the pattern, such as 1, 2, 3 or Jan, Feb, Mar, Apr.

2. Select the cells that define the pattern.

3. Click the fill handle in the bottom-right corner of the last cell (see Figure 19.14) and drag it to create the series.

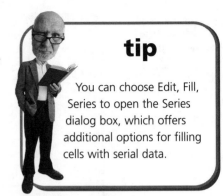

**tip**

You can choose Edit, Fill, Series to open the Series dialog box, which offers additional options for filling cells with serial data.

**FIGURE 19.14**

You can drag a cell's fill handle to create a series.

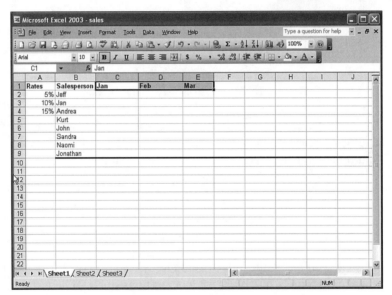

# Using Automatic Formatting

You can spend a lot of time improving the appearance of a worksheet by adding font formatting, borders, shading, and so on. A better approach is to let Excel handle the formatting for you automatically.

Excel includes an AutoFormat command and several predefined formats that enable you to quickly apply a formatting style to a range of cells. Here's how you use AutoFormat:

1. Select the range of cells you want to highlight.

**tip**

You can remove automatic formatting as easily as you add it. You simply select the range, choose Format, AutoFormat to open the AutoFormat dialog box, choose the format labeled None at the bottom of the list, and click OK.

2. Choose Format, AutoFormat to open the AutoFormat dialog box.

3. Click the Options button to expand the dialog box, as shown in Figure 19.15.

**FIGURE 19.15**

You can apply formatting by using the AutoFormat dialog box.

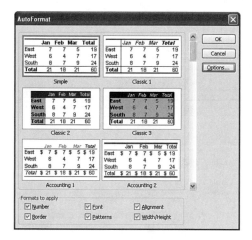

4. Click a predefined format to select that format.

5. Clear the check boxes for any items you don't want to format and then click OK to apply the format.

# Adding Comments to a Worksheet

It's often useful to add comments to a worksheet. For example, you might include comments about special commission goals for each salesperson. Or maybe you need to explain some results on the worksheet, such as why sales were down over the previous quarter.

Comments do not appear by default. Instead, Excel places a small red triangle in the upper-right corner of the cell where a comment is inserted, as shown in Figure 19.16. If you rest the cursor over the triangle, Excel displays the comment in a pop-up window.

Comments are also useful for reviewing documents. For example, you might send a worksheet to a manager for review and comment. The manager can add comments in the worksheet and send it back to you for further comment or action.

**tip**

You can turn on comments so that they show in the worksheet. You choose View, Comments to turn on or off display of comments.

**FIGURE 19.16**

You can let the cursor hover over a comment mark to view the comment.

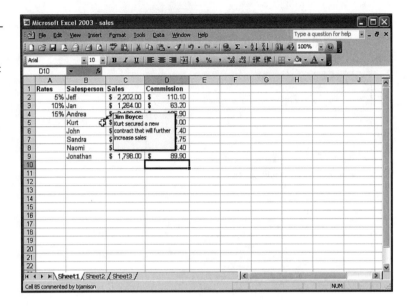

**FIGURE 19.16**

You can let the cursor hover over a comment mark to view the comment.

## Adding Comments

Follow these steps to add comments to a cell:

1. Click a cell to select it.

2. Choose Insert, Comment to open a comment window that is attached to the cell.

3. Type the comment text, pressing Enter to start a new line if needed.

4. Click any other cell to close the comment window.

## Editing and Deleting Comments

Letting the cursor hover over a comment mark displays the comment but doesn't give you the capability to edit the comment. Instead, you need to right-click the cell and choose Edit Comment to open the comment window. You can also choose Insert, Edit Comment to open the comment window.

To delete a comment, right-click the cell that contains the comment and choose Delete

**tip**

You can choose View, Toolbars, Reviewing to open the Reviewing toolbar, which includes buttons that help you view, edit, and delete comments.

Comment. You can also select a cell and click the Delete Comment button on the Reviewing toolbar.

## Reviewing Comments

It can be difficult to review comments if a worksheet contains lots of them or the comments overlap one another. Rather than turn on comments, you can let Excel cycle through the comments one at a time:

**tip**

You can use the Previous Comment button to move back through the comments.

1. Open the worksheet and choose View, Toolbars, Reviewing to turn on the Reviewing toolbar.

2. Click the Next Comment button to open and read the next comment. If you need to edit the comment, either click the Edit Comment button or simply click in the comment window and make the necessary additions or changes.

3. Click Next Comment again to view the next comment. Repeat this step to review all the comments.

# THE ABSOLUTE MINIMUM

This chapter explains how to format numbers and text in a worksheet, add borders and shading, and format cells in other ways. These types of changes not only make a worksheet look more appealing (in most cases), but can also make the worksheet more useful. This chapter also explains how to use automatic formatting to change a worksheet's appearance.

Excel's capability to fill a series of cells can be very handy because Excel can recognize several patterns and add information to a worksheet with very little effort. Finally, the capability to add comments to a worksheet can help you explain values or add other explanatory or supporting information.

The next chapter explores other types of information you can add to a worksheet to make it more useful, including charts, labels, legends, and other elements. That chapter also explains how to print charts.

**20**

# PiES, BARS, AND OTHER SWEET ADDiTiONS

A picture really is worth a thousand words, and in the case of a spreadsheet, a graph is worth, well, several hundred numbers.

You can easily add charts and graphs to Excel worksheets, use those charts in documents, print them, and so on. In this chapter you'll learn how to create and print charts and graphs in Excel. You'll also learn how to adjust fonts, legends, and other chart properties to suit your needs.

# Inserting a Chart Quickly

It takes very little effort to insert a simple chart into a worksheet. In general, all you need to do is select the cells to include in the chart and click a few buttons, and you have your chart.

## Adding a Chart

Follow these steps to see how easy it is to insert a chart:

1. Open a new worksheet and enter numbers in several cells.

2. Select the cells and click the Chart Wizard button on the Standard toolbar to start the Chart Wizard (see Figure 20.1).

**FIGURE 20.1**

You can insert charts by using the Chart Wizard.

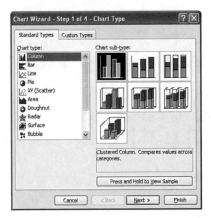

3. Select a type of chart from the Chart Type list.

4. Select a specific chart type from the Chart Sub-Type list.

5. Click and hold the Press and Hold to View Sample button to preview the chart.

6. Click Finish to insert the chart.

It's easiest to insert a chart from cells that contain only numbers because there aren't many options to worry about. However, in many cases you need to include other information in the chart.

Using the commission example from the Chapter 19, "Jazzing Up Worksheets in Excel," let's say you want to insert a chart that shows commissions for each salesperson. Using Figure 20.2 as a guide, you'll discover that you need to pull information from Column B and Column D to create the chart.

**FIGURE 20.2**

Two ranges will be used to create a commission chart.

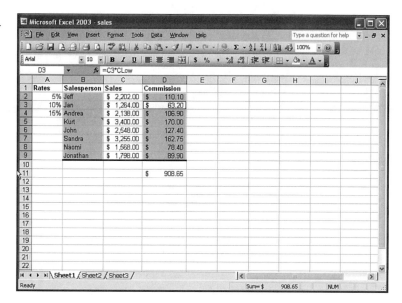

Follow these steps to create a pie chart based on this example:

1. Click and drag the range of cells from B2 to B9 to select the salespeople.
2. Hold down the Ctrl key and click and drag from D2 to D9 to select the commissions.
3. Click the Chart Wizard button on the toolbar or choose Insert, Chart to start the Chart Wizard.
4. Select the Pie type from the Chart Type list.
5. Select the 3D Pie (the second subtype).
6. Click Finish. The pie chart shown in Figure 20.3 appears.

You can control many other properties of a chart, such as the legend. These properties are covered later in this chapter.

**tip**

Make sure to click in a blank area inside the box rather than on the chart itself.

## Positioning and Resizing a Chart

You can position a chart anywhere you want on a worksheet. A chart includes a box around it, and you can easily reposition a chart by clicking inside the box and dragging the chart to the new location.

**FIGURE 20.3**

You can create this pie chart by using two columns.

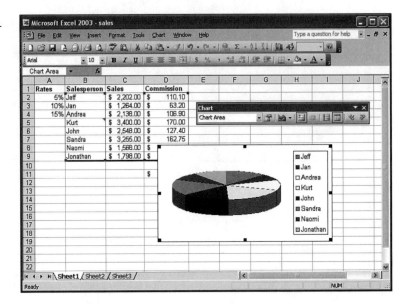

It's also easy to resize a chart so that it's larger or smaller, to fit the area available for it. The box around the chart includes eight control points, one at each corner and one in the middle of each side. You click the chart to select it and then click and drag a control point to resize the chart.

## Changing Chart Type

After you insert a chart, you might decide that a different chart type would be better. For example, say you insert a bar chart and later decide that a pie chart will show the information more clearly.

Changing an existing chart type is easy:

1. Right-click the chart and choose Chart Type or select the chart and choose Chart, Chart Type. The Chart Type dialog box appears.

2. In the Chart Type dialog box, select the chart type and subtype and then click OK.

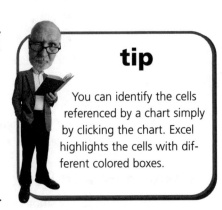

**tip**

You can identify the cells referenced by a chart simply by clicking the chart. Excel highlights the cells with different colored boxes.

## Moving a Chart to a Different Worksheet

One of the options in the Chart Wizard enables you to specify that a chart is inserted either in the current worksheet or on a new worksheet. You can move a chart around after you insert it, regardless of its location. Here's how:

1. Right-click the chart and choose Location to open the Location dialog box.

2. Choose As Object In and select a worksheet if you want the chart to appear in a particular worksheet. Or choose As New Sheet and specify a sheet name to create a sheet and move the chart to the specified sheet.

# Working with Other Chart Properties

To this point this chapter has explained only the very basics of adding a chart. There are lots of other properties you can change to control the way a chart looks. For example, you can use different fonts, change the chart legends, and change the colors used.

## Changing Fonts

Excel uses a default font when you create a chart, but you can easily change the font characteristics for the text in a chart:

1. Double-click the chart to open the Format Chart Area dialog box or select the chart and choose Format, Selected Chart Area.

2. Select the Font tab (see Figure 20.4).

**FIGURE 20.4**

You can use the Font tab to change chart fonts.

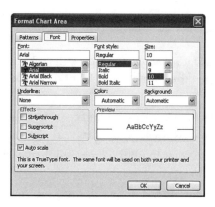

3. Select the font and other properties, such as font size, and click OK to apply the changes.

## Adjusting Colors and Shading

Excel automatically chooses the colors to use in a chart, but you can certainly change colors to achieve the look you want. Follow these steps to change the color of individual elements of a chart:

1. Click the chart to select it.

2. Click the area of the chart (the data point) you want to change, as shown in Figure 20.5.

Select a data point

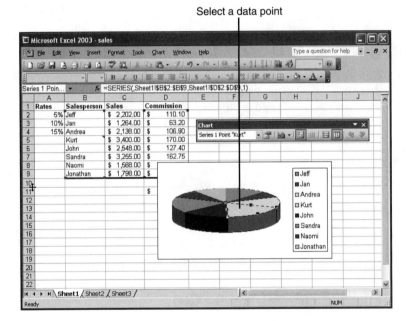

**FIGURE 20.5**

You select the area of the chart to change.

3. Choose Format, Selected Data Point or right-click the selection and choose Format Data Point to open the Format Data Point dialog box (see Figure 20.6).

4. In the Border group, select the border type and color to outline the selection, or choose Automatic to let Excel set the border.

5. In the Area group, select a color to fill the area and then click OK to apply the change.

6. Repeat steps 2 through 5 for other data points until you have the chart looking the way you want.

**FIGURE 20.6**

You can use the Format Data Point dialog box to change colors.

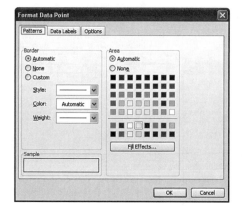

Excel doesn't limit chart fills to solid colors. You can use gradient fills and other options to produce outstanding-looking charts.

To use advanced options, follow steps 1 through 3 of the previous procedure to select a data point and open the Format Data Point dialog box. Then click Fill Effects to display the Fill Effects dialog box (see Figure 20.7).

**FIGURE 20.7**

You can assign custom patterns by using the Fill Effects dialog box.

Use the Gradient tab, shown in Figure 20.7, to apply a gradient pattern to a data point. Use the Texture tab, shown in Figure 20.8, to assign a texture map to a data point. Excel provides several textures, and you can click Other Texture to select an image to use for the fill texture. You can use Windows bitmap (BMP) files, Windows

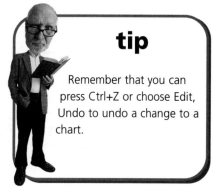

**tip**

Remember that you can press Ctrl+Z or choose Edit, Undo to undo a change to a chart.

metafile (WMF) files, and any other graphics type, such as JPG files, for which you have import filters installed.

**FIGURE 20.8**

You can use the
Texture tab to
apply a texture
to a data point.

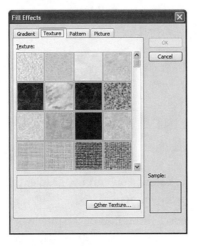

If you prefer to use a pattern rather than a color or texture, you can select the Pattern tab (see Figure 20.9). Then you can choose a foreground and background color, choose a pattern type, and click OK to apply the selected pattern.

**FIGURE 20.9**

You can use the
Pattern tab to
apply a pattern
to a data point.

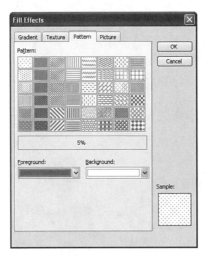

# Working with Titles, Legends, and Data Labels

Depending on your selections when you create a chart, Excel might include a title on the chart. Figure 20.10 shows an example of a chart with a

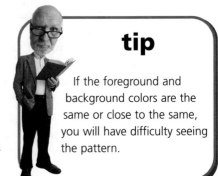

**tip**

If the foreground and background colors are the same or close to the same, you will have difficulty seeing the pattern.

title. When the chart was created, the Sales column was selected, so Excel used "Sales" as the chart title. Excel also includes a legend to show what the various parts of the chart mean.

**FIGURE 20.10**

In this example Excel uses the Sales column header for the chart title.

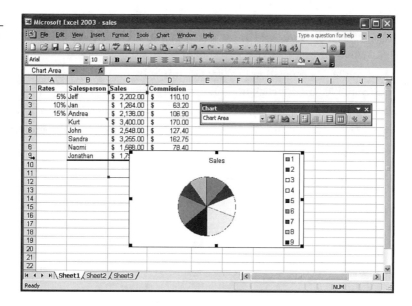

## Changing Titles

If Excel doesn't add a title to a chart, or if you want to change the title, follow these steps:

1. If there is a title, click the title to select it. Then highlight the text and change it. If there is no title, or if you prefer to use a dialog box to change an existing title, right-click the chart and choose Chart Options or click the chart and choose Chart, Chart Options. Excel opens the Chart Options dialog box, shown in Figure 20.11.

**FIGURE 20.11**

You can change a chart title and other properties by using the Chart Options dialog box.

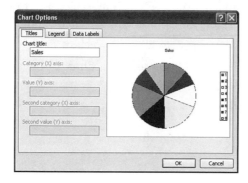

2. Click in the Chart Title field and change the chart title.

3. Use the additional fields to set the axis titles, if any.

## Changing a Chart Legend

A *chart legend* identifies the chart data points. You have some control over the legend and how it appears in the chart.

You can easily reposition the legend simply by dragging it in the chart. You can also resize the legend by clicking and dragging one of its control points.

To change other legend properties, select the chart and choose Chart, Chart Options to open the Chart Options dialog box. Then you select the Legend tab (see Figure 20.12).

**FIGURE 20.12**

You can use the Legend tab to change legend properties.

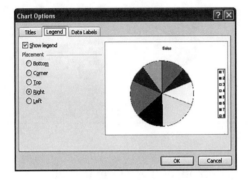

You should clear the Show Legend check box if you don't want a legend on the chart. Use the Placement options to control the location and layout of the legend on the chart.

## Using Data Labels

*Data labels* provide additional information about data points in a chart. For example, you might want to include percentage labels on a pie chart to show the percentage used by each element. Figure 20.13 shows an example of data labels.

Follow these steps to add or change data labels for a chart:

1. Click the chart to select it and choose Chart, Chart Options. The Chart Options dialog box appears.

2. Click the Data Labels tab (see Figure 20.14).

**FIGURE 20.13**

You can use data labels to add information about data points.

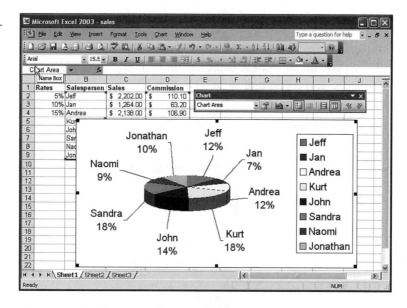

**FIGURE 20.14**

You can set data labels by using the Data Labels tab.

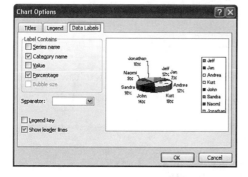

3. In the Label Contains group, select the information you want to include with the data label.

4. Choose from the Label Contains group the items you want to include in the label.

5. From the Separator drop-down list, choose the character to use to separate multiple items in the label (if you chose more than one from the Label Contains group box).

6. Select the Legend Key check box to include the legend values in the data labels.

7. Select the Show Leader Lines check box to have Excel draw leader lines from the data labels to their respective data points on the chart.

8. Click OK to apply the changes.

# Printing Charts

Unless you specify otherwise, Excel prints charts along with a worksheet. In some situations you might want to print a chart by itself. For example, maybe you are putting together a report and want a chart to fill a page in the report.

Printing a chart by itself is easy:

1. Click the chart to select it.

2. Choose File, Print to open the Print dialog box. Excel automatically chooses the Selected Chart option for you (see Figure 20.15).

**FIGURE 20.15**

You can use the Selected Chart option to print just the chart.

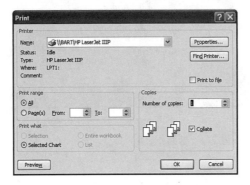

3. Set other options and then click Preview to see how the chart will print.

4. Adjust margins and other settings as needed and click Print to print the chart.

# THE ABSOLUTE MINIMUM

It won't be long after you begin using Excel that you will want to add charts to your worksheets. This chapter explains how to insert graphs and bar charts in a worksheet, position and resize them, change from one chart to another, and add legends and other text to charts. You also learned how to change colors and other properties of charts.

The next chapter explains how to save, print, and email spreadsheets.

21

# SAVING, PRINTING, AND EMAILING WORKBOOKS

Like any other type of document, a workbook needs to be saved and, in many situations, printed. You have a few options for saving workbooks, and Excel gives you a handful of different file formats from which to choose.

You can also exercise some control over how a worksheet prints, printing the entire worksheet or just a selection. As explained in Chapter 20, "Pies, Bars, and Other Sweet Additions," you can also print a chart by itself, if needed.

Finally, as you can with Word documents, you can email an Excel workbook. This chapter explains how to accomplish all these tasks.

# Saving Excel Workbooks

The process for saving a file in Excel is essentially the same as the process of saving files in most other Windows applications. You choose File, Save As to open the Save As dialog box (see Figure 21.1).

Where to save the file isn't your only choice, however. You also need to decide on a file format.

## Choose a File Format

Excel 2003 offers several file formats, most of which you will never use—guaranteed. The following list concentrates on just a few of them:

- **Microsoft Excel Workbook**—This file format is Excel's native format and is compatible with Excel version 2000 and later.

- **Template**—You use this format to save an Excel workbook as a template, which you can use to create other workbooks. For example, you might create an Expense Report workbook and then save it as a template so that you can quickly create a monthly expense report. See the section "Using Templates," later in this chapter, for more information.

- **Other Excel formats**—Excel offers several earlier native Excel formats to support

note

Excel 2003 supports a couple Extensible Markup Language (XML) data file formats. Support for XML provides compatibility and portability of your Excel data, making it easy to use the data in other ways. XML is a relatively advanced topic, so it is not covered in this book. See the Excel Help documentation for more information on XML and how Excel 2003 makes use of it.

earlier versions of Excel. You can use these formats if you need to send your workbooks to people who use earlier versions of Excel.

# Using Templates

A *template* in Excel, as in Word, is a document that you use to create other documents. For example, assume that you want to start using Excel to submit your monthly expense reports. You could open last month's expense report workbook, make changes to it, and save it as a new document. The potential problem with this is that you might accidentally save this month's report over last month's report, losing its data if you don't have a backup.

To avoid this problem, you can create a workbook that contains the bare bones of your expense report, such as column or row heads, formulas, and so on, without the actual expense data. Then, choose File, Save As to open the Save As dialog box, specify a filename, choose Template from the Save As Type drop-down list, and click Save.

Excel suggests the Template folder of your user profile as the storage location when you choose the Template format in the Save As dialog box. Excel uses this folder as the default location for the Templates dialog box (see Figure 21.2), which it displays when you choose to create a new document from a template.

**FIGURE 21.2**

You can choose a template from the Templates dialog box.

When you need to create a new document from a template, choose File, New to open the task pane, and then click On My Computer under the Templates group. From the Templates dialog box that appears, select the template and click OK. Excel starts a new document that has all the contents of the template.

# Printing Worksheets and Workbooks

It's a good bet that you will need to print worksheets at least some of the time. As you can with other types of documents, you can print an entire worksheet, a selection of a worksheet, or individual chart. The following sections explain the printing options in Excel.

## Printing a Worksheet or Workbook

Printing an entire worksheet is much like printing any other document. Open the document and choose File, Print to open the Print dialog box (see Figure 21.3).

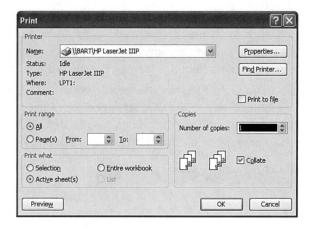

The Print Range group in the Print dialog box lets you choose between printing the entire document and printing only a certain number of pages.

The Print What group lets you choose how much of the workbook to print. The Active Sheet(s) option, if selected, causes Excel to print only those sheets that are active. How do you make multiple sheets active for printing? That's easy: Hold down the Ctrl key and click the sheet tabs for the sheets that you want to print. Then choose File, Print to open the Print dialog box, select the Active Sheet(s) option, and click OK.

You might want to print an entire workbook, not just one or two worksheets in the workbook. In that case, you choose File, Print to open the Print dialog box, select the Entire Workbook option, and click OK to print the entire workbook.

## Printing Just a Selection of a Worksheet

Many times, particularly with complex worksheets, you want to print only a selection within a worksheet. Here is one way to print just a selection:

1. Use the mouse to select a range of cells.

2. Choose File, Print to open the Print dialog box.

3. Select the Selection option in the Print What group.

4. Set other printing options, as needed, and click OK.

## Designating Printing and Nonprinting Information by Using Print Areas

In many cases, the information you want to print in the worksheet is the same from one day to another. For example, the worksheet might include supporting figures, notes, or other information that is useful for creating or working with the worksheet but it not useful on a printed copy.

**tip**

You can hide columns and rows that you don't want to print rather than exclude those rows and columns from a print area.

You can use a *print area* to specify the areas in a worksheet that you want printed. The print area is saved with the workbook, so the next time you need to print the document, the same print area will apply.

You can specify only one print area in a worksheet, but that print area can contain multiple ranges. However, each range in the print area prints on its own page.

The following example creates a print area with a single range:

1. Select the range A1 to D11.

2. Choose File, Print Area, Set Print Area. Excel puts a dashed line around the print area to identify it, as shown in Figure 21.4.

You can clear the print area if needed, such as when you need to print the entire worksheet. To clear the print area, choose File, Print Area, Clear Print Area.

## Making It Fit

When you work with lots of information in a worksheet, fitting that information on a printed sheet can be difficult. One way to fit more on a page is to reduce the margins. Another is to specify landscape mode instead of portrait mode. You can also direct Excel to fit a worksheet to the available paper width or print it on a specified number of pages. You accomplish all these tasks by setting page properties. Here's how:

**tip**

Setting a new print area clears the old one.

1. Choose File, Page Setup to open the Page Setup dialog box and then select the Page tab (see Figure 21.5).

**FIGURE 21.4**

A dashed line indicates a print area.

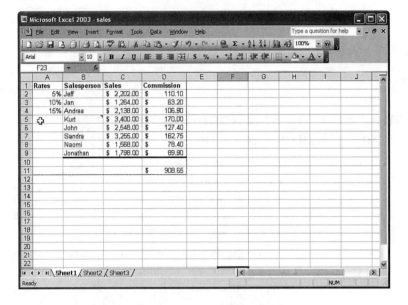

**FIGURE 21.5**

You can use the Page tab of the Page Setup dialog box to fit a worksheet on a printed page.

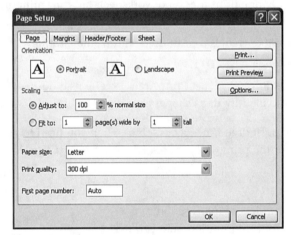

2. Select Landscape if you need to print in landscape mode (sideways on the page).

3. Select the Fit To option to fit the data on a specified number of pages.

4. Click the Margins tab (see Figure 21.6) and set the margins for the printed page.

**FIGURE 21.6**

You can set page margins on the Margins tab of the Page Setup dialog box.

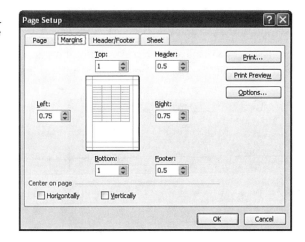

5. Click Print Preview to check the results and then click Print in the Print Preview window to print the document if the settings are acceptable.

# Adding Headers and Footers

Just as you can with Word documents, you can add headers and footers to an Excel worksheet. The header appears at the top of the page and the footer appears at the bottom. You might use headers to include a title for the worksheet and footers for page numbers, for example.

Follow these steps to set the header or footer:

1. Choose File, Page Setup to open the Page Setup dialog box and click the Header/Footer tab (see Figure 21.7).

**FIGURE 21.7**

You can add headers or footers by using the Header/Footer tab.

| Page Setup | ? X |
| --- | --- |

Page | Margins | Header/Footer | Sheet

Sheet1    **Jim Boyce, Inc. Confidential**    Page 1

Print...
Print Preview
Options...

Header:

Sheet1, Jim Boyce, Inc. Confidential, Page 1

Custom Header...    Custom Footer...

Footer:

(none)

OK    Cancel

2. Select from the Header drop-down list the header you want to include or that most closely matches what you need.

3. Click Custom Header to display the Header dialog box (see Figure 21.8) if you want to specify a custom header or modify the standard header you selected.

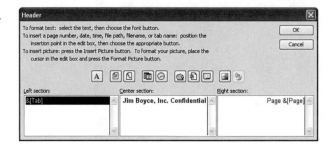

4. In each section, edit the text you want included and then click a button to add a dynamic element, such as a page number.

5. Click OK to close the Header dialog box.

6. Choose a footer from the Footer drop-down list on the Header/Footer tab of the Page Setup dialog box and then click Custom Footer to customize it as you did for the header.

7. Click OK to close the Footer dialog box, and then click OK to close the Page Setup dialog box.

## Specifying Row and Column Titles

The Sheet tab of the Page Setup dialog box (see Figure 21.9) enables you to specify rows and columns to repeat in a printed document. For example, assume that Row A includes column headers that identify each column, and you want those headers to print on each page. You can configure the Page Setup dialog box options so that Excel will repeat Row A on each page.

You follow these steps to specify row or column titles:

1. Choose File, Page Setup to open the Page Setup dialog box and then click the Sheet tab.

2. Click in the Rows to Repeat at Top field and then click in the row you want repeated.

3. Click in the Columns to Repeat at Left field and then click in the column you want repeated.

4. Click OK.

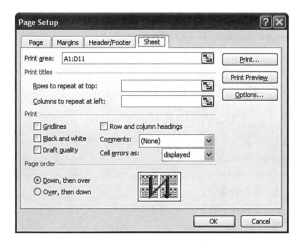

## Setting Miscellaneous Print Options

The Sheet tab of the Page Setup dialog box offers some miscellaneous options that bear mentioning:

- **Gridlines**—You can choose this option to have Excel print gridlines that define the cell boundaries. You can clear this option to omit the gridlines.

- **Black and White**—You can use this option to print a worksheet in black and white even if it contains color. This option has no effect on a noncolor printer, but it can reduce printing time on a color printer.

- **Draft Quality**—You can use this option to print a draft without gridlines or graphics.

- **Row and Column Headings**—You can use this option to include the row and column headings on the printed document.

- **Comments**—You can use this option to specify how comments are printed, if at all.

- **Cell Errors As**—You can use this option to specify how you want errors to print within a cell.

- **Down, Then Over and Over, Then Down**—These two options determine the order in which Excel prints the document, which affects the page order.

# Emailing a Workbook

In some situations you might want to email a workbook file to someone. You can embed the information in a message so that the Excel data appear in the body of the message, or you can send the workbook as an attachment.

Your options for emailing an Excel workbook are essentially the same the options as for emailing a Word document. Rather than repeat the information here, I'll point you to the section "Easy Ways to Email a Document" in Chapter 14, "Saving, Printing, Emailing, and Faxing Documents," which explains the process.

# THE ABSOLUTE MINIMUM

This chapter explains how to save Excel workbooks in various formats, print all or part of a worksheet or workbook, and fit a large worksheet on a page. In this chapter you also learned how to set page properties such as headers and footers to change the way a document looks when printed. At the end of the chapter, you got a quick overview of emailing workbooks.

The next chapter explains the most common settings you are likely to want to change as you become more proficient with Excel.

## IN THIS CHAPTER

- Controlling how comments appear
- Specifying how the cursor and mouse work
- Specifying custom file locations and opening files automatically
- Creating custom fill series and controlling other options

# 22

# EXCEL SETTINGS TO CHANGE

Like the other Office applications, Excel offers many options you can set to control the way the program works and the way worksheets appear. For example, you can change the default file location for templates, add more recently used files to the File menu, and turn AutoComplete on or off for text entries.

This chapter examines several of the most common settings you are likely to change as you become more comfortable using Excel.

# Changing How Comments Appear

By default, Excel shows a small, red triangle in the upper-right corner of a cell to indicate that the cell contains a comment. You can rest the cursor over the comment indicator to view the comment in a pop-up window.

You can change the way Excel handles comments, either hiding the comment indicator altogether or showing the indicator and comment. To change these settings, choose Tools, Options to open the Options dialog box, and then select the View tab (see Figure 22.1). You can choose one of the following options:

**FIGURE 22.1**

You can set comment appearance on the View tab.

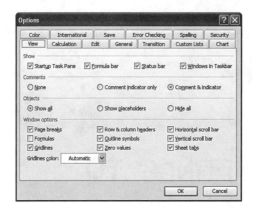

- **None**—If you select this option, Excel does not show the comment or the comment indicator. You can use the Reviewing toolbar to view the comments: Just click Next Comment or Previous Comment.

- **Comment Indicator Only**—If you select this option, Excel shows the triangle comment indicator on the cell where the comment is inserted.

- **Comment & Indicator**—If you select this option, Excel shows the comment indicator and the comment.

# Turning Off Automatic Calculation

By default, Excel automatically recalculates a worksheet when you change a value in the

> **tip**
>
> You can click and drag the edge of a comment box to move it. The leader remains attached to the cell and adjusts accordingly. You can right-click a comment and choose Format Comment to change the font properties for the comment.

worksheet. As the worksheet grows more complex, calculation takes more time. For very complex worksheets, you might want to change the way Excel handles recalculation.

You can choose Tools, Options to open the Options dialog box and then select the Calculation tab (see Figure 22.2).

**FIGURE 22.2**

You can control how Excel recalculates a worksheet by using the Calculation tab.

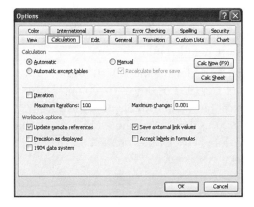

The following options control calculation:

- **Automatic**—You can select this option to calculate dependent values every time you change a value.

- **Automatic Except Tables**—If you select this option, when you change a value, you calculate all dependent formulas except data tables.

- **Manual**—You can select this option to calculate the workbook only when you direct Excel to do so by clicking the Calc Now button or pressing F9.

- **Recalculate Before Save**—You can choose this option to have Excel automatically recalculate the workbook when you save it.

- **Calc Now (F9) and Calc Sheet**—You can click Calc Now (F9) to initiate a manual recalculation of the workbook. You can click Calc Sheet to recalculate only the current sheet and any associated charts.

- **Iteration**—You can choose this option to limit the number of calculation iterations Excel performs for goal seek and resolving *circular references* (that is, formulas that point to each other). You use the Maximum Iterations and Maximum Change options to control iteration.

- **Update Remote References**—You can select this option to recalculate formulas that reference data in other applications.

- **Save External Link Values**—You can enable this option to save the values of linked cells with the workbook. You can clear this option to require Excel to update those values from the source instead. Clearing this option can speed up the saving and opening of large workbooks.

■ **Precisions as Displayed**—If this option is enabled, Excel changes values stored in the workbook from full precision of 15 decimal places to whatever is specified for the cell format. Decreasing precision reduces file size but naturally makes the values less precise.

■ **Accept Labels in Formulas**—If you select this option, you can use row and column labels in formulas. See Chapter 18, "From Simple Addition to What-ifs: Formulas," for more detailed information.

■ **1904 Date System**—Excel for the Macintosh uses the 1904 date system, which means it treats 1/2/1904 as day 1. If you enter 1 in a date-formatted cell, for example, Excel for Macintosh displays the date 1/2/1904. Excel for Windows uses 1/1/1900 as day 1. You should have to enable this option only if you cut and paste date between files created for the Macintosh and files created under Windows.

# Zooming/Scrolling by Using the Mouse Wheel

If you have a Microsoft IntelliMouse or another mouse with a compatible scroll button, Excel scrolls the worksheet up or down when you move the scroll button. If you are working with a very complex worksheet or one with lots of graphs that have fine detail, you might prefer to use the scroll button to zoom in and out of the worksheet.

To change the zooming and scrolling options, choose Tools, Options to open the Options dialog box, and then select the General tab (see Figure 22.3). You can select the option Zoom on Roll with IntelliMouse if you want Excel to zoom instead of scroll. You should leave this option cleared if you want Excel to scroll with the mouse.

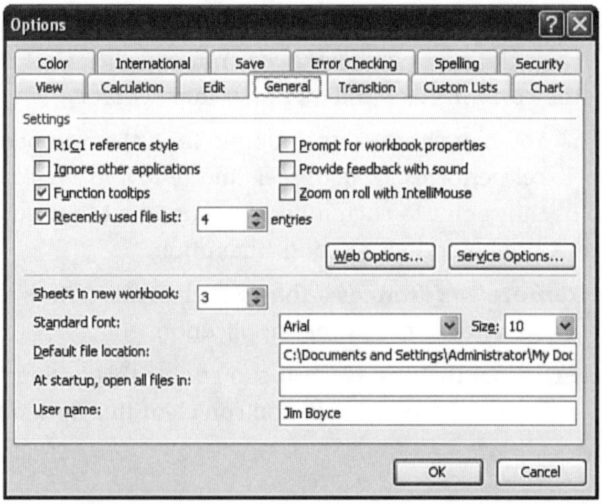

**FIGURE 22.3**

You can configure mouse scrolling or zooming on the General tab.

# Setting AutoRecover Time

By default, Excel automatically saves changes in an AutoRecover file every 10 minutes. If Excel or your system hangs, Excel reads the AutoRecover data when Excel restarts, enabling you to restore the document to the point of the last AutoRecover save. If you make lots of changes, 10 minutes could be too long. Use the Save AutoRecover Info Every n Minutes option on the Save tab of the Options dialog box to turn AutoRecover on or off and change the AutoRecover period.

**tip**

You can choose the option Disable AutoRecover on the Save tab to prevent AutoRecover saves for the current workbook. This setting is saved with the document.

# Changing the Direction Excel Moves the Cursor After You Press Enter

Excel's default behavior is to move the cursor down one cell when you press Enter. You might want to change that behavior, depending on the layout of the worksheet. For example, you might prefer to work bottom-to-top in a column.

To make such changes, you choose Tools, Options to open the Options dialog box, select the Edit tab (see Figure 22.4), and select a direction—Down, Up, Left, or Right—from the Direction drop-down list box. You can choose between.

**FIGURE 22.4**

You can configure cursor movement by using the Edit tab.

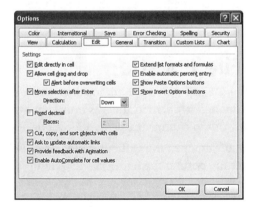

**tip**

If you don't want Excel to move the cursor at all but want Excel to keep it in the current cell, you should clear the option Move Selection After Enter.

# Turning AutoComplete On and Off for Text Entries

Like Outlook and other applications, Excel provides an AutoComplete feature that enables it to automatically complete text information when you type the first part of the text. For example, if you have entered Expenses somewhere in a worksheet and click in another cell and type Exp, Excel automatically completes the word for you.

If you prefer to not use AutoComplete, you can turn it off. To do so, you choose Tools, Options to open the Options dialog box, select the Edit tab, and clear the option Enable AutoComplete for Cell Values. Then you click OK.

# Adding More Recently Used Files

Excel, like many other Windows applications, maintains a most recently used file list in the File menu. Excel keeps track of the last four documents you opened in Excel. You can increase or decrease this number to show more or fewer recently used documents.

To change the number of recently used documents shown in the File menu, you choose Tools, Options to open the Options dialog box and then select the General tab. You then increase or decrease the number in the Recently Used File List spin control.

# Setting the Default File Location

Like other Office applications, Excel uses a default location for workbooks—the user's My Documents folder. If you frequently open documents from a network share instead of My Documents, you might want to change the default location.

To do so, choose Tools, Options to open the Options dialog box, and then select the General tab. You then enter the path to the folder in the Default File Location field and click OK.

# Opening Files Automatically at Startup

Let's assume that you work with the same three workbooks all day, every day. Every morning you have to open the workbooks one at a time. You can save yourself some time and trouble by having Excel open them automatically.

The option At Startup, Open All Files In on the General tab of the Options dialog box enables you to have Excel open all documents in a specified folder when Excel starts. You just enter the full path to the folder and click OK.

# Changing the Default Font

The General tab of the Options dialog box includes two options, Standard Font and Size, that define the font Excel uses by default for text in a workbook. You can use these options to change the font or size if you prefer a different font or font size.

# Creating Custom Fill Series Lists

If you read the section "Quickly Filling Cells with a Series" in Chapter 19, "Jazzing Up Worksheets in Excel," you know that Excel can automatically extend a selection to fill that selection with a series, such as days of the week or months of the year.

Excel includes a handful of predefined series lists. You can define your own custom lists in order to quickly fill cells with your own series data. Follow these steps to define a custom list:

1.  Choose Tools, Options to open the Options dialog box and then select the Custom Lists tab (see Figure 22.5).

**FIGURE 22.5**

You can add a custom list by using the Custom Lists tab.

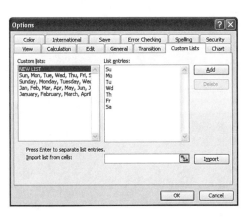

2.  Click NEW LIST in the Custom Lists list and click in the List Entries list.
3.  Type the items in the series and press Enter after each list element.
4.  Click Add to add the list.

# The Absolute Minimum

This chapter explains some of the most common settings you will likely want to change as you begin to become more comfortable using Excel. There are many others, so you should take the time to explore the Options dialog box to discover others that might suit your needs.

This chapter completes the coverage of Excel. The next chapter introduces you to Microsoft PowerPoint, which you can use to create presentations for meetings, classes, reports, and even online presentations.

# PART V

# CREATING PRESENTATIONS IN POWERPOINT

## IN THIS CHAPTER

- Creating a quick, basic slide show
- Starting a presentation by using the AutoContent Wizard
- Adding text to a presentation
- Navigating, inserting, moving, and deleting slides
- Switching slide orientation between portrait and landscape
- Saving a presentation
- Controlling look and feel by using a slide master
- Adding and removing slide numbers and dates

**23**

# QUICKLY CREATING A BASIC SLIDE SHOW

PowerPoint is used for creating presentations or slide shows. You can make PowerPoint presentations very complex, but all presentations boil down to a series of slides. The slides can contain text, but they can also contain graphics and pictures, animation, videos, and other advanced features. These advanced features are covered in later chapters in Part V, "Creating Presentations in PowerPoint."

This chapter explains how to create a basic presentation in Microsoft PowerPoint.

# A Quick Tour of Microsoft PowerPoint

Figure 23.1 shows the main PowerPoint window, which is used to edit and preview a slide show and typically shows one slide at a time. The slide is shown in the center of the main window. The Navigation pane, on the left side of the main window, is used to move between slides in a presentation.

**FIGURE 23.1**

The default PowerPoint window has the Navigation pane on the left, the slide being edited in the middle, and the task pane on the right.

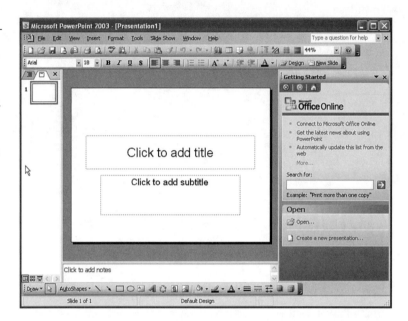

The Drawing toolbar, shown at the bottom of the main PowerPoint window, is used for drawing on slides and adding pictures, graphics, and other objects to slides. Finally, the task pane is shown by default on the right side of the PowerPoint window. By default, the task pane is used to open existing presentations and create new presentations as well as to search the Microsoft Web site. The task pane's purpose changes, depending on what is happening in the main window.

# Starting a Presentation by Using the AutoContent Wizard

The easiest way to start building a presentation in PowerPoint is by using the AutoContent Wizard. The AutoContent Wizard walks you through the creation of a slide show so that you don't need to know the intricacies of PowerPoint. After you use the wizard to create the skeleton of a presentation, you must add content, as discussed in the remaining sections of this chapter. To begin using the AutoContent

Wizard, you select File, New. The New Presentation task pane appears, as shown in Figure 23.2.

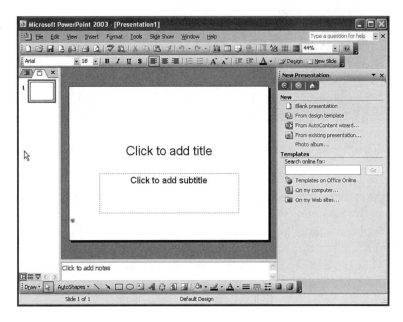

You click From AutoContent Wizard in the New Presentation pane to open the AutoContent Wizard and begin creating a presentation. The opening page in the AutoContent Wizard is a Welcome page. You should read the introduction to the Wizard and click Next to continue. The next step in the wizard (see Figure 23.3) enables you to select the type of presentation to create. You should select a presentation type from the available lists and click Next to continue.

The next step in the AutoContent Wizard is to select the presentation output—that is, the type of media that will be used to display the presentation. You can select On-screen Presentation (which means the slide show will be shown directly on the computer screen or a projector) Web Presentation, Black and White Overheads, Color Overheads, or 35mm Slides. Many PowerPoint presentations are onscreen presentations because they are shown on the computer or by using a projector, but Web presentations are becoming much more common. You need to select an output type and click Next to continue.

**tip**

Using each type of presentation in the AutoContent Wizard results in a different layout of slides when the wizard is complete. You might want to create a few types of presentations by using the wizard to see how the end results differ.

**FIGURE 23.3**

You can create a number of different types of presentations by using the AutoContent Wizard.

The last step in the AutoContent Wizard, shown in Figure 23.4, is to assign a title to the presentation and set any recurring data to be included. First, you enter a title for the presentation in the Presentation Title text box. You can then select whether to display the date the presentation was last modified on each slide and whether to display an incremental slide number on each slide. You can also use this step of the wizard to indicate in the Footer text box whether any text should be shown at the bottom of each slide. When you're done making selections, you click Next to continue.

**FIGURE 23.4**

You can enter a presentation title and an optional footer, and you can select whether the modified date and slide numbers should be displayed on each slide.

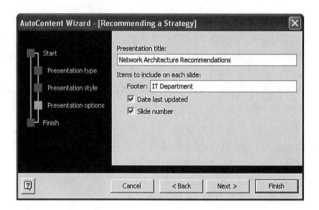

After you have entered all the required information in the AutoContent Wizard, you click Next, and the Finish page is displayed, informing you that the wizard has everything it needs to create the presentation. You click Finish to complete the wizard. The new presentation is then displayed in the main PowerPoint window, and the Navigation pane has the Outline tab selected. The first page of the presentation is the title page, which contains the title you specified in the final AutoContent Wizard step.

# Adding Text to a Presentation

When you have a rough skeleton created by the AutoContent Wizard, the next step in creating a basic PowerPoint presentation is to add text. Text makes up the main content of most presentations.

The easiest way to add text to a presentation, especially to a presentation created with the AutoContent Wizard, is to do it directly in the Outline tab of the Navigation pane. You click the text in one of the existing slides in the Outline tab, as shown in Figure 23.5. Then you select the text to be replaced and type the desired text. The existing text is overwritten, and the new text is shown in both the Outline tab and the presentation itself.

**FIGURE 23.5**

You select the text to be replaced and type the new text to be shown in the presentation.

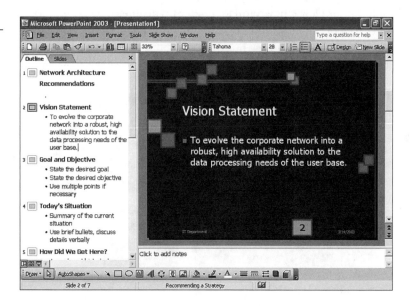

In addition to selecting and typing text in the Outline tab, you can do it directly in the presentation itself. If all text is removed from a slide, the text "Click to add text" is shown. Clicking this text allows you to add text to the slide. You can also change the title of each slide in addition to the body text of the slide.

# Navigating, Inserting, Moving, and Deleting Slides

You navigate between the slides in a presentation by using the Navigation pane on the left side of the PowerPoint window. The Navigation pane has two tabs, Outline and Slides. The Slides tab shows a graphical representation of each slide, and the Outline tab shows an outline of the text on each slide. You navigate to a specific slide by clicking the slide in either tab. The selected slide is then shown in the main PowerPoint window. If there are more slides than fit in the Navigation pane, you use the scrollbar to move up and down through the list.

# Using the Slide Sorter View

Besides using the Navigation pane, you can navigate through slides by using the Slide Sorter view (shown in Figure 23.6). This method is useful for getting an overview of a presentation and organizing slides. To use the Slide Sorter view, you click the Slide Sorter View button at the bottom of the Navigation pane. To go back to the Normal view in the Navigation pane, you click the Normal View button.

**FIGURE 23.6**

The Slide Sorter view gives an overview of a presentation.

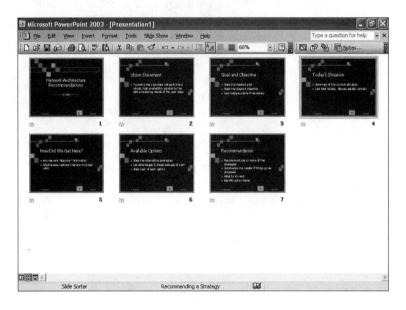

Although the AutoContent Wizard creates a useful rough presentation for you to use, you might want to add or remove some slides or move slides within the presentation. You do this by using either the Outline tab or the Slides tab of the Navigation pane.

# Inserting a Slide

To insert a slide, you start by right-clicking the slide that appears immediately before where you want to insert the new slide and then select New Slide. For example, if you want to insert a slide between Slide 2 and Slide 3, you right-click Slide 2 in the Navigation pane and select New Slide. By default, when you select New Slide, the Slide Layout pane appears. By using the Slide Layout pane, you can select a predefined layout for the slide, so you don't need to format the slide yourself. Figure 23.7 shows a newly added Slide 3 and the Slide Layout pane. You can select a slide layout from the Slide Layout pane, if required, and then you add text to the new slide.

**FIGURE 23.7**

A new slide has been inserted.

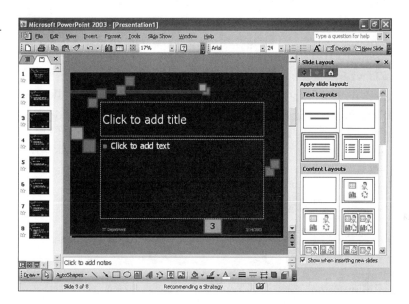

# Moving a Slide

The procedure for moving a slide is simple. In the Navigation pane, you simply click and drag a slide in order to move to a new location. You can do this in either the Outline tab or the Slides tab of the Navigation pane or in the Slide Sorter view. As you drag a slide, a line appears to show where the slide will be inserted. You need to ensure that the line is between the two slides that you want preceding and following the slide being moved, and then you release the mouse button.

# Deleting a Slide

If you have a slide that you don't want in a presentation, you can easily remove it. You commonly do this when creating a presentation by using the AutoContent

Wizard because the wizard creates a number of slides based on a sample presentation, but you might not need all of them. To delete a slide, you simply right-click the slide in either tab of the Navigation pane or in the Slide Sorter view and select Delete Slide. The slide is then removed.

# Switching Slide Orientation Between Landscape and Portrait

Slides in a new presentation are oriented in landscape by default. You might want to show slides in portrait orientation instead. This can be useful if slides contain long lists of text. Slides can be either all landscape or all portrait orientation, but not a combination of both.

To change the orientation of slides, you select File, Page Setup. In the Page Setup dialog box that appears (see Figure 23.8), you select Portrait or Landscape under Slides in the Orientation section. When you click OK, the changes are applied to the presentation.

**FIGURE 23.8**

You select an orientation for slides in the Page Setup dialog box.

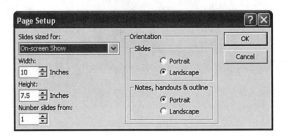

You have an option to print notes and an outline for a presentation in PowerPoint, as well. This is covered in Chapter 25, "Organizing, Printing, and Presenting." You can set the orientation for these additional documents from the Page Setup dialog box by changing the Notes, Handouts & Outline setting, which is set to Portrait by default.

# Saving a Presentation

After you have created a presentation and added the required text, you should save it. PowerPoint presentations are saved to .PPT files. To save a presentation the first time, you select File, Save As. In the Save As dialog box that appears, you navigate to the location where you want to save the presentation, enter a name for the presentation in the File Name box (the presentation title is used by default), and click Save. After you have saved your presentation once by using the Save As dialog box, you can save it again in the future by simply selecting File, Save.

# Controlling Look and Feel by Using a Slide Master

A *slide master* is used to control the fonts, colors, and other styles globally across all slides in a presentation. By working with a slide master, you can change the look of all the slides in a presentation from a central location. A slide master allows you to maintain consistency across a presentation.

To work with a slide master, you select View, Master, Slide Master to open the Slide Master view (shown in Figure 23.9). The presentation in Figure 23.9 has two slide masters; holding the mouse cursor over each slide master in the Navigation pane shows to which slides each slide master applies. In this example, Slide Master 1 applies to Slides 2–7, the body of the presentation, and Slide Master 2 applies to Slide 1, the presentation title page.

**FIGURE 23.9**

You use the Slide Master view to edit a slide master.

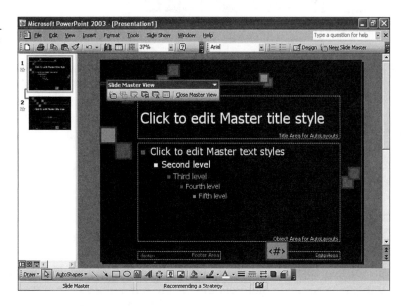

Editing a slide master is simple. In the Slide Master view, you click the style to change in the slide master. You can change the font, color, or any other formatting you want to change for each style. You click Close Master View in the Master View toolbar to close the Slide Master view. Your changes are then applied to the entire presentation.

# Adding or Removing Slide Numbers and Dates

**tip**

Some styles are shared across slide masters. In the example shown in Figure 23.9, the Master Title style is shared between both slide masters and is applied to all slides that are affected by either of the two masters.

Earlier in this chapter, in the section "Starting a Presentation by Using the AutoContent Wizard," you learned how to use the wizard to add to each slide a slide number and the date the presentation was last modified. You can also add and remove these features manually. To add slide numbers and dates to all slides or remove them from all slides, you select View, Header and Footer to display the Header and Footer dialog box, which is shown in Figure 23.10.

**FIGURE 23.10**

You use the Header and Footer dialog box to add slide numbers and dates.

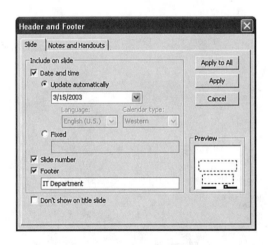

In the Include on Slide section of the Header and Footer dialog box, you select what items you want included on the slides. The first option is Date and Time, which can be updated automatically based on the last modified time for the presentation, using the format selected from the Update Automatically drop-down list box or a fixed time and date that you enter in the Fixed text box. The second option, Slide Number, adds an automatically incrementing slide number to each slide.

The final option in the Header and Footer dialog box, Footer, displays the specified text at the bottom of each slide. You also have the option to not show the footer, slide number, and date on the title slide (the first slide in the presentation). When you have selected the appropriate options, you can click the Apply to All button to apply the options to all slides. Clicking the Apply button applies the changes to only the current slide.

# THE ABSOLUTE MINIMUM

Microsoft PowerPoint is used to create slide show presentations that can later be presented to an audience, printed and handed out, published to a Web site, or any combination of these. Using PowerPoint presentations is an effective way to disseminate information to groups. In this chapter you learned how to create a basic slide show by using the AutoContent Wizard, add text, organize slides, save your presentation, and customize the look of your presentation.

In the next chapter you will learn how to add to a presentation more advanced features, such as tables, pictures, videos, and sounds. You will also learn how to animate slide shows and add more advanced text formatting. By using these features, you can make a presentation more lively and interesting.

# In this Chapter

- Adding tables
- Adding pictures and video clips
- Adding sounds
- Animating slides
- Using slide transitions
- Creating a table of contents or summary slide
- Adding bullets and numbered lists
- Using special text formatting

**24**

# Adding Graphics and Other Flashy Stuff

In addition to creating a simple slide show, as discussed in Chapter 23, "Quickly Creating a Basic Slide Show," you can use PowerPoint to add to a presentation a number of advanced features, such as tables, pictures, and animation.

Adding tables, pictures, videos, and sounds to a presentation is similar to the process for adding objects to other document types that you've seen in previous chapters. Slide transitions enable you to animate your presentation to grab the audience's attention.

# Adding Tables

Adding a table to a PowerPoint slide is similar to adding a table to Microsoft Word, as discussed in Chapter 11, "Organizing with Tables and Columns." To add a table, you first navigate to the slide to which you want to add the table. You place the cursor at the location where you want the table to be added in the slide and select Insert, Table. The Insert Table dialog box appears, as shown in Figure 24.1.

**FIGURE 24.1**

The Insert Table dialog box is used to set the initial table size.

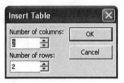

You can set the number of columns and rows for the table by using the Insert Table dialog box and click OK to insert the table. The table is inserted and automatically scaled to fit the area in which the table is added.

After a table has been added to a presentation, the Tables and Borders toolbar (see Figure 24.2) is shown any time the table has the focus (that is, when you click the table). You use the Tables and Borders toolbar to change options for the table. Selecting the line type and weight from the drop-down boxes sets the border type for the table. You can use the options in the Table menu to add and remove rows and columns in the table. Finally, a few alignment options are available on the toolbar for aligning text within table cells and aligning table cells within the table.

The size of a table is not fixed; you can add columns and rows after you add a table to a presentation. The Insert Table dialog box is just used to set the initial size of a table.

**FIGURE 24.2**

You use the Tables and Borders toolbar to set options for a table.

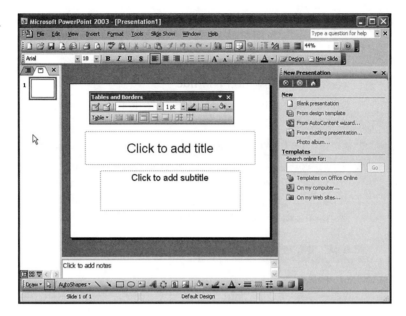

# Adding Pictures and Video Clips

Pictures and video clips can be useful additions to a presentation. Pictures can include charts or photographs or any other graphics you want to add to slides.

## Adding Pictures

To insert a picture in a presentation, you first navigate to the slide where you want to insert the picture and place the cursor at the location to insert the picture. Then you select Insert, Picture, and you see that there are a number of ways to insert a picture. You can insert clip art from the Microsoft Office clip art, pictures from a scanner or digital camera, and organization charts from the Office tool. However, the most common way to insert a picture is from a file. You can select From File to open the Insert Picture dialog box. Then you locate the picture to insert and click Insert. The picture is inserted into the slide and scaled to fit appropriately. You can then use the handles on the edges of the picture to change the size or use the Picture toolbar to modify the picture.

## Adding Video Clips

Inserting a video clip into a slide is as simple as inserting a picture:

1. Navigate to the slide into which the video clip will be inserted and place the cursor at the insertion point.

2. Select Insert, Movies and Sounds, Movie from File to open the Insert Movie dialog box.

3. Locate the movie to insert and click OK to insert the movie.

4. When you insert the movie, you are prompted for how to start the movie, as shown in Figure 24.3. You can have the movie start automatically when the slide opens, or you can have the movie start when it is clicked. Make a selection, and the video clip insertion is complete.

**FIGURE 24.3**

When you insert a video clip, you must choose how the clip will start.

# Adding Sounds

Adding sounds to a slide is similar to adding pictures and movies. You can insert sounds from a file or cause a CD track to be played when the slide opens. To insert a sound, you navigate to the slide in which to insert the sound and select Insert, Movies and Sounds. Choose the source from which you will insert the sound. The following sections explain the steps for the most common types.

## Inserting a Sound from a File

To insert a sound from a file, select Insert, Movies and Sounds, Sound from File to open the Insert Sound dialog box. Then you locate the sound file to insert and click OK. You are presented with a dialog box similar to the one shown in Figure 24.3. You can choose to have the sound start automatically when the slide opens or only when the sound icon is clicked. When you make your selection, the sound is inserted.

## Playing a CD Track

To play a CD track in a slide show, you select Insert, Movies and Sounds, Play CD Audio Track to open the Insert CD Audio dialog box, which is shown in Figure 24.4.

You select the CD tracks and start and end points, set the volume level, and select whether the controls should be hidden when the CD track is not playing. After you have set the options, you click OK. You then need to select whether the track should play automatically or when the icon is clicked. You make a selection, and the CD track is placed in the slide.

**FIGURE 24.4**

When you insert a video clip, you must choose how the clip will start.

# Animating Slides

You can add animation to a slide to create a more dynamic presentation or to draw attention to certain items on a slide. The simplest way to animate slides is to use an animation scheme. It is also possible to animate slides by using custom animations, but that is more complex and is not covered here. The main difference between these two methods is that an animation scheme is predefined and applies to all items on the slide, whereas custom animation can be used to give different animations to each item on a slide.

The first step in animating slides by using an animation scheme is to select the slides to animate. You can apply the same animation scheme to multiple slides by selecting the first slide in the navigation pane and then holding down the Ctrl key and selecting more slides. When you have selected the slides to which you want to apply the scheme, you select Slide Show, Animation Schemes to open the Slide Design pane, which is shown in Figure 24.5.

As you can see in Figure 24.5, there are a number of predefined animation schemes you can use for slides. These schemes are categorized into Subtle, Moderate, and Exciting. Subtle schemes have less animation and are less obvious than the other schemes; for example, they might cause text to fade into view. Exciting schemes have lots of motion; for example, they might have text spiral into view from off to the side of the slide.

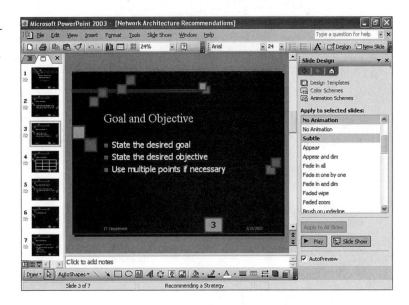

You can select a scheme from the list to apply that scheme to the selected slides. The AutoPreview box is checked by default, and it allows you to see the results of your selection in the main PowerPoint window on the selected slide. If AutoPreview is off or you want to see the results of the animation scheme again, you can click the Play button. You can also click the Apply to All Slides button to apply the selected animation scheme to all slides in the presentation—not just to the selected slides.

# Using Slide Transitions

Whereas slide animation controls how objects are displayed on the slide when it is shown, slide transitions control how a presentation moves from slide to slide. No transition is used by default, but you can apply a transition if you use the AutoContent Wizard to create a presentation. To configure slide transitions, you first select the slides for which you want to configure transitions by selecting the first slide and then selecting more slides by holding down the Ctrl key and selecting Slide Show, Slide Transition. The Slide Transition pane appears, as shown in Figure 24.6.

**tip**

Slide transitions control how a presentation moves into a selected slide. For example, if you select only one slide and apply a transition, the transition is used as the presentation moves to the selected slide and not as it moves from the selected slide to the following slide. You should keep this in mind as you are selecting slides to which to apply transitions.

**FIGURE 24.6**

Slide transitions are applied from the Slide Transition pane.

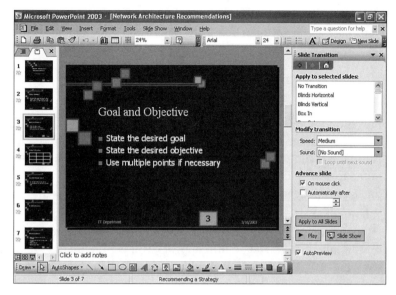

You select the transition to use for the selected slides from the list in the Slide Transition pane. The AutoPreview box is selected by default, so the selected transition is previewed in the main PowerPoint window on the selected slide. From the Slide Transition pane, you can also use the Sound drop-down box to set the speed of the selected transition and apply a sound to the transition. In addition, you can select how the slide will advance. By default, slides advance on mouse click, but you can instead have slides advance after a specified period of time. If you want to apply the selected slide transition configuration to all slides, you click the Apply to All Slides button.

# Creating a Table of Contents or Summary Slide

The Slide Sorter view makes it simple to add a table of contents or summary slide to a presentation. A table of contents or summary slide contains a list of the titles of the slides in a presentation. A table of contents slide is the same as a summary slide, but a table of contents slide is added to the beginning of a presentation, and a summary is added to the end. You use the same procedure to create both table of contents and summary slides. You open the Slide Sorter view by clicking the Slide Sorter View button in the navigation pane.

In the Slide Sorter view, you select the first slide to add to the table of contents or summary. You hold down the Ctrl key and select the remaining slides to add to the table of contents. When you have selected all the slides you want to summarize, you click the Summary Slide button in the toolbar. The summary slide is inserted immediately preceding the first slide you selected to summarize. You move the summary slide to the location you want by clicking and dragging it to the new location.

⇨ How to move slides is explained in Chapter 23.

# Adding Bullets and Numbered Lists

Bullets and numbered lists work the same way in PowerPoint as they do in other Office applications, such as Microsoft Word. To apply bullets or numbering to text in PowerPoint, you select the appropriate text and click the Bullets or Numbering icon in the toolbar. Or you can click the Bullets or Numbering icon while in a blank line, and a new bullet or number is added each time you enter some text and press Enter.

You might want to change the style of bullets or numbering for text. To do this, you select the text to modify and select Format, Bullets and Numbering. In the Bullets and Numbering dialog box that appears, you use the Bullets tab to select a bullet style and set the bullet size and color and you use the Numbered tab to set numbering style, size, color, and starting point.

# Using Special Text Formatting

Text formatting works the same in PowerPoint as in other Office applications. To change the format of text, you simply select it and then select Format, Font. You select the font, style, size, and color, as well as any effects, and then you click OK to change the text style. In addition, you can change the alignment of a line by placing the cursor on the line and selecting Format, Alignment and then selecting the appropriate option. Finally, you can select Format, Line Spacing to open the Line Spacing dialog box, where you can set the spacing between lines as well as the spacing preceding and following a paragraph.

# THE ABSOLUTE MINIMUM

This chapter covers some of the rather advanced features in Microsoft PowerPoint that haven't been covered until now. These include the addition of tables, pictures, videos, sounds, animation, table of contents or summary slides, and advanced text formatting. These extra components, used sparingly, can spice up a presentation, make it more aesthetically pleasing, and make it more interesting to the audience.

In the next chapter you will learn how to add notes to a presentation, create handouts, package a presentation on a CD, print a presentation, and present a slideshow. Using these features, you can create handouts for your audience and a set of annotated printed slides for your use during the presentation. You'll also learn how to use the presentation tools so you can give a more effective presentation.

## IN THIS CHAPTER

- Using personal notes in a presentation
- Creating a set of handouts
- Packaging a presentation on a CD
- Printing slides
- Running a slide show

**25**

# ORGANIZING, PRINTING, AND PRESENTING

After you create a slide show by using the procedures described in Chapters 23, "Quickly Creating a Basic Slide Show," and 24, "Adding Graphics and Other Flashy Stuff," the next step is to present the slide show. There are a number of ways to give a PowerPoint presentation, including showing it on the Web, showing it on printed overhead transparencies, and (the most common way) showing it directly onscreen or through a projector.

# Using Personal Notes in a Presentation

PowerPoint allows you to add notes to a presentation. Notes are not included when you show the presentation, but they are printed on notes pages. *Notes pages* show a small version of the presentation, along with the notes you add to the presentation, as shown in Figure 25.1.

**FIGURE 25.1**

This example of a printed notes page shows the presentation slide above and the associated notes below.

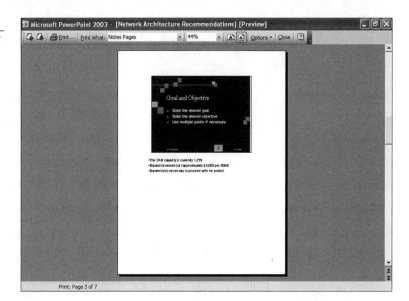

## Adding Notes

You add notes to each slide of a presentation by using the Notes pane. The Notes pane appears immediately below the main PowerPoint window and contains the text "Click to add notes" when there are no existing notes.

Click in the Notes pane for the first slide into which you want to add notes. Then you begin typing your notes, pressing the Enter key after each one. You can use bullets and numbers in the Notes pane by clicking the Bullets and Numbering icons in the toolbar while the cursor is in the Notes pane. The AutoFormat feature also applies to the Notes pane, so if you begin your

**tip**

It is often helpful to expand the size of the Notes pane when you are adding notes to a presentation. You click and drag the border between the Notes pane and the main PowerPoint window to change the height of the Notes pane.

notes with a hyphen or a number, bullets or numbering are enabled automatically. After you enter your notes for a slide in the Notes pane, you navigate to the next slide into which you want to add notes and follow the same procedure.

## Printing Notes Pages

After you have added notes to a presentation, you can print the notes pages so that they look as shown in Figure 25.1. To print notes pages, you select File, Print to open the Print dialog box. Then you select Notes Pages from the Print What drop-down box, set any other print options you want, and click OK. Your notes pages are then printed.

# Creating a Set of Handouts

Printing handouts is a way of printing a presentation in a concise manner for distribution to an audience or to others who may not be able to see the presentation onscreen. You can print handouts with one, two, three, four, six, or nine slides per page. Figure 25.2 shows an example of a handout with six slides on a page.

**FIGURE 25.2**

A handout with six slides on a page.

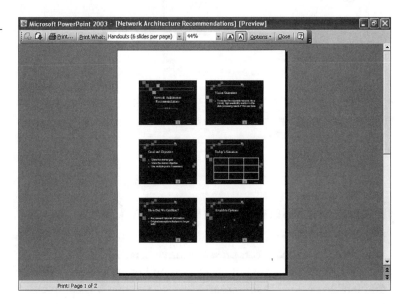

Printing handouts is simple. You select File, Print to open the Print dialog box, and then you select Handouts from the Print What drop-down box, as shown in Figure 25.3. You select the number of slides per page from the Slides per Page drop-down box in the Handouts section and select whether they should be ordered horizontally or vertically if you are printing four or more slides per page. If they are ordered horizontally, Slide 1 will be in the upper left and Slide 2 in the upper right. If they are ordered vertically then Slide 1 will be in the upper right and Slide 2 will be immediately below it. You should click OK when you are ready to print the handouts.

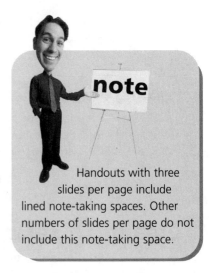

note

Handouts with three slides per page include lined note-taking spaces. Other numbers of slides per page do not include this note-taking space.

**FIGURE 25.3**

You use the Print dialog box to configure handout printing options.

# Packaging a Presentation on a CD

PowerPoint provides a feature that enables you to package a presentation and place it on a CD so that you can present it anywhere. The PowerPoint Viewer can even be included so that you are not dependent on having PowerPoint installed at your destination. To package a presentation on a CD when it is complete, select File, Package for CD to open the Package for CD dialog box, which is shown in Figure 25.4.

**FIGURE 25.4**

You use the Package for CD dialog box to create a CD that contains your presentation and, optionally, a PowerPoint Viewer.

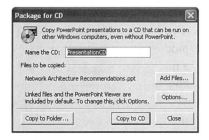

You need to give the CD a name. The name should reflect the content of the presentation, but it's not vital. Next, you need to decide which files to copy to the CD. The current presentation is copied to the CD by default, but you can add additional presentations to the CD by clicking the Add File button, selecting the PowerPoint presentation to add, and clicking OK. This is useful if you want to be able to show a few different presentations from a single CD. Finally, you can set the options for the CD by clicking the Options button to open the Options dialog box, which is shown in Figure 25.5.

**FIGURE 25.5**

The Options dialog box enables you to set options for a presentation CD.

The PowerPoint Viewer and any files that are linked (for example, graphics and sounds) to the presentation are included on the CD by default. You definitely want to include linked files, but you might not want to include the PowerPoint Viewer if you're sure the system on which you will be giving the presentation has PowerPoint. However, it is prudent to include the viewer just in case. You can also choose to include any embedded TrueType fonts in case they are not installed on the system that will be used for the presentation, but this is a less likely scenario than not having the linked files or PowerPoint.

If you choose to include the PowerPoint Viewer, you can select how the presentation will be presented when the CD is inserted into the computer used for the presentation. By default, all presentations that are included by using the Add Files button on the Package for CD dialog box are played automatically, in the order in which they are specified in that list. The other options are to play only the first specified presentation, allow the presenter to select the presentation to play, or do nothing. If you choose the option to do nothing, the presenter must run the presentation manually.

You can also use the Options dialog box to set passwords for the presentation. This is useful if you don't want anyone to be able to view the presentation if the CD gets lost or stolen. You can specify optional passwords to open and modify a presentation. When you have set all the options, you click OK.

After you have configured the options in the Package for CD dialog box, you can create the CD by clicking the Copy to CD button. You must have a CD recording device in your system for this to work. The other available option is to save the presentation and associated files with the CD package to a folder on the system. You can do this by clicking the Copy to Folder button, assigning a name to the presentation folder, selecting a location for the folder, and clicking OK. This is useful if you want to save a presentation to a shared network drive and show the presentation on another system on the network.

# Printing Slides

Printing slides is a simple process. First, you select File, Print. When the Print dialog box appears, you need to ensure that the Print What drop-down box is set to Slides. You select a printer, a number of copies, the range of slides to print (all slides are printed by default), and any other print options, and then you click OK. The slides then print to the selected printer.

# Running a Slide Show

Running a presentation is fairly simple, but you might want to set some options for the slide show before you start.

## Configuring Slide Show Options

To configure options for a presentation, select Slide Show, Set Up Show to open the Set Up Show dialog box, which is shown in Figure 25.6. There are a number of options for running a slide show. The Show Type section allows you to specify whether the show will be presented by a person and shown in full-screen mode, browsed by a user and shown in a window, or browsed at a kiosk. Setting these options can override some of the other options in the dialog box. For example, the Browsed at a Kiosk setting forces the presentation to run in a loop.

The Show Options section allows you to have the presentation loop continuously,
and it allows you to disable any narration you might have recorded or to disable
animation for the show. The Show Slides section is used to configure the presentation
to show only a subset of slides in the presentation. The Advance Slides section is
used to override any automatic slide advance timers that may be set and only allow
slide advancing manually. The Multiple Monitors section is available only if you
have multiple monitors, and it allows you to select on which monitor the presentation is shown. Finally, the Performance section is used to enable hardware graphics
acceleration and configure the screen resolution in which the presentation is shown.
You should change these settings only in special cases. You click OK when you've set
the options you want.

## Running a Presentation

After you have configured any options needed for your slide show, you can begin the
presentation. You need to make sure you're ready to present the show, and then you
select Slide Show, View Show or press the F5 key to begin the presentation. To pro-
ceed through the slides in the presentation—assuming that you didn't set automatic
timers for the slides—you click the left mouse button. When you get to the final slide
and click the left mouse button, you see a message that the final slide has been
reached. One more click returns you to PowerPoint. You can exit from the slide show
before the last slide is shown by pressing the Esc key or right-clicking and selecting
End Show.

While the slide show is running, you can right-click to bring up a context menu.
From this menu you can do a few useful things, the first of which is to move to the
next slide or the previous slide. You can also go to a specific slide by using the Go to
Slide option. You can bring up a black or white screen or your notes, or you can

switch to another program from the Screen submenu. Finally, the Pointer Options submenu allows you to change your pointer (an arrow, by default) to a ballpoint pen, felt-tip pen, or highlighter. These pointer options allow you to draw freehand on the slide to make notes or point out important information. You can also bring up a black or white screen to use as a "virtual whiteboard" from the Screen submenu. The Pointer Options submenu also has an eraser option and an option to erase all drawing from the slide. You can also open the Pointer Options menu by clicking the arrow icon at the bottom left of the slide show.

# THE ABSOLUTE MINIMUM

In this chapter you learned how to present and print a PowerPoint presentation. This is the most important part in most presentations because it is when your audience gets to see the result of your work. In PowerPoint you can add notes to your slides and print annotated copies of your slides or create handouts to go along with your presentation. You can also print slides individually. In addition, there are many extra features available while you're running a slide show, such as pen tools for drawing notes or diagrams on your slides as they're being shown.

In the next chapter you will learn about many of the available configuration options in Microsoft PowerPoint. The configuration options enable you to customize PowerPoint's behavior to better suit your needs.

**26**

# PowerPoint Settings to Change

There are a number of settings you can change to customize PowerPoint's operation. Most of these settings are configured in PowerPoint's Options dialog box, which you access by selecting Tools, Options.

# Setting Default File Location

By default, PowerPoint saves files in your My Documents folder. You might want to change this setting in the Options dialog box if you always need to save your files to a network drive, for example. To do so, you select Tools, Options to open the Options dialog box and then click the Save tab, as shown in Figure 26.1. Then you set the Default File Location setting to the desired location and click OK to save your changes.

**FIGURE 26.1**

The Save tab of the Options dialog box is used to configure settings related to saving files.

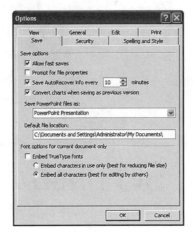

# Setting the AutoRecover Interval

Like other Microsoft Office applications, PowerPoint uses the AutoRecover feature to automatically save your work at a specified interval; the default is 10 minutes. If your system crashes, when you open PowerPoint again, your presentation is recovered automatically from the last AutoRecover save. You might want to change the AutoRecover interval if you are worried about losing a significant amount of work in a 10-minute period. AutoRecover causes your system to slow somewhat every time the interval is reached and an automatic save is performed, but it does not cause any other significant overhead.

To change the AutoRecover interval, first open the Options dialog box by selecting Tools, Options, and then click the Save tab. Then set Save AutoRecover Info Every X Minutes to the desired value by using the arrow buttons. You can also disable AutoRecover by deselecting the Save AutoRecover Info Every X Minutes check box, but it is not advisable. Then click OK to save your settings.

# Adding More Files to the Recently Used Files List

PowerPoint stores a list of recently used files in the File menu; by default, it stores four files in this list. If you find that you edit or view a lot of presentations in PowerPoint, you might want to increase the number of recently used files for convenience. You can also disable the recently used file list completely if you never use it.

To change the settings for the recently used file list, open the Options dialog box by selecting Tools, Options and clicking the General tab, shown in Figure 26.2. Then you set the Recently Used File List option to the desired number by using the arrow buttons or disable the list by deselecting the Recently Used File List check box. You save your changes by clicking OK.

**FIGURE 26.2**

The General tab of the Options dialog box is used to configure general PowerPoint settings.

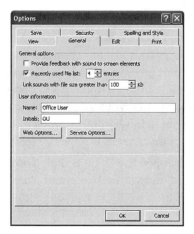

# Setting the Link/Embed File Size Limit

As explained in Chapter 24, "Adding Graphics and Other Flashy Stuff," you can link or embed sounds, graphics, and videos in a presentation. Linking and embedding are different in that *embedding* saves the object inside the presentation file whereas *linking* links the presentation to the outside file. By default, graphics and videos are linked and sounds are embedded if they're smaller than 100KB but linked if they are larger than 100KB. You can change this value if you want larger sounds to be embedded in a presentation. This results in a larger presentation file, but it eliminates the need to keep the linked sounds with the presentation. You can also change this value if you want smaller sounds to be linked, resulting in a smaller presentation file.

To change the link/embed file size limit, you open the Options dialog box by selecting Tools, Options and clicking the General tab. Then you set the link/embed threshold by changing the Link Sounds with File Size Greater Than value by using the arrow buttons. You then click OK to save your changes.

# Controlling Chart Fonts

By default, new charts inserted into a slide take on the font used in the slide. If you want new charts to maintain their original font, you open the Options dialog box by selecting Tools, Options, clicking the Edit tab, and deselecting the New Charts Take on PowerPoint Font option. Then you click OK to save your changes.

# Adding More Undo Levels

If you are working on a slide show and make a mistake, you can click the Undo icon in the toolbar to step backward through your last few changes. Each change is known as an *undo level*, and PowerPoint gives you 20 undo levels by default. You might want to be able to step back more than 20 undo levels, and you can configure this in the Options dialog box. The only disadvantage of enabling more undo levels is increased memory usage, but this shouldn't become a problem unless your system has limited memory or the number of undo levels is set very high.

To change the number of undo levels, open the Options dialog box by selecting Tools, Options. Then click the Edit tab and set the Maximum Number of Undos value to the desired number. Then you click OK to save your changes.

# Adding and Removing Navigation Controls for Web Viewing

When you're showing a presentation on the Web, a set of navigation controls that is similar to those on a regular onscreen presentation is displayed. You might want to remove those controls so that the viewer is forced to watch the presentation at the rate at which it was designed to run. To do this, you open the Options dialog box by selecting Tools, Options, clicking the General tab, and then clicking the Web Options button. When the Web Options dialog box appears, you click the General tab (see Figure 26.3) and deselect the Add Slide Navigation Controls check box. You can also change the color of the navigation controls if desired.

**FIGURE 26.3**

The General tab of the Web Options dialog box can be used to enable Web navigation controls and animations in Web presentations.

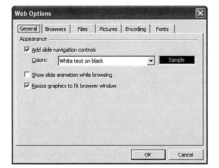

# Turning On and Off Animations for Web Viewing

Slide animation is disabled by default for Web viewing of presentations to save bandwidth and make Web presentations more responsive. You can enable animations by selecting Tools, Options to open the Options dialog box and then clicking the General tab. Then you click the Web Options button to open the Web Options dialog box. Finally, you click the General tab and select the Show Slide Animation While Browsing check box.

# THE ABSOLUTE MINIMUM

This chapter covers many of the available configuration options for Microsoft PowerPoint. Changing these options enables you to customize your PowerPoint environment. Settings such as the default file location, AutoRecover interval, and recently used files list enable you to control how you work with your PowerPoint files. Other settings, such as chart fonts and undo levels, allow you to change how the PowerPoint editing environment functions.

In the next chapter you will begin to learn about what a database is and then learn how to use Microsoft Access, a database application. You will learn how to start a new database, add data, navigate and search the database, and set formatting.

# PART VI

# ORGANIZING DATA WITH ACCESS

## IN THIS CHAPTER

- Taking a look at databases in general and Access in particular

- Starting a new database

- Working in the Access interface

- Accomplishing simple searches in a database

- Formatting fields in a database

**27**

# DATABASE BASICS

Many people who are new to Office are not familiar with databases, which you can use to store, analyze, and retrieve information. You can use a database such as an Access database to keep track of all kinds of information.

This chapter explains the function a database plays and how Microsoft Access fits into the picture. By the end of the chapter, you should have a good understanding of databases and how to work in the Access interface to create and modify a database.

# What Is a Database and Why Use One?

A *database* is a collection of data of some kind. For example, you might create a database of clients, products, product components, or something more mundane, such as your DVD collection or recipe collection.

An Access database is a relational database. A *relational database* stores information in *tables*, which are sets of data stored in rows and columns. The columns represent the individual *fields*, and the rows represent *records*. Figure 27.1 shows a simple database in Access.

**FIGURE 27.1**

Access stores data in database tables.

Employees : Table

| First | Last | EmpID | Hired | Payrate | Phone | Current |
|---|---|---|---|---|---|---|
| Gordon | Nodrog | 123456788 | 1/5/1999 | $2,500.00 | | ☑ |
| Dan | Burns | 123456789 | 1/1/1999 | $1,750.00 | | ☑ |
| Sally | Johnson | 124234878 | 9/22/2001 | $3,000.00 | | ☐ |
| Benson | Jones | 213457896 | 1/8/2001 | $1,200.00 | | ☐ |
| David | Jones | 231456789 | 2/2/2000 | $2,250.00 | | ☑ |
| Shelly | Snow | 234567890 | 2/8/2000 | $1,200.00 | | ☐ |
| Jeff | Barry | 453542121 | 2/2/2003 | $750.00 | | ☐ |
| | | 0 | | $0.00 | | ☐ |

Record: 1 of 7

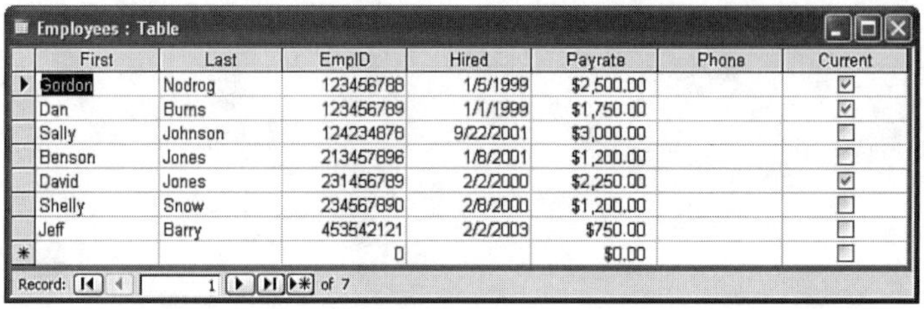

For example, let's assume that you want to maintain a customer database that not only keeps track of your customers' address and phone information but also tracks recent sales, discount rates, information about which company division handles the customer, and so on.

In this example, each customer would be stored in a record (row). Within each record you might have the fields `Company Name`, `Contact Name`, `Address`, `Phone`, `Region`, `Division`, `Discount Rate`, and so on. Each of these is a field in the record.

You might be wondering why you wouldn't simply use Microsoft Excel to store this information in rows and columns in a workbook. After all, Excel probably looks a bit less intimidating to the beginning Office user. You would want to use a relational database in such an instance because you can use it to easily relate data from one table to another.

For example, let's say you create one table to contain the customer contact information, including name, address, phone, and other information. You create a second table to keep track of your products. You create a third table to keep track of sales. You then establish relationships between these tables to build a system whereby you track the sales to each customer. Putting the data in separate tables reduces the amount of data in each table and reduces duplication. For example, you don't need to enter the customer information for each sale in the `Sales` table. Instead, you just link it to the appropriate record in the `Customers` table.

The capability to associate data from one table to another offers a lot of flexibility. For example, let's say you launch a completely new product line. You can create a separate table or even a separate database to keep track of that product. You don't need to duplicate the information from the Customers table because it doesn't change—you're just marketing a new product line to the same customers.

Like other database applications, Access gives you considerable power and flexibility for analyzing and organizing data. For example, you might query a database to determine which products are selling well and which ones are not, which customers bought certain products, where the majority of your sales are going in geographical terms, and so on.

In a nutshell, if you need to keep track of data and retain the flexibility to organize and analyze that data, you should consider keeping it in an Access database.

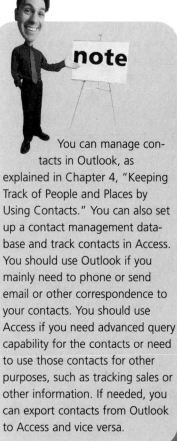

**note**

You can manage contacts in Outlook, as explained in Chapter 4, "Keeping Track of People and Places by Using Contacts." You can also set up a contact management database and track contacts in Access. You should use Outlook if you mainly need to phone or send email or other correspondence to your contacts. You should use Access if you need advanced query capability for the contacts or need to use those contacts for other purposes, such as tracking sales or other information. If needed, you can export contacts from Outlook to Access and vice versa.

# Creating and Working with a New Database

When you open Access, the program opens the Getting Started pane (see Figure 27.2), which helps you open an existing database or create a new one.

To start a new database, click the Create a New File link near the bottom of the Open area of the Getting Started pane. Access displays the New File pane (see Figure 27.3).

The following are the options in the New File pane:

- **Blank Database**—You can use this option to create a new database file that contains no tables or other data.

- **Blank Data Access Page**—A *data access page* is a Web page that has a connection to a database. Data access pages provide a means of viewing and editing database records from a Web page.

**FIGURE 27.2**

You can use the Getting Started task pane to start a new database.

**FIGURE 27.3**

Access offers a handful of options for starting a new database.

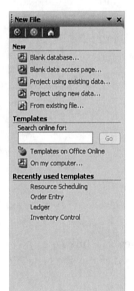

- **Project Using Existing Data**—An Access *project* is an Access file that connects to a SQL Server database and is used to create client/server applications. You can choose this option to create a project that is linked to an existing SQL Server database.

- **Project Using New Data**—You can use this option to create a new Access project that is linked to a new SQL Server database.

- **From Existing File**—You can use this option to create a new database from an existing one.

- **Templates**—You can create an Access database from a database template. Access provides several templates to help you create specific types of databases (customer management, order entry, and so on).

As a beginning Access user, perhaps the easiest way for you to start working with Access is to use one of the many templates included with Access to start a database. These templates create tables, reports, forms, and other items to let you start working with the database right away. You can tailor these databases to suit your specific needs.

It isn't very difficult to create and use a database from one of Access's templates because Access provides most of the forms and reports you need in order to work with the data. These template-based databases are covered later in this chapter, in the section "Using Templates: Access's Canned Databases." The following sections show you how to make your way around a blank database to become familiar with Access.

## Creating a Blank Database

I bet you're ready to start learning how to enter and sort data, so we'll start with something simple. First, let's create a database:

1. Open Access, click the Create a New File link near the bottom of the Open area of the Getting Started pane, and click Blank Database in the New File pane. Access displays the File New Database dialog box (see Figure 27.4).

**FIGURE 27.4**

You specify the path and file-name for the database.

2. Enter the name `Employees` in the File Name field and click Create. Access displays the window shown in Figure 27.5.

Objects list     Database window

**FIGURE 27.5**

This database contains no tables or other objects.

The Database window (refer to Figure 27.5) is your jumping off point to objects such as tables, queries, forms, and reports. You can use the Database window to open an existing table, create new tables, and so on.

## Creating and Saving a Table

A database isn't much good without somewhere to place the data. Now let's create a simple table in the database:

1. Click Tables, which is the first option in the Objects list of the Database window (refer to Figure 27.5).

2. Double-click Create Table in Design View to open the Table1 window shown in Figure 27.6.

**FIGURE 27.6**

This blank table is ready for fields.

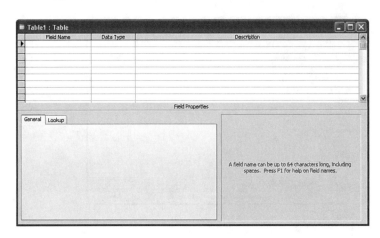

3. In the `Field Name` column, type **First** and press Tab.

4. Accept the default data type `Text` in the `Data Type` column by pressing Tab.

5. In the `Description` column, type **First Name**.

6. Press Enter to create the field (see Figure 27.7).

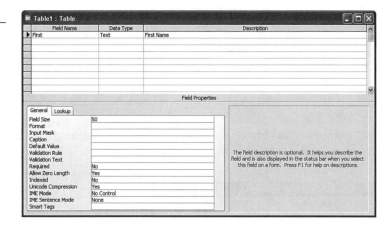

7. Type **Last** in the `Field Name` column, press Tab twice, type **Last Name** in the `Description` column, and press Enter.

8. Type **EmpID** in the `Field Name` column and press Tab.

9. Select Number from the Data Type drop-down list box and press Tab.

10. Type **Employee ID** in the `Description` column and press Enter.

11. Type **Hired** in the `Field Name` column, press Tab, choose Date/Time, press Tab, type **Date Hired**, and press Enter.

Your table should look like the one shown in Figure 27.8.

Next, you need to save the table:

1. Click the Save button on the toolbar to open the Save As dialog box.

2. Type **Employees** and click OK. Access displays the dialog box shown in Figure 27.9.

**FIGURE 27.9**

Access asks if you want to specify a key.

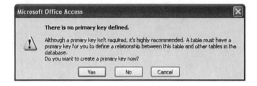

3. Click No.

4. Click the Close button to close the table, which should now appear in the Database window (see Figure 27.10).

**FIGURE 27.10**

The new table appears in the Database window.

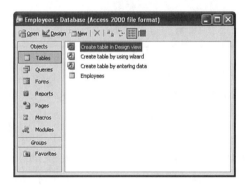

## Understanding Keys

When you saved the table in the preceding section, Access asked if you wanted to assign a primary key to the table. A *primary key* uniquely identifies a record in the database. You can define any field as the primary key, but the value must be unique from one record to another.

In many cases you can let Access create the primary key field for you as an *AutoNumber* field. Access automatically uses the next available value for the key when you create a new record in a table with an AutoNumber primary key.

In our sample Employees table, let's use EmpID—the employee ID field—as the primary key field because the employee ID should be unique:

1. In the Database window, click the Employees table and then click the Design button on the toolbar.

2. Click in the EmpID row and then from the top toolbar choose Edit, Primary Key. Access adds a key icon beside the row (see Figure 27.11).

**FIGURE 27.11**

You can set EmpID as the primary key.

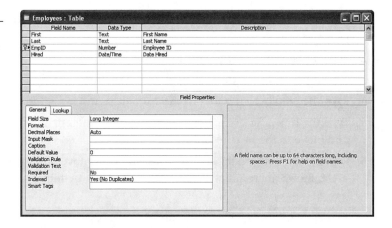

3. Close the table window and click Yes when prompted to save changes.

How are you going to use the primary key in this example? Let's assume that you create another table to store other information, such as the projects being worked on by all your employees. Rather than enter all the employee information in this new table, you can simply link the tables by the primary key, which is the EmpID field.

# Switching Between Design View and Datasheet View

When working with a table, you can work in a handful of different views. The two covered in this chapter are Datasheet view and Design view.

Design view is the one that you used earlier in this chapter, in the section "Creating and Saving a Table," to add fields to a database. Figure 27.8 shows Design view.

You can use Datasheet view to actually enter data in a table. Figure 27.12, in the next section, shows Datasheet view.

To switch between Datasheet view and Design view, you click the View icon on the toolbar or choose View and then choose the type of view you need.

# Entering Data in Datasheet View

The best way to enter data in a complex database is to use a form.

➪ Chapter 28, "Beyond the Basics," explains how to create and use forms.

Forms are not really necessary for simple databases such as the Employees table example in this chapter. Instead, you can enter data right in Datasheet view. Here's how:

1. In the Database window, double-click the Employees table to open it in Datasheet view.

2. Type a first name in the First field and press Tab to move to the Last field.

3. Type a last name in the Last field and press Tab.

4. Type the employee number in the EmpID field and press Tab.

5. Type the hire date in the Hired field and press Enter or Tab to add the record and move to the next record (row).

6. Repeat steps 2 through 5 to add three more employees to the table. Figure 27.12 shows the result of adding four records to the table.

**FIGURE 27.12**

The Employees table contains four records.

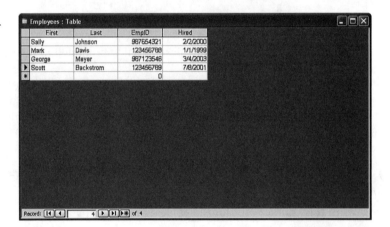

You can easily change the information in a record. You just click in the field, highlight the data you want to change, and type the new data. Then you press Enter to change the record.

Access saves the changes to a table as you enter data. You don't need to choose File, Save or take any other action to save the changes. You just close the table when you are finished working with it.

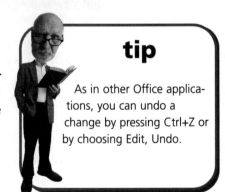

**tip**

As in other Office applications, you can undo a change by pressing Ctrl+Z or by choosing Edit, Undo.

# Moving Around a Database

The Database window, shown in Figure 27.5, is your means of navigating a database. The Objects list groups the types of objects that you can create in the database. When you want to open a particular table, just open the Database window and then double-click the table you want to open. You open the other objects in the database, such as queries or reports, in the same way. Click the object type in the list and then double-click the object in the right pane of the Database window to open it.

You can also open objects for editing from the Database window. Rather than double-click the object in the Database window, you click the object to select it and then click the Design button on the toolbar in the Database window.

You need to be able to move around within a table as you work with a database. At the bottom of the screen in Datasheet view (see Figure 27.13) are table navigation controls. You can use these controls to move forward through the records in the table. You can move forward and back one record at a time, move to the first or last record in the table, or add a new record by using these buttons.

**FIGURE 27.13**

You can use the record navigation buttons to move through a table.

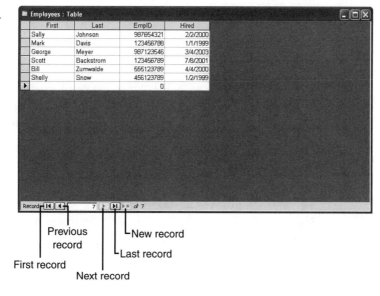

You can also use the scrollbar and arrow keys on the keyboard to move through a table. In addition, you can use simple searches to move through a table. The following section explains how to perform simple searches in a table.

# Performing Simple Searches

It's easy to find data in a small table. Finding data becomes more difficult as the table grows in size. Fortunately, it's easy to search a table for specific data. You just need to perform a simple search.

To perform a search, you follow these steps:

1. Open the table and, if you want to search a particular field, click in that field in the first record.

2. Choose Edit, Find or press Ctrl+F. Access displays the Find and Replace dialog box, as shown in Figure 27.14.

**FIGURE 27.14**

You use the Find and Replace dialog box to find data in a table.

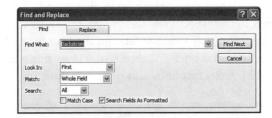

3. In the Find What field, type the text you want to find.

4. From the Look In drop-down list box, select the part of the table to search. By default Access searches the selected field, but you can select the table to search all fields.

5. From the Match drop-down list box, select one of the following:

   ■ **Whole Field**—When you select this option, the contents of the entire field must match the text in the Find What field.

   ■ **Any Part of Field**—When you select this option, the search text can be located anywhere within the field.

   ■ **Start of Field**—When you select this option, the search text must be at the beginning of the field.

6. From the Search drop-down list box, choose the direction to search, whether up, down, or the entire table.

7. Choose one or both of the following options:

   ■ **Match Case**—This option makes the search case sensitive.

   ■ **Search Fields as Formatted**—You can search for data based on the way it is formatted, not on its absolute value. For example, you can search for a specific data as 23-Sep-03 rather than the way it was entered, 9/23/03.

8. Click Find Next to start the search. Access searches for the text, and if it finds it, it highlights the data.

9. When you complete your search, click Cancel to close the dialog box.

# Forcing a Particular Format for a Field

It's often important that the information in a particular field of a database be formatted to display a certain way. For example, a phone number should usually be entered in the form *(nnn) nnn-nnnn*. Or perhaps you want a Yes/No field to be formatted as True/False or On/Off. You might want a date to display as 23-Sep-03 rather than 9/23/03.

The following sections focus on two ways to control data format: by using the Format property and input masks.

## Using the Format Property

A field has several properties that control the way Access accepts and processes the data. The Format property is one of them. You can use the Format property to specify the way numbers, dates, times, and text are displayed in a database.

For example, maybe you want a specific number field to display as currency, with a $ sign in the front, commas as separators, and two decimal places. However, you want to be able to enter the data just by typing the numbers.

To set a field's Format property, you open the table in Design view and then click on the field. In the Table window (see Figure 27.15), you click in the Format field on the General tab.

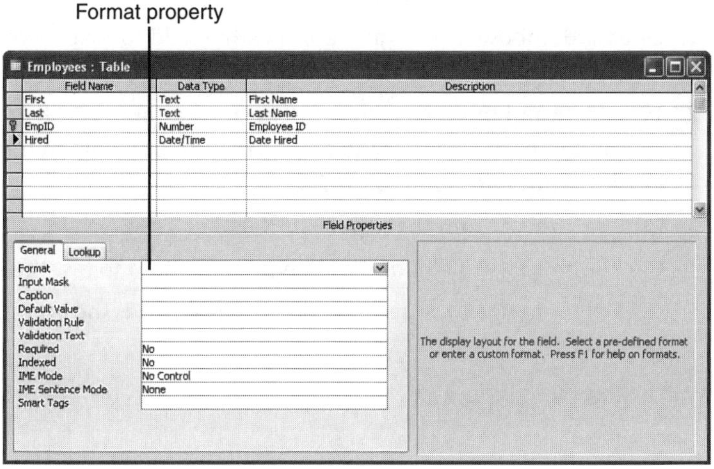

Format property

**FIGURE 27.15**

The Format property is one of several properties for a field.

Most field types have predefined formats that you can select from the drop-down list button to the right of the Format property field. You can manually define a format for any field type by typing a format code in the field. There are many format codes you can use for the various data types. We don't spend time discussing them here, but you can view them in Help by clicking in the Format property field and pressing F1.

If one of the predefined formats suits your needs, you can just select it from the drop-down list. Otherwise, you just type the format string, using the format codes specified in Help for your selected data type. For example, the Yes/No data type offers three formats: Yes/No, True/False, and On/Off. You could enter the following to use a bit of Russian in your database:

`;"Dah"[blue],"Nyet"[red]`

**tip**

As you enter data in the Format property field, Outlook uses a check box by default in Datasheet view. You don't see your custom formatting for the Yes/No field unless you display the field in a text box (such as in a form).

## Using Input Masks

Whereas the Format property controls the way data appears, an *input mask* controls the way the user puts data into the field to begin with. For example, you might want a phone number field entered with the area code in parentheses, with the exchange prefix separated from the number by a dash, like this:

`(123) 555-8932`

You specify an input mask in much the same way that you specify the Format property because Input Mask is a field property, also. Here's how:

1. Open a database in Design view, click the field for which you want to create an input mask, and then click in the Input Mask property field.

2. Type the input mask code to define a custom input mask or click the ellipsis (...) button at the right of the Input Mask property field to open the Input Mask Wizard (see Figure 27.16).

3. Choose a mask from the Input Mask list.

4. Click in the Try It field, and then type some data to test the input mask.

5. Click Next to open the second page of the wizard, shown in Figure 27.17.

**FIGURE 27.16**
Access provides
several prede-
fined input
masks.

**FIGURE 27.16**
Access provides
several prede-
fined input
masks.

**FIGURE 27.17**
You can edit an
input mask, if
needed.

6. From the drop-down list select the character to use as the placeholder when
   data is being entered and then click Next.

7. Choose one of the following options:

   ■ **With the Symbols in the Mask**—When you select this option, the
      mask characters become part of the data and are stored in the database
      with the data.

   ■ **Without the Symbols in the
      Mask**—When you select this
      option, you can use the mask char-
      acters only to format data input;
      the mask characters are not stored
      with the data.

8. Click Finish.

In most situations it is easiest to use the wizard
to specify and test the input mask. However, you
can enter your own input mask or customize one
in the wizard by changing the mask string. I

**tip**

The Input Mask Wizard
works only for Text and
Date fields.

don't cover all the characters and what they do here, but to learn more, you can click in the `Input Mask` property field and press F1 to open Help and view the allowable characters for the `Input Mask` property.

## Using the `Format` and `Input Mask` Properties Together

Generally, you use the `Format` and `Input Mask` properties together to control how data goes into a database and how it is displayed. Using an input mask forces the data into the format you want stored in the database and helps ensure that the user enters the appropriate data. For example, using the Phone Number input mask helps ensure that the user enters an area code along with the number. You might modify the Phone Number mask to make the user also enter an extension number.

Although you might think that the `Input Mask` and `Format` properties do essentially the same thing, they do not. The `Format` property has no effect on the actual data—it only controls how the data appears. The data itself can be quite different from how it appears.

# Using Templates: Access's Canned Databases

Setting up a database can be a difficult task for a newcomer to Access, but fortunately, Access provides templates that help you easily create specific types of databases.

To start a new database from a template, choose File, New. Under the Templates area in the New File task pane, click the On My Computer link. When the Templates dialog box appears, click the Databases tab (shown in Figure 27.18), select the template for the type of database you want, and click OK.

**FIGURE 27.18**

You can choose a database template from the Databases tab.

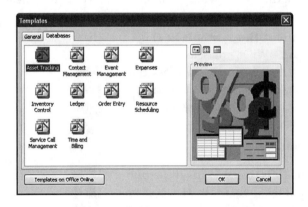

The templates include the following:

- **Asset Tracking**—You can use this type of database to keep track of assets, depreciation, maintenance, employees, departments, and vendors.

- **Contact Management**—You can use this type of database to manage contacts, including names, addresses, and phone numbers.

- **Event Management**—You can use this type of database to track events, attendees, registration information, event pricing, and other properties associated with one or more events.

- **Expenses**—You can use this type of database to enter and manage expense reports for a group of employees.

- **Inventory Control**—You can use this type of database to track product information, supply and sales information, quantity on hand and on order, information about suppliers, and other properties for managing inventory.

- **Ledger**—You can use this type of database to keep track of accounts, transactions, and transfers.

- **Order Entry**—You can use this type of database to manage customer information and product information, take orders for products, and keep track of sales.

- **Resource Scheduling**—You can use this type of database to manage scheduling and maintenance for one or more resources, such as equipment or meeting rooms.

- **Service Call Management**—You can use this type of database to track customer or staff service call requests.

- **Time and Billing**—You can use this type of database to track time and billing for one or more projects.

These canned databases are a great resource for new and experienced Access users alike because they are complete and ready-to-use, with data tables, entry forms, reports, and queries already set up. Figure 27.19 shows an example of a database created from the Expenses template. In many cases you can use them as-is without any modifications, but you can certainly open any of the tables or other items in Design view and change them as needed.

**tip**

Microsoft offers additional Access templates on its Web site. You can choose File, New, On My Computer and then click Templates on Office Online to open a Web browser at the Office Web site and download additional templates.

**FIGURE 27.19**

The templates in
Access help you
create ready-to-
use databases.

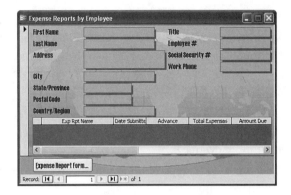

Before you start using a database from one of the templates included with Access,
you should consider reading the remaining chapters in this part of the book to learn
more about Access. With that information in hand, you'll be better prepared to take
advantage of the template-based databases.

# THE ABSOLUTE MINIMUM

A database application such as Access is a great tool for gathering and analyzing all
sorts of data. In this chapter you stuck a toe in the water and learned how to create
a database, work within the Access user interface to view tables and other objects,
and accomplish a simple search in a database. You also learned how to format fields
in a table.

Now it's time to wade a little deeper. The next chapter takes you beyond the basics
to learn how to create forms for entering and viewing data. You'll also learn how to
create and use queries, perform calculations, and bring data into a database from
other sources.

- Creating data forms to enter and view data
- Sorting and searching through a database
- Creating a query to find specific data
- Performing calculations by using queries
- Importing data into a database from other sources

28

# BEYOND THE BASICS

Setting up a database and adding records are just two aspects of working with Access. The real power of a database comes in the capability it gives you to sort and analyze the information it contains.

In Chapter 27, "Database Basics," you learned how to take the first steps in creating a database. Now it's time to take a look at some of the tasks you can accomplish with a database. This chapter explains how to create forms for entering and viewing data, how to perform simple queries, and how to import data from other sources into a database.

# Using Forms for Data Entry and Viewing

It certainly is easy to add records in Datasheet view, particularly in a table that contains few fields. As the number of fields increases, however, Datasheet view becomes less and less desirable as the main means for entering data in a database.

The solution is to create *forms* to enter and view data. Forms (see Figure 28.1) enable you to put data into a logical format and group related fields. You can also add instructions, labels, and other information on a form to help the user understand the purpose or required format for a particular field or fields.

**FIGURE 28.1**

You can use forms to enter data into a complex table.

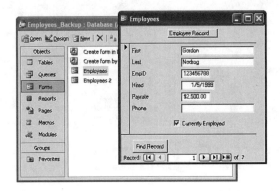

As you'll see in the next section, Access provides the Form Wizard, which makes it relatively easy to create forms. When you create a form, you can *lock* some or all of the controls on the form. Locking a control prevents the user from using the form to change the contents of the field associated with the control. It's often a good idea to lock fields on forms that are used for displaying data to prevent unwanted changes.

You can create forms manually by dragging controls to a blank form and associating controls such as text boxes and list boxes on the form with specific fields in a table. Even experienced Access users often use the Form Wizard as a starting place, however, because adding controls and associating them with fields can be very time-consuming. Therefore, this chapter focuses on using the Form Wizard.

## Creating a Form by Using the Form Wizard

You can create forms from existing tables or queries by using the Form Wizard. Follow these steps to create a simple form, using the Employees database as an example:

1. Open Access and open the Employees database.

2. In the Database window, click Forms in the Objects list.

3. Double-click Create Form by Using Wizard to start the Form Wizard.

4. In the first wizard page (see Figure 28.2), select Table:Employees from the Tables/Queries drop-down list box.

**FIGURE 28.2**

You can create data entry forms by using the Form Wizard.

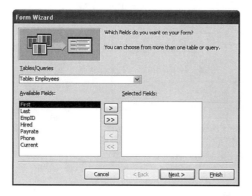

5. Click the double-right-arrow button to add all fields to the Selected Fields list and then click Next.

6. Choose the Columnar Layout option (the default) and click Next.

7. Select the style you want to use for the form. For this example, choose the Standard style (see Figure 28.3).

**FIGURE 28.3**

You can choose a style for a form.

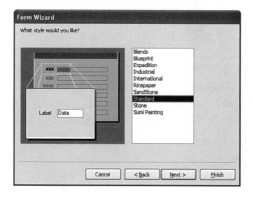

8. Click Next, enter a name for the form, and click Finish. Figure 28.4 shows the resulting form.

As with other Access objects, with forms you can switch to Design view to change the layout of a form. You open the Database window, click Forms in the Objects list, select the form, and click Design on the toolbar. Figure 28.5 shows the Employees form in Design view.

**tip**

You can create your own form style. To do so, choose a blank style in the wizard and then set the background property for the form and controls to create the look you want.

**FIGURE 28.4**

This is a simple
employee data
entry form.

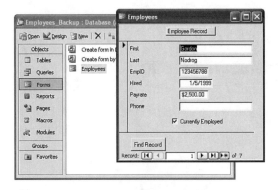

**FIGURE 28.5**

The Employees
form is now
open in Design
view.

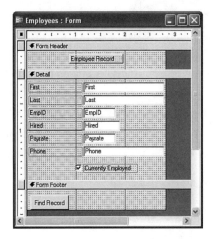

With the form opened in Design view, you can rearrange fields on the form, change or add labels, and make other changes to fine-tune the form. The following section explains how to lock controls on a form to prevent changes to those controls.

# Locking Controls on a Form

Locking a control makes the control read-only, preventing the user from changing the data associated with the control. For example, you can lock the text box associated with the EmpID field in the Employees database to cause Access to display the employee ID but prevent the ID from being changed.

Follow these steps to lock the EmpID field:

1. Open the Employees form in Design view.

2. Click the EmpID text box.

3. Choose View, Properties to open the properties window for the control (see Figure 28.6).

**FIGURE 28.6**

You can set properties for a control to change its appearance or behavior.

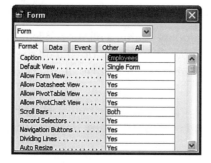

4. Click the Data tab, click in the Locked property field, click the drop-down list, and choose Yes.

5. Close the properties window.

6. Click the View button on the Form Design toolbar or choose View, Form View to change to Form view.

7. Choose a record with the form and click in the EmpID field. Then try to change the data. Access prevents you from doing so.

Although you don't have to disable a control to prevent users from making changes to the data associated with it, disabling a control provides a visual indicator that a field is locked. This visual cue can also serve as a reminder to the user that the field is not supposed to be changed.

Now you should disable the EmpID control:

1. Switch back to Design view, select the EmpID field, and open the properties window.

2. On the Data tab, find and set the Enabled property to No and then close the properties window.

3. Switch back to Form view.

Now try to click in or tab to the EmpID field. Access doesn't let you select the field. What about that visual cue? In this case, I would set the Back Color property on the Format tab to gray to indicate that the field is locked. You can use your own formatting choices to indicate locked and/or disabled fields.

**tip**

You can also press Alt+Enter or click the Properties button on the toolbar to open the properties window.

## Adding Controls and Associating Controls with Fields

It's a good idea to make sure a database contains all the needed fields and even to enter a few records before you start creating forms. Having all the fields in the database to start with ensures that the Form Wizard makes all the fields available when you create the form.

It seldom works out that a database is perfect when you start creating forms. Sooner or later, you have to manually add controls to a form and perhaps associate them with fields in the database.

Adding form controls is easier than you might think. In the following steps, you add a Yes/No field to the Employees table and then add a corresponding check box to the form:

1. Open the Employees table in Design view.

2. Add a field named Current, make it a Yes/No field, and use **Currently Employed** as the description.

3. Open the Employees form in Design view.

4. Click at the top of the Form Footer bar (see Figure 28.7) and drag the bar down to extend the bottom of the form.

**FIGURE 28.7**
You can drag the Form Footer bar down to make room on the form for a new control.

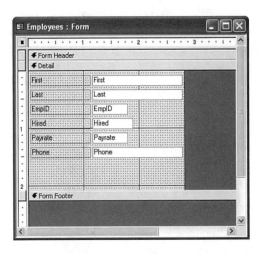

5. If the Toolbox window is not already open, choose View, Toolbox to open the control toolbox.

6. Click the CheckBox control in the toolbox and then click and drag in the form to add a check box (see Figure 28.8).

**FIGURE 28.8**

This check box needs to be associated with the Current field.

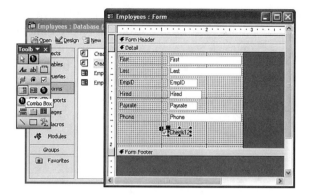

7. With the CheckBox control's text selected, choose View, Properties to open the properties window.

8. On the Format tab, set the Caption property to **Currently Employed**.

9. Close the properties window and click the check box itself (not the text). Then press Alt+Enter to open the properties window.

10. On the Data tab, click the drop-down list in the Control Source property field and select Current from the list (see Figure 28.9).

**FIGURE 28.9**

You can choose a field to associate with a control.

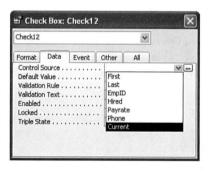

11. Close the properties window and switch the form back to Form view.

12. Set the Current field for a couple records by clicking the check box in those records.

13. Close the form and open the Employees table in Datasheet view. You should see that the records you modified with the check box have the Current field set to Yes (checked).

You have a lot more capability to associate a control with data than you might think from this example. In the Data tab of the properties window, you can click the ellipsis (...) button to the right of the Control Source property field rather than click the drop-down list. Access displays the Expression Builder dialog box (see Figure 28.10), which you can use to create complex expressions and calculations, link to other database properties, and associate other data with the control.

**FIGURE 28.10**

You can use the
Expression
Builder dialog
box to change
the control asso-
ciation.

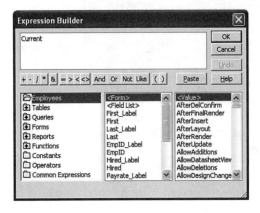

Using the Expression Builder goes a bit beyond the beginner level, but now that you know it's there, you can start to experiment with it in your forms.

## Using the Form Header and Footer

This chapter focuses mainly on the Detail area of the form. Forms have other areas to consider. Take a moment to look at the Header and Footer areas. In Figure 28.5, the Form Header bar appears at the top of the form, and the Form Footer bar appears at the bottom. Both the header and footer are empty. Figure 28.11 shows controls added to both the header and footer.

**FIGURE 28.11**

The header and
footer now con-
tain controls.

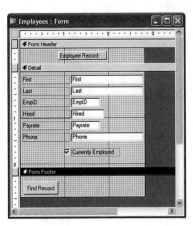

To increase or decrease the size of the header, you click the line between the Form Header and Detail bars and drag the line up or down. You can click and drag the bottom of the Form Footer bar to change the footer size.

You add controls to a header or footer in the same way you add them to the Detail area: You just click the control type in the toolbox and then click and drag in the header or footer. Figure 28.12 shows the header and footer, with their new controls, in Form view.

> **tip**
>
> The size of the form window in Design view determines the size of the finished form in Form view. You can adjust the size of the form in Design view by dragging its borders and then switch to Form view to see the results.

**FIGURE 28.12**

The header and footer appear in the form in Form view.

## Building a Database Interface with a Switchboard Form

A rather advanced topic that you should know about but that isn't covered in detail in this book is the use of a switchboard form. In general, a *switchboard form* contains buttons that open other forms. You use a switchboard as a launching place for a database. Figure 28.13 shows a switchboard form created with the Contact Management template.

You follow these steps to start a simple switchboard form for the Employees database and add a button that will open the Employees form:

1. Open the Employees database and click Forms in the Objects list of the Database window.

> **tip**
>
> It's a good idea to add a Find button to a form when the user will need to locate specific records. The form's footer is a good place for the Find button. You can add a command button to the footer, and in the Command Button Wizard, choose Record Navigation from the Categories list and Find Record from the Actions list. Then you follow the wizard's remaining instructions to complete the wizard and add the button.

2. Click New, click Design View, and click OK.

3. In the toolbox, click Command Button and then click in the form.

4. In the Command Button Wizard (shown in Figure 28.14), choose Form Operations from the Categories list, choose Open Form from the Actions list, and click Next.

**FIGURE 28.13**

This switchboard was created with the Contact Management template.

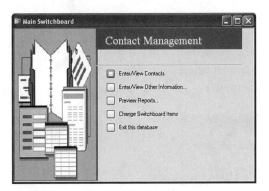

**FIGURE 28.14**

You use the Command Button Wizard to add buttons to a form.

5. Select the Employees form and click Next.

6. Click Next, choose the Text option, and click Finish. The result is a button with the text Open Form that when clicked opens the Employees form.

# Sorting and Filtering Records

Sometimes you might need to sort the records in a database. For example, you might want to view the Employees table sorted by last name.

**tip**

You can do far more with buttons than just display forms. You can read in the Help documentation about events and event procedures to learn how to add program code to buttons.

Or you might want to view only employees who are currently employed. You can use Access's sort and filter features for these tasks.

# Sorting a Table

Sorting a table often makes it easier to work with the information in the table, particularly if you are viewing a long table in Datasheet view. It's really easy to sort a table:

1. Open the table in Datasheet view.

2. Click in the field (any record) you want to use as the sort field. For example, to sort by last name in the Employees table, click in the Last field.

3. Choose Records, Sort, Sort Ascending or Sort Descending to sort the table based on the selected field.

4. Close the table. Access prompts you to save changes. If you click No, the table's sort order is not changed.

# Filtering a Table

As the amount of data in a table grows, it may become more important to limit the data that shows. For example, you might want to filter the Employees database so it shows only employees currently on staff.

You have a handful of ways to filter a table:

- **Filter by Form**—When you use this method, Access displays a simple table form, and you select criteria from a drop-down list in each field. For example, you would place a check mark in the Current field and apply the filter to view only employees currently on staff.

- **Filter by Selection**—When you use this method, you can select a field or range of fields and view only the records that match the selected criteria.

- **Filter Excluding Selection**—When you use this method, you can select a field or range of fields and view only records other than those that match the selected criteria.

- **Advanced Filter/Sort**—When you use this method, you can specify criteria manually to define the filter.

The following sections describe how to filter by form and how to do advanced filtering and sorting.

## Filtering by Form

Follow these steps to filter by form:

1. Open the Employees database and choose Records, Filter, Filter by Form or click the Filter by Form button on the toolbar. Access displays a simple table form (see Figure 28.15).

**FIGURE 28.15**

You can use a form to filter a table.

2. Click the drop-down list under the field for which you want to specify a condition and select a value. Or place a check mark in a Yes/No field to select that as a condition.

3. Click Filter, Apply Filter/Sort.

You can also enter the search condition yourself. For example, you can click in the Last field and type **Jones** or **Smith** and then apply the filter to view records for all employees whose last name is either Jones or Smith.

## Using Advanced Filters

Setting a filter manually is almost as easy as filtering by form, but it requires a little more work:

1. Open the table and choose Records, Filter, Advanced Filter/Sort to open the Filter window (see Figure 28.16).

**FIGURE 28.16**

You can use the Filter window to define filter conditions.

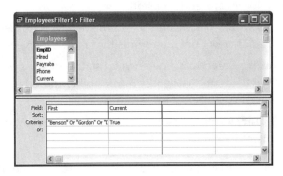

2. From the Field row, click the drop-down list and select a field.

3. Click in the Criteria field and type the criterion, such as **Smith** or **Jones**.

4. To sort the results, click the drop-down list in the Sort field and choose either Ascending or Descending.

5. Repeat steps 2 through 4 to specify other fields and criteria, as needed.

6. When you are satisfied with the filter criteria, choose Filter, Apply Filter/Sort.

**tip**

To remove a filter and display the entire table again, you choose Records, Filter, Remove Filter/Sort.

# Searching for and Selecting Data by Using Queries

Using a filter is one way to filter a table, but using a *query* is a much better option when you need to do more than just view records that fit your search conditions. For example, you might want to purge the records for all employees no longer working for the company. In this case, you would create a query for records where the Current field is equal to No and then extract those records to a separate database.

There are several types of queries:

■ **Select queries**—This type of query retrieves data from the database and displays it in a datasheet for viewing or editing. You can also perform calculations such as sums and totals by using a Select query.

■ **Parameter queries**—This type of query displays dialog boxes that prompt the user to enter information that defines the search criteria. A parameter query is useful because it can be flexible, searching the database for varying information, according to the user's current needs.

■ **Crosstab queries**—A Crosstab query locates data and performs calculations that result in a spreadsheet-like datasheet.

■ **Action queries**—Action queries perform actions on the database such as deleting or appending records, updating records, or creating another table containing the records that match the search criteria.

■ **SQL queries**—You can build queries by using Structured Query Language (SQL). SQL queries can display or modify data. Using SQL queries requires an understanding of SQL commands and syntax. See www.sql.org for more details.

The following sections focus mainly on using a wizard to create select queries, but they also explain how to modify a query and change its type.

## Creating a Select Query

To create a simple query, you follow these steps:

1. Open the Employees table and click Queries in the Objects list of the Database window.

2. Double-click Create Query by Using Wizard.

3. Access prompts you to select where the data should come from and which fields should be included. Select the Employees table, select all fields, and click the double-right-arrow button to add all fields to the Selected Fields list. Then click Next.

4. With the Detail option selected, click Next.

5. Enter a name for the query and click Finish. Access displays a datasheet that contains all of records in the table.

6. Choose View, Design View to open the query in Design view (see Figure 28.17).

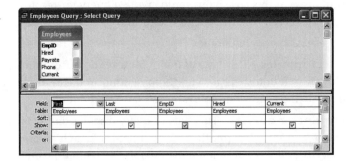

7. Under the Last field column, choose Sort Ascending from the Sort row. This causes the query to sort by last name.

8. Click in the Criteria row under the Last column and type **Smith** or **Jones**.

9. Close the Query window and click Yes when you're prompted to save the changes.

10. Double-click the query in the Database window to run the query and view its results.

**tip**

To add a field that is not already in the query, you click the field in the field list above the query and drag the field to the query.

## Modifying a Query

You can change a query simply by opening it in Design view and changing the items shown in the Query window. For example, assume that you want to view only the employee's last name, first name, and employee ID. Here's how you remove the other fields from the query:

1. Open the query in Design view.
2. Clear the Show check box under each field you want to exclude from the query.
3. Close the query and save changes.
4. Run the query to view the results of the changes.

## Changing a Query's Type

When you create a query, you're not stuck with the query type you specify initially. You can change the query type. In the following example you create a select query that shows only noncurrent employees, and then you change the query to a Make-Table query. The result is a new table that contains all noncurrent employees in the database. Let's get started:

1. In the Database window, click Queries and start a new query by using the Simple Query Wizard.
2. Select Table:Employees as the source and add all fields to the field list. Then click Next.
3. Click Next and type the name **Noncurrent**.
4. Select the option Modify the Query Design and click Finish.
5. Scroll over in the Query window and find the Current field. Click in the Criteria row under the Current field and type **False**.
6. Close the query and save changes.
7. Run the Noncurrent query to view the results. You should see the employees who are not currently employed (the Current field should be unchecked).
8. Open the query again in Design view.
9. Choose Query, Make-Table Query to open the Make Table dialog box (shown in Figure 28.18).

10. Enter Old Employees in the Table Name field.

11. With Current Database selected (the default), click OK.

12. Close the query and save changes.

13. Run the query. Access displays a dialog box that asks you to allow data to be modified. Click Yes to create the new table.

The next logical step might be to create a Delete query (or modify this one) to delete the noncurrent records from the existing table.

# Performing Calculations by Using Queries

Access makes it possible to perform all sorts of calculations in a query. You can count the number of records that match a query, sum the value of a particular field, calculate averages, and much more. You can also create your own formulas to calculate values based on the data in a table.

For example, perhaps you want to create a query that calculates the total annual salary for each employee. The query needs to multiply the Payrate field by 12 to come up with an annual value.

You follow these steps to create a new query to show annual pay rate:

1. Open the Employees database.

2. Click Queries in the Database window and start a new query by double-clicking Create Query by Using Wizard.

3. Select the Employees table and add the Last, First, and Payrate fields to the field list. Then click Next.

4. Select the Detail option and click Next.

5. Enter the query name Annual Payroll, choose Modify the Query Design, and click Finish.

6. Click in the Field row of the fourth column (the first empty column) and then type Annual:[Payrate]*12 and press Enter.

7. Close and save the query.

8. Run the query. Figure 28.19 shows the results.

**FIGURE 28.19**

This query includes a calculated field.

| First | Last | Payrate | Annual |
|-------|------|---------|--------|
| Sally | Johnson | $3,000.00 | 36000 |
| Gordon | Nodrog | $2,500.00 | 30000 |
| David | Jones | $2,250.00 | 27000 |
| Dan | Burns | $1,750.00 | 21000 |
| Benson | Jones | $1,200.00 | 14400 |
| Shelly | Snow | $1,200.00 | 14400 |
| Jeff | Barry | $750.00 | 9000 |
| * | | $0.00 | |

*Employees Query2 : Select Query*

Record: 1 of 7

In this example, the following expression created the Annual field:

Annual:[Payrate]*12

The first part of the expression, Annual:, specifies the new field name. The field on which the calculation operates—Payrate—is enclosed in square brackets ([]). The *12 portion of the expression multiplies Payrate by 12 to determine an annual value.

Next, let's sort the query by annual salary from highest-to-lowest and format the Annual field to display as currency:

1. Reopen the Annual Payroll query in Design view.

2. Under the Annual field, click the Sort row and choose Descending.

3. Right-click the Annual field and choose Properties. The Field Properties dialog box appears (see Figure 28.20).

**FIGURE 28.20**

You can use the Field Properties dialog box to format the field.

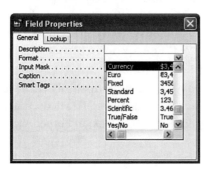

4. Click in the Format property field and choose Currency from the drop-down list.

5. Close and save the query.

6. Run the query. Figure 28.21 shows the results.

**FIGURE 28.21**

The query now sorts by annual pay rate.

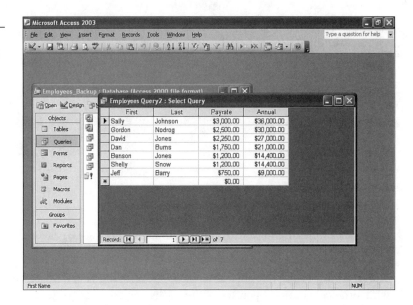

This section just scratches the surface of what you can do with calculations in Access. For more information about using calculations—particularly the predefined calculations for sum, average, and so on—you can search the Access Help documentation on the phrase *calculate query*.

# Importing Data from Other Sources

Building a database can be very time-consuming, especially if you have to enter every record yourself. You can sometimes ease that burden by importing data from other applications. For example, if you have been using Outlook to manage your customer list but now want to move it to Access, you can easily import the contacts into a database.

Access supports data import from a wide variety of applications, including Excel, other database applications, Outlook and Exchange Server, HTML documents, and other sources. The following sections focus on two: Outlook and other Access databases.

## Importing Data from Outlook

You can import data from any Outlook folder, but it is most likely that you will import contacts from the Contacts folder. That's the example we use here:

1. Open Access and open the database in which you want to import the data.

2. Choose File, Get External Data, Import to open the Import dialog box, which is shown in Figure 28.22.

**FIGURE 28.22**

You can select the type of data to import by using the Import dialog box.

3. From the Files of Type drop-down list box, choose Outlook. Access starts the Import Exchange/Outlook Wizard. Outlook prompts for an Outlook profile if more than one exists and Outlook is configured to prompt for a profile.

4. In the wizard, select the folder from which you want to import (see Figure 28.23).

**FIGURE 28.23**

You can choose the Contacts folder as the source.

5. Choose the Contacts folder, either from the Address Books branch or the Personal Folders branch, and then click Next.

6. Choose In a New Table to specify a new table in the current database for the incoming data. Or select In an Existing Table and choose an existing table in the database. Then click Next.

7. The wizard prompts you to specify how each field is imported (see Figure 28.24). Click each field in the table and then specify the data type and field name in the options at the top of the dialog box. Choose the Do Not Import Field (Skip) option to prevent Access from importing the selected field from Outlook.

**FIGURE 28.24**

You can specify how you want fields to be imported.

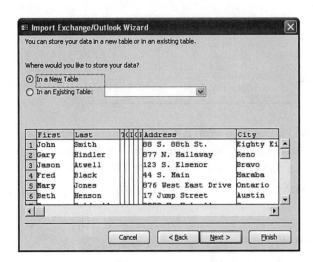

8. Click Next, choose Let Access Add Primary Key, and click Next.

9. Enter a name for the new table (if you did not specify an existing table for the import) and click Finish.

## Importing Data from Other Access Databases

You can import data from other Access databases. This is a good approach when you need to reuse information from one database in another and are not concerned that you are duplicating the data.

➪ The following section, "Linking Tables," explains how to link tables and not duplicate data.

Follow these steps to import from another Access database:

1. Open Access and open the database into which you want to import the data.

2. Choose File, Get External Data, Import.

3. With Microsoft Access selected in the Files of Type drop-down list box (the default selection), browse to and select the database that contains the data to be imported. Click Import to open the Import Objects dialog box, which is shown in Figure 28.25.

**FIGURE 28.25**

You can use the Import Objects dialog box to specify which objects to import.

4. Click each tab and select on each tab the items you want imported.

5. Click Options to expand the dialog box and choose from the following options:

   ■ **Relationships**—You can use this option to import existing relationships between tables and queries in the source database.

   ■ **Menus and Toolbars**—You can use this option to import custom menus and toolbars contained in the source database.

   ■ **Import/Export Specs**—You can use this option to import the import/export specifications from the source database. You create import/export specifications by using the Import Text Wizard or the Export Text Wizard or by creating a Schema.ini file for the database.

   ■ **Definition and Data**—You can use this option to import the table structures and the data from the source database.

   ■ **Definition Only**—You can use this option to import only the table structure but not the data contained in the table. (This results in empty tables with the same structure as the source database.)

   ■ **As Queries**—You can use this option to make queries in the source database become queries in the target database.

   ■ **As Tables**—You can use this option to make queries in the source database create tables in the target database.

   When you're done selecting options, click OK.

In most cases you can accept the default options when you import data from another database.

## Linking Tables

In some cases you don't want to duplicate the data from one database in another, but instead you want to link to the data. When you *link* to a table in another database, the data remains in the source database, and only a representation of the table appears in the target database. If you change the data from what is in the target database, the data is updated in the source database.

For example, assume that you have a Customers database that contains contact information for all your customers. You want to create an Orders database that uses information from the Customers database, but you don't want to duplicate the customer information that is in the Orders database. The solution is to link the required table(s) from the Customers database into the Orders database.

**tip**

Linked tables have an arrow icon beside them in the Database window to indicate that they are linked.

Here's how you link tables from one database to another:

1. Open the target database into which you want to link the external tables.

2. Choose File, Get External Data, Link Tables to open the Link dialog box.

3. Select the database that contains the tables you want to link into the target database and click Link.

4. In the Link Tables dialog box (see Figure 28.26), select the tables to link and click OK.

**FIGURE 28.26**

You can use the Link Tables dialog box to choose which tables to link.

# THE ABSOLUTE MINIMUM

Databases are very useful for storing many different types of data, but more importantly, they enable you to analyze, sort, merge, and create reports about the data in many different ways.

In this chapter you learned how to simplify data entry and viewing by creating simple forms. You also learned how to sort the records in a database and search for particular information by using queries. This chapter also explains how to perform calculations in queries and import data from other sources.

The next chapter moves from the screen to the printer to help you create printed reports from databases.

**29**

# FROM TABLE TO PRINTER: REPORTS!

It seems like we have been chasing a paperless office for decades. We have made a lot of progress, but paper reports are still a fact of business life. It's a safe bet that at some point, you will need to print reports from Microsoft Access.

This chapter explains not only how to create reports in Access, but also just what an Access report is. Understanding what reports are will help you more effectively control and generate them.

# What Is an Access Report?

If you have read Chapters 27, "Database Basics," and 28, "Beyond the Basics," you should now understand the role that forms and queries play in an Access database. Each represents a different way to display information from the database. Both also offer a means for adding data to a database.

I think of Access reports as sort of a cross between forms and queries. A *report* extracts information from a database, just like a query, and it displays information much like a form. The main difference is that a report is designed for output to a printer.

As you will learn in the following section, you create and save reports in a database in much the same way you create forms and queries. A report is saved by name as a separate Access object.

When you open the Reports object, the report extracts the data from the database in much the same way a query extracts data from a database when you run the query. So the report isn't a static representation of the data. Instead, it is a dynamic object that changes each time you open it. For that reason, you can create a single report to extract certain information from a database and use that single report to report on the data at different times and achieve different results. The report changes to reflect the contents of the database at the time the report is run.

Access reports are not fixed objects, either. After you create a report, you can open it in Design view and modify it to add or change headers, change page layout properties, add or remove data fields, and so on.

# Creating a Report by Using the Report Wizard

You would likely have a difficult time—at least at first—creating reports in Access if you had to build them manually, field by field. Fortunately, Access provides a wizard that steps you through the process of creating a report. Before you start creating reports, however, you need to understand from where the data for a report will come.

When you create a report, you can specify either a table or a query as the data source. The wizard doesn't give you the option of setting conditions to filter the data. You can modify the report in Design view and add expressions, but initially the report contains everything that is in the data source.

If you want to include in a report all records in a particular table, use the table as the data source. You should create a query, however, if you want to extract only certain records from the database. For example, assume that you are creating a phone list but want to extract only customers whose company names start with the letter B. You would create a query that extracts that information and then use the query— not the table—as the data source for the report.

Now that you have some understanding of the mechanics of a report, you're ready to create one. You follow these steps to run the Report Wizard to create a simple report:

1. Open Access and open a database. Use the Employees database for this example.

2. In the Objects list on the Database window, click Reports and then double-click Create Report by Using Wizard. Access starts the Report Wizard (see Figure 29.1).

**FIGURE 29.1**

You can use the
Report Wizard
to create reports
in Access.

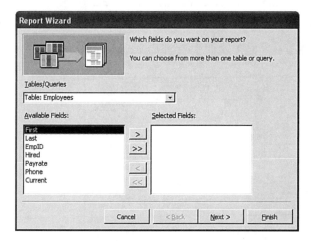

3. From the Tables/Queries drop-down list box, choose the table or query that will be the source for the report. Use the Employees table for this example.

4. Select fields from the Available Fields list and add them to the Selected Fields list. The selected fields appear in the report.

   At this point the wizard asks if you want to add any grouping levels (see Figure 29.2). Groups determine how information is organized in a report. For example, the employees report should organize the employees by last name and then sort each last name group by first name.

5. Click Last and then click on the right-arrow button to specify the Last field as a grouping field. Then click Next.

6. From the sort page (see Figure 29.3), select First from the first drop-down list box to specify that within each last name group, the records should be sorted by first name. Then click Next.

**FIGURE 29.2**

You can add grouping levels in a report to organize records.

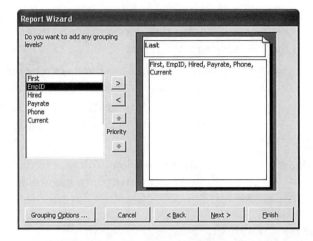

**FIGURE 29.3**

You can easily sort records within a group.

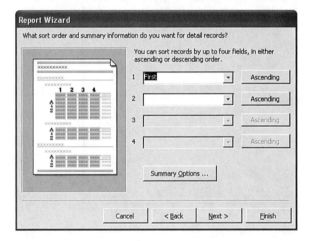

7. Choose the initial layout from the Layout group box (see Figure 29.4) and choose the report orientation. Then click Next.

8. Choose one of the predefined styles for the report and click Next.

9. Type a name for the report and click Finish to preview the report onscreen (see Figure 29.5).

**FIGURE 29.4**

You need to choose an initial layout for a report.

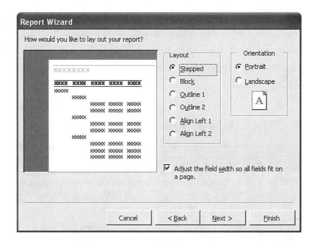

**FIGURE 29.5**

Access shows you a preview of a report onscreen.

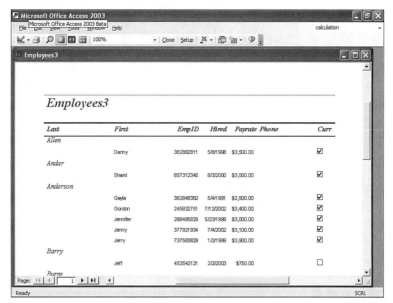

# Viewing and Modifying Reports

As explained earlier in this chapter, Access reports are named Access objects in the same way that tables and queries are named objects. Reports appear under the Reports object in the Database window.

It's simple to view a report. You simply click Reports in the Database window and then double-click the report you want to view. Or you can select the report and click Preview on the toolbar.

With a report open, you can zoom in and out of the report in much the same way you can zoom in and out of a Word document. You just click in the report to zoom in or zoom out. You can also specify the zoom percentage in the Zoom combo box on the toolbar. The toolbar also offers controls that enable you to display multiple report pages onscreen.

## Changing a Report's Layout and Design

As with other Access objects, you can work with a report in more than one view. You can use Layout Preview view and Print Preview view to see how a report will look onscreen and when printed. You can use Design view when you need to modify the report's contents or layout. Figure 29.6 shows the Employees report in Design view.

**FIGURE 29.6**

You can switch to Design view to modify a report.

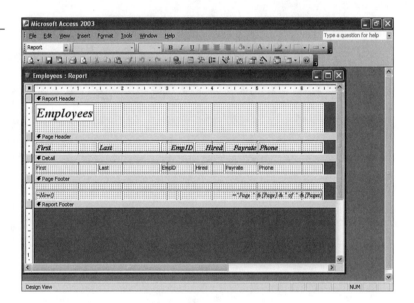

Design view offers access to several report components:

- **Report header**—The report header appears at the top of the first page of the report and generally includes the report's title. You can include other information, such as the date the report was generated and summary information for the data.

- **Page header**—The page header appears at the top of each page. In many cases it is used to display the headings for the columns in a tabular report, but you can include other information in the page header, as well.

■ **Group headers**—Group headers display information for each group of data when you include grouping in the report. Access provides a header for each defined group.

■ **Detail**—The Detail area shows the data extracted from the database table or query. It's the body of a report.

■ **Page footer**—The page footer by default includes the current date and page number. You can add other information, as needed, including summary information. The page footer appears at the bottom of each page of the report.

■ **Report footer**—The report footer appears at the end of the report, immediately after the last data item in the Detail area. By default, the report footer is not visible and contains no data.

> **tip**
>
> You can turn on or off these areas of a report simply by setting the `Visible` property for each one. To do this, you open the report in Design view, click the object, and press Alt+Enter to open its properties window. On the Format tab, you select No from the Visible drop-down list to hide the object on the report.

Modifying a report (or even creating one from scratch in Design view) is a lot like modifying a form. When you use the Report Wizard to create a report, the wizard adds the headers and objects to display the data based on your selections in the wizard. You can then reposition these existing controls and add others.

The field list (see Figure 29.7) makes it easy to add table fields to a report. You simply drag a field from the field list to a spot in the report. Then you choose View, Field List to turn the Field List window on or off.

**FIGURE 29.7**

You can add fields to a report by using the field list.

You can also open the toolbox to add labels, text boxes, and other elements to a report. You choose View, Toolbox to display the toolbox, and then you click a control on the toolbox and click in the form. To change the properties for a control, you select the control and press Alt+Enter to open the properties window for the control. From the properties window you can access and change properties that control the control's format, visibility, color, font, data source, and so on.

## Adding or Modifying Grouping and Sorting

When you create a report by using the Report Wizard, you have the option of grouping and sorting the data. For example, in the Employees report example earlier in this chapter, the report was grouped by last name and sorted by first name within each group.

You follow these steps to change the grouping of an existing report:

1. Open the database and open the report in Design view.

2. Choose View, Sorting and Grouping to open the Sorting and Grouping dialog box (see Figure 29.8). Fields assigned as group headers have a special grouping icon to the left of the Field/Expression column.

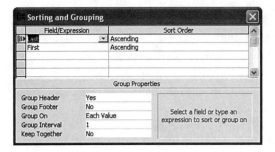

3. To change the field used to sort within a group, select the field from the drop-down list in the Field/Expression column. For example, choose Phone instead of First to sort the Employees list by phone number instead of by first name.

4. To remove a group header, click in the field or expression's row of the Field/Expression column and then choose No from the Group Header drop-down list in the Group Properties area.

5. To add a group header, add the field or expression on a new row and choose Yes from the Group Header drop-down list.

6. To rearrange the order of group headers or sort elements in the report, click an item in the Sorting and Group dialog box and then drag it to a new location. Do the same for other elements, until you have the order you need.

7. Close the Sorting and Grouping dialog box and then change to Layout Preview view to see the results.

# Using Summary Information

When you create a report by using the Report Wizard, you have the option of adding summary information within the report. To see the summary options, you run the wizard, and when the wizard prompts you to select the sort order, you click the Summary Options button to open the Summary Options dialog box (see Figure 29.9).

The Summary Options button is available in the wizard only if you specify at least one grouping level.

**FIGURE 29.9**

You can summarize data in a report by using the Summary Options dialog box.

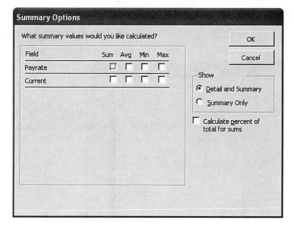

For example, assume that you have an Inventory database that lists all the items you sell, along with information about each item, such as cost, warehouse location, and quantity on hand. The items are stored at three different warehouse locations. Figure 29.10 shows this database in Design view.

**FIGURE 29.10**

The Inventory database stores information about items in stock at various warehouse locations.

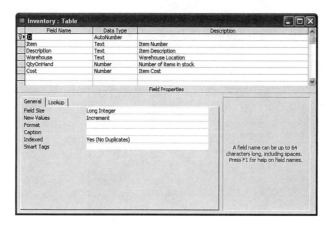

Say you want to view a report that shows the total quantity on hand so you can see which items should be reordered or so you can move items from one warehouse to another for better distribution. In this case, you would likely create a report that groups the data based on the Item field, sorts by the Warehouse field, and sums the QtyOnHand field. The result would be a report that lists each item under its own group, shows the quantity on hand at each warehouse, and totals the quantity on hand for all locations. The following steps describe how to do this:

1. Open the Inventory database and start a new report by using the Report Wizard.

2. Add all database fields to the Selected Fields list and click Next.

3. Add the Item field as a grouping level (see Figure 29.11) and click Next.

**FIGURE 29.11**

The Item field is added as the grouping level.

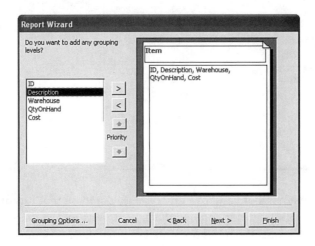

4. Select the Warehouse field as the sort field (see Figure 29.12).

**FIGURE 29.12**

You can select the Warehouse field as the sort field.

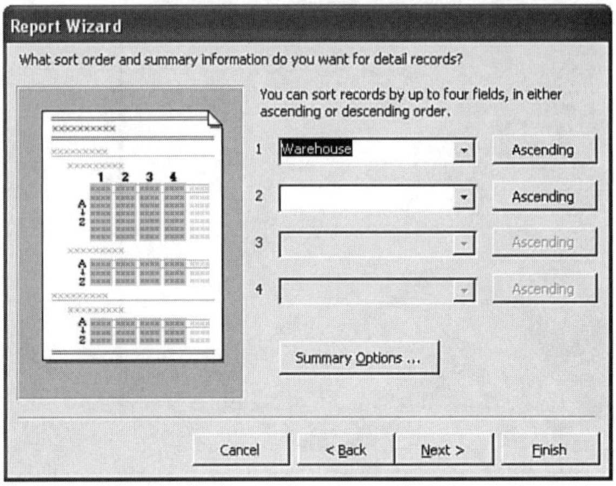

5. Click Summary Options, and in the Summary Options dialog box that appears, which is shown in Figure 29.13, place a check mark in the Sum column for the QtyOnHand field.

**FIGURE 29.13**

You can sum the QtyOnHand field.

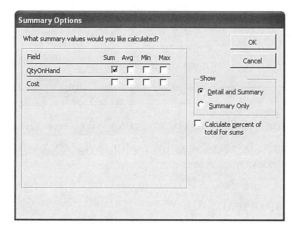

6. Click OK, click Next, and choose a report layout.
7. Click Next, choose a report style, and click Next.
8. Type the report name **Quantity on Hand** and click Finish.

When you preview the report, you see that it summarizes the quantity on hand for each item, as shown in Figure 29.14.

**FIGURE 29.14**

This report totals the quantity on hand for each item.

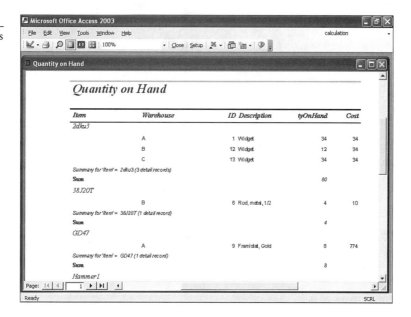

## Adding Calculations to a Report

Let's add a few more bits of information to the Quantity on Hand report started in the previous section: a total value for each item and a total value for all items in stock. You can do this by adding some expressions in the right places on the report:

1. Open the Inventory database and open the Quantity on Hand report in Design view.

2. Choose View, Toolbox to open the toolbox.

3. Click on the TextBox control and then click and drag in the item header to add the text box.

4. Click on and select the label text and change it to **Item Total.**

5. Click on the text box portion of the control and press Alt+Enter to open the properties window for the text box.

6. Click the Data tab, click in the Control Source field, and type **=sum([QtyOnHand]*[Cost])**, as shown in Figure 29.15.

**FIGURE 29.15**

You can add an expression to perform a calculation in a report.

7. Add another text box control, this time to the report header. Set the label text to **Total Inventory Value,** and set the Control Source property to **=sum([QtyOnHand]*[Cost]).**

8. Switch to Layout Preview view to view the report.

Now the report shows a total value for the quantity on hand for each item. It also includes a total inventory value in the report header. You could have put the total value in the report footer, but putting it in the report header makes it available on page 1.

You probably realized that the formula is the same for both expressions. What makes the results different is the location where you place the expression. If you place the expression within the Group Header area, Access applies the calculation to the group. If you place the expression in the report header or report footer, Access applies the calculation to the entire report.

# Printing and Exporting Reports and Labels

You can certainly view and analyze reports onscreen, but you will probably want to have a paper copy of some reports or perhaps export them to Word for inclusion in longer reports. This section explains both of these topics, as well as how to create labels from a database.

## Setting Page Layout Options

Before you print a report, you should review its page layout and adjust such settings as margins and page orientation. In Access, you open the Reports page of the Database window and double-click a report to open it. You can click the Setup button on the toolbar or choose File, Page Setup to display the Page Setup dialog box (see Figure 29.16).

**FIGURE 29.16**

You can config-ure report layout by using the Page Setup dia-log box.

Use the Margins tab to set the page margins, the Page tab to set page orientation and printer options, and the Columns tab to configure options for multicolumn reports. All these settings are generally self-explanatory.

## Printing a Report

You print an Access report in much the same way you print any Windows document. You open the report and choose File, Print to display the Print dialog box, which is the same in Access as in other Office applications. Then you set the necessary options, such as number of copies or target printer, and click OK to print.

## Using a Report in Word

It's likely that at some point you will want to use an Access report in a Word document. For example, you might need to include the report in a larger document that you've created in Word.

> **tip**
>
> To insert an Access report in another Word document, you export it to Word and save the RTF file. Then you open the Word document in which you want to insert the report and choose Insert, File. Finally, you browse to and select the RTF file, and then you click Insert.

When you view the report in Access, the OfficeLink button appears in the toolbar. You can click the arrow beside this button and choose Publish It with Microsoft Word to export the report to a Word rich text format (RTF) document that you can edit, print, or include in another Word document.

## Printing Labels

If you use Access to manage contacts, at some point you will probably want to print a set of labels from those contacts. However, you can create a set of labels for almost any database. For example, if you have an extensive CD or tape collection and use Access to manage it, you might want to print a set of labels for the cases. Or maybe you need to print item labels for a parts inventory database.

Labels are just another type of report in Access. You follow these steps to create a set of labels:

1. Open Access and open the database that contains the contacts.

2. Choose Insert, Report to open the New Report dialog box.

3. Select Label Wizard from the report type list and then choose the source for the labels from the drop-down list. Choose the table or query that contains the contacts list and click OK.

> **tip**
>
> To print a subset of your contacts (such as everyone in a particular state), you create a query that extracts that information from the database. Then you use that query as the source for the Label Wizard.

4. In the Label Wizard (see Figure 29.17), choose the label manufacturer and the label type.

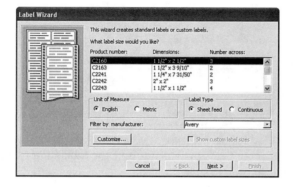

5. If the Label Wizard doesn't include the type of label you have, click Customize and then click New to open the New Label dialog box (see Figure 29.18). Click in the boxes and type the dimensions for the labels. Then click OK.

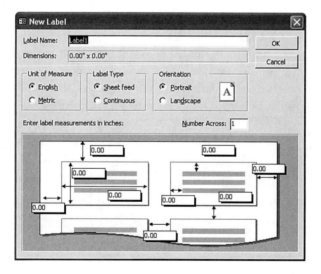

6. Back in the Label Wizard, click Next to select font properties and view a sam- ple. Click Next when you are satisfied with the font and sample.

7. Select fields (see Figure 29.19) and click the right-arrow button to add the fields to the label. Use the spacebar to add spaces between fields and the Enter key to start a new line. Add any other text, as needed, in addition to the Access fields. Click Next when the layout is correct.

**FIGURE 29.19**

You can add
fields to a label.

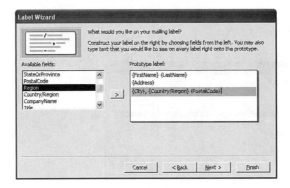

8. Choose one or more fields by which to sort the labels. For example, you might sort by zip code to save on postage. Click Next after you specify the sort field(s).

9. Type a name for the report and click Finish.

10. Insert the blank labels in the printer and choose File, Print to print the labels.

# THE ABSOLUTE MINIMUM

This chapter rounds out the tutorial chapters on Access with an explanation of how to extract the data from a database and show it in a report. You learned in this chapter how to create, modify, format, and print reports. You also learned how to accomplish a handful of related tasks, including sorting data and using calculations in a report.

Although Access lets you create reports, it's not the best solution when you need a polished and professional-looking document. This chapter explains how to export reports to Microsoft Word to spruce them up or create mailing labels.

The next chapter concludes the chapters on Access by explaining the most common settings in Access that you will want to change as you become more familiar with the program.

## IN THIS CHAPTER

- Changing the way you open Access objects
- Controlling how Access moves the cursor when you enter data
- Setting default fonts and colors
- Configuring miscellaneous Access options

# 30

# ACCESS SETTINGS TO CHANGE

Like other Office applications, Access offers many options you can set to control the way the program looks and functions. There are not as many options available in Access as in some of the other Office applications, but the ones that are available control a wide range of features.

This chapter examines the settings you are most likely to want to change and how to use them.

# Enabling Single-Clicking to Open Tables and Other Items

The Database window is a single point of access (pun intended) to all the objects in a database. You can open tables, reports, and other objects from the Database window.

By default, in the Database window you must double-click an object to open it. You can also select an object and then click Open, Design or click Preview (for reports) to open the object.

If you prefer to click once on an object in the Database window to open the object, you follow these steps to change the setting:

1. Choose Tools, Options to open the Options dialog box and then click the View tab, shown in Figure 30.1.

2. Choose the Single-Click Open option.

**FIGURE 30.1**

You can enable single-clicking to open objects by using the View tab.

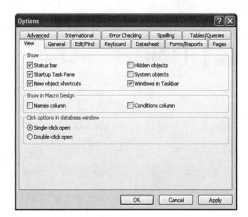

3. Click OK.

With the Single-Click Open option enabled, each object in the Database window acts like a link in a Web page. You just click the underlined link once to open the object.

# Adding More Recently Used Files

Like other Office applications, Access displays recently used databases in the File menu to make it easy to open frequently or recently used databases. You can increase the number of recently used databases in the File menu by following these steps:

1. Choose Tools, Options to open the Options dialog box and then click the General tab (shown in Figure 30.2).

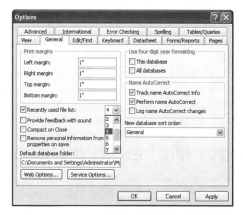

2. Make sure the Recently Used File List option is selected and then choose a number from its drop-down list box.

3. Click OK.

# Changing the Default Search Method

As you gain experience performing searches in a database, you are likely to find that you perform the same type of search often. Access defaults to searching the current field and attempting to match the entire field. However, you might prefer that Access search the entire table and match any part of the search string.

To change the default search behavior, you choose Tools, Options to open the Options dialog box and then click the Edit/Find tab, shown in Figure 30.3.

Then you choose one of the following options:

- **Fast Search**—Search the current field and match the entire field.
- **General Search**—Search all fields and match any part of the field.
- **Start of Field Search**—Search the current field and match the first few characters of the field.

**FIGURE 30.3**

You can use the Edit/Find tab to change the default search behavior.

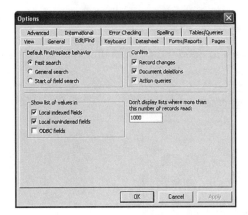

# Controlling How Access Moves in a Record

By default, Access moves to the next field when you press Enter in Datasheet view. This works great when you are entering data because you generally enter each field in a record before you move to the next record.

However, if you are reviewing an existing table and perhaps changing just the contents of one field in each record, you might prefer to have Access move to the next record when you press Enter.

To change this setting, you choose Tools, Options to open the Options dialog box and then click the Keyboard tab, shown in Figure 30.4. You can use the Move After Enter options to specify how Access should move the cursor when you press Enter. You can use the Behavior Entering Field options to specify how Access should select within the record when you move to a new record. You can use the Arrow Key Behavior options to specify what action Access should take when you press an arrow key on the keyboard.

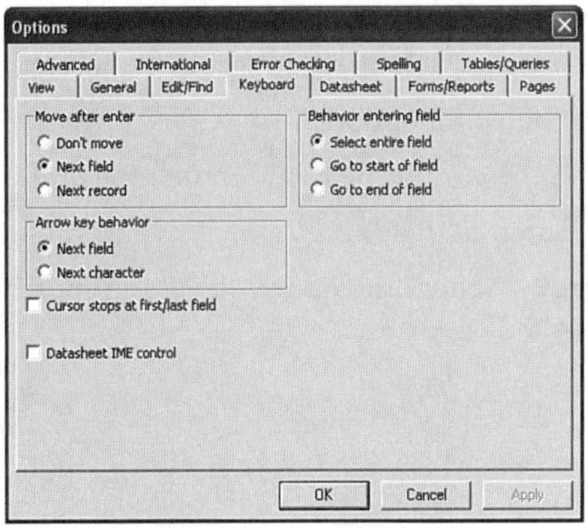

**FIGURE 30.4**

You can configure keyboard options by using the Keyboard tab.

# Setting Default Fonts and Colors

Access uses the Arial font by default, as well as default colors for font, background, and grid lines. You can change these if you prefer a different font or colors. You can also turn off the grid lines between fields and records, and you can choose a raised or sunken effect for Datasheet view.

To make such changes, you choose Tools, Options to open the Options dialog box and then click the Datasheet tab (see Figure 30.5). You can use the Default Colors options to set colors, the Default Font options to specify the default font, and the Default Gridlines Showing options to set the grid options. You can choose Flat, Raised, or Sunken effects in the Default Cell Effect group.

**FIGURE 30.5**

You can configure the way Datasheet view looks.

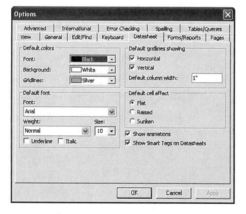

# Setting the Default Folder Location

By default, Access looks in My Documents when you open a database. If most of your databases are stored in a different location—such as a network server—you can change the default file location in order to locate files more quickly.

To do this, you choose Tools, Options to open the Options dialog box and then click the General tab. You enter the path in the Default Database Folder text box and click OK. The Pages tab of the Options dialog box (shown in Figure 30.6) includes a couple settings that let you specify the default location for database project files and Open Database Connectivity (ODBC) connection files.

**FIGURE 30.6**

You can configure default folders by using the Pages tab.

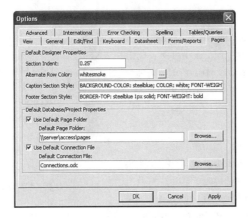

# THE ABSOLUTE MINIMUM

This chapter explains a few of the most common settings you will likely want to change as you become comfortable using Access. There are many others not explored here, so take some time to browse through the other options to learn more about them.

# Index

*How can we make this index more useful? Email us at indexes@quepublishing.com*

worksheets
absolute cell references, 296-298
automatic formatting, 322
cell references, 296-298
cells, hiding, 320-321
cells, locking, 320-321
cells, merging, 319-320
cells, series fills, 321-322
cells, splitting, 319-320
charts, data labels, 336-337
charts, legends, 336
charts, printing, 338
charts, titles, 335
column titles, specifying, 346
comments, adding, 323-324
comments, deleting, 324
comments, editing, 324
comments, reviewing, 325
fitting to printed sheets, 343-345
footer additions, 345-346
functions, 302
functions, inserting, 302-303
header additions, 345-346
numbers, formatting, 312-313
range references, 296-298
relative cell references, 296-298
row titles, specifying, 346
simple formulas, creating, 301-302
text, aligning, 315-316
text, formatting, 314
XML support, 340

**Exchange Server**
Contacts folder, sharing contacts with other users, 77-78
mailboxes, opening others, 117-118

**existing documents, opening (Word), 170**
**expanding message groups (Inbox), 84**
**Expenses template (databases), 411**
**exporting Contacts folder (Outlook) to Personal folder file (PSI), 79**
**Expression Builder, fields, control associations, 419**

## F

**F1 key, Help features, 50-51**
**Fax Wizard (Word), 254**
**faxing documents (Word), 17, 254**
**fields (databases)**
control associations
Expression Builder, 419
Form Wizard, 418-420
format control via Format property, 407-408
format control via input masks, 408-410
**file attachments in messages (Inbox), 89-91**
**file extensions**
.DOC files (Word), 9
.DOT files (Word), 9
.MDB files (Access), 10
.OST files (Outlook), 10
.PPT files (PowerPoint), 10
.PST files (Outlook), 10
.XLS files (Excel), 10
**file formats**
documents, saving (Word), 245
workbooks, saving, 340
**File menu commands (Excel)**
Page Setup, 343
Print Area, 343
Save As, 340

**File menu commands (Outlook)**
Close, 41
Import and Export, 68
Save, 41-42
**File menu commands (Word)**
Options, 272
Page Setup, 188-189
Send To Mail Recipient, 251
**files**
default storage location, setting (Access), 455
embed size limits, setting (PowerPoint), 389-390
link size limits, setting (PowerPoint), 389-390
presentations, save location (My Documents folder), 388
Recently Used Files List option, number settings, 389, 452
searching by types, 9-10
**filling cells with serial data (Excel), 321-322**
**Filter by Form option (database records), 424**
**filtering**
junk mail, 109
list options, 111-112
protection levels, 110-111
records in database tables, 423-424
**FIM-A courtesy reply mail bar code, 265**
**Find and Replace dialog box (Access), 406-407**
**Find and Replace dialog box (Word), 180-182**
**finding text in documents (Word), 180-181**
**fitting worksheets on printed sheets, 343-345**
**fixed column width option (tables), 211**

*How can we make this index more useful? Email us at indexes@quepublishing.com*

# Q - R

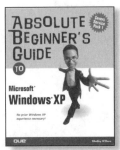